P9-DMI-491

Flowers on Grave.

Why so much fear of tears? Because the masks we use are made of salt. A stinging, red salt which makes us beautiful and majestic but devours our skin.

Luisa Valenzuela

WHO WAS THAT MAN?

WHO WAS THAT MAN?

A Present for Mr Oscar Wilde

Neil Bartlett

The publishers thank Kathy Acker, Mark Ainley, Martin Chalmers, Bob Lumley, Enrico Palandri, Kate Pullinger for their advice and assistance.

British Library Cataloguing in Publication Data
Bartlett, Neil
    Who was that man?: a present for Mr.
    Oscar Wilde
    1. Wilde, Oscar — Biography 2. Authors,
    Irish — 19th century — Biography
    I. Title
    828'.809 PR5823

Copyright © 1988 by Neil Bartlett

First published 1988 by
Serpent's Tail
3a Exmouth House
Pine Street
Exmouth Market
London EC1R 0JH
www.serpentstail.com

Layout and design by Fiona Keating

Cover design by Roy Trevelion
Typeset by Theatretexts, London

Printed in the United States

CONTENTS

PERMISSIONS AND ILLUSTRATIONS

All quotations from Wilde's letters © the Estate of Vyvyan Holland and reproduced by kind permission of Merlin Holland; all quotations from the work of H. Montgomery Hyde by kind permission of the author.

ILLUSTRATIONS

By permission of the British Library: Portraits of Lord Alfred Douglas, the *Border Standard*, 15 December 1923 (pp. 75, 191); twelve portraits from the *Illustrated Police News* 1870, 1884, 1889, and 1890, two portraits from the *North London Press* and photographs by Frederick Rolfe and Anon., *The Studio*, vols. i & v 1893 (pp. 65–75); engraving by Simeon Solomon, *Leisure Hour*, 1866 (p. 73); illustration of "Philip and Gerald", E.I. Stevenson, 1893 (p. 66); portraits of H.M. McDonald (p. 65), Solomon (p. 65), Whitman (p. 71), Wilde by Beardsley (p. 72); plates from the *Orchid Album* by John Nugent Fitch, London, B.S. Williams 1882 (pp. 41, 43, 47, 51, 55).

By permission of the National Portrait Gallery: Portraits of Wilde (p. 25, 62, 239), Symonds (p. 62), Kitchener (p. 69), Burnaby (p. 69) and Burton (p. 74).

Thanks to Bob Lumley for the photograph of Wilde's grave (frontispiece and endpiece).

Not to find one's way in a city may well be uninteresting and banal. It requires ignorance — nothing more. But to lose oneself in a city...

...city crowd pushing wrestling shouldering, against the tide face after face, breath of liquor, infidel skin, shouts, threats, greetings, smiles, eyes and breasts of love, breathless, clutches of lust, limbs, bodies, torrents, bursts, savage onslaughts, tears, entreaties, tremblings, stranglings, suicidal, the sky, the houses, white faces from afar bearing down nearer nearer, almost touching, and glances unforgotten and meant to be unforgotten...

This book is in loving memory of Jack Saul of Lisle Street, Private Flower, Fanny and Stella, La Princesse Salomé and her sisters and lovers, Mr Gibbings, the eighteen-year-old fisherman, the Euston Road queen, Clibborn and Allen, and, of course, all The Boys.

WHO WAS THAT MAN?

I wrote this book in London in 1985 and 1986, and I suppose that's what it's about. I wanted to write a book about what it feels like, because I think that's what people always want to know, really, what does it feel like...

Tell me your story from the very beginning, and how you got acquainted with him.

Well, first... you know I haven't always lived in London. I moved here in the early summer of 1981, but I suppose I always assumed that I'd live here. When I was sixteen I used to come up here on the train to go to the museums, to stand and look at the pictures, and also to be looked at, picked up, and then when I was twenty I would come up here to meet someone. It was always the place to be. I used to get an erection just waiting for the train.

The London I live in now seems very different. I go to different places, take different routes to get there. I wear different clothes when I walk the same streets; 1975 now seems a very long time ago. I don't think anybody's life changes as fast as a gay man's when he moves to a big city.

(There is a pause while he lights a cigarette.)

I think you're right when you say I should tell my story from the very beginning, but I'm sorry, this can't be a simple confession, I mean it's not even my story at all. Coming to London (and that isn't something you do just by stepping off the train; it takes years, believe me, it's taken me years), coming to London meant moving into a life that already existed — I started to talk to other people for the first time, to go to places that already had a style, a history if you like. What I've done, I suppose, is to connect my life to other lives, even buildings and streets, that had an existence prior to mine. This is in itself remarkable, because for the longest time imaginable I experienced my gayness in complete isolation, just like any other gay child in a small town. And now, gradually, I've come to understand that I am connected with other men's lives, men living in London with me. **Or with other, dead Londoners. That's the story.**

The connection, at first, was simple. Of course it didn't feel simple — looking back, I think I must have been scared all the time. I matched my life with the patterns of other men around me. I taught myself the pleasure of being like other people. I went to the same places, I had the same sort of sex life, I talked about roughly the same things and in roughly the same language. I didn't either need or want to know anybody's name. More recently I've started experimenting with the other extreme, matching the patterns of my life with those of just one other man. It feels like another variation on the same strategy, just as necessary and just as pleasurable. All the time, I think, we want to find out about each other, to know if we really belong to each other, belong together.

1981 was the first year that I actually lived here, and that was when I discovered that a city has nights as well as days. That summer the city was full of men, hidden, just waiting for me. I'd be walking up the Strand, dressed to kill, and then I'd find myself looking up from the street to all the nineteenth-century façades above me, and fantasize that all the buildings of the West End had seen other men before me living a life after dark, that somehow the streets had a memory. What if I rounded the corner of Villiers Street at midnight, and suddenly found myself walking by gaslight, and the man looking over his shoulder at me as he passed had the same moustache, but different clothes, the well-cut black and white evening dress of the summer of 1891 — would we recognize each other? Would I smile at him too, knowing that we were going to the same place, looking *for the same thing? Would our eyes meet? What would we talk about?*

I suppose I realize how ignorant I am. If we don't learn anything from history then it is because we don't know any history.

So I began to try and learn my own history, and I did it in exactly the same way as I learnt my way around contemporary London. You hear a man talking about a pub, or you read an address in a paper, or sometimes you simply follow someone you fancy and discover a whole new part of town. You know that your knowledge is quite arbitrary. Your knowledge of the city is shaped by the way ex-lovers introduce you to their friends, by the way you hear someone's story simply because he happened to be in the same place as you at the same time. And eventually you build up a network of places and people, perhaps you discover a particular group of people, or you look for, or accidentally find, one man who focuses your life. I moved from clue to clue, from name to name and from book to book. I started collecting pictures and anecdotes. I bought four big scrapbooks and filled them with whatever texts or images I could find from the London of a hundred years ago. I went back to the picture galleries and museums I used to haunt when I was sixteen. Gradually I began to learn the geography and language of 1895 or 1881, to redraw my map of the city, to recognize certain signs, certain words. I began to see this other London as the beginning of my own story — and up till then, like a lot of other men, I'd seen America and 1970 as the start of everything.

In writing this story I've had some particular difficulties that have to do with the fact that I'm writing as a gay man. These difficulties are characteristic of a city, in which our lives are lived, at best uneasily, alongside a culture which either ignores or hurts us. It was very difficult to sit in a library, or stand in front of a picture or contemplate a face in an old newspaper, and wonder what the people around me would think if they knew the reason why I was suddenly so intent. It was very odd to leave the streets full of men and sit in quiet rooms — libraries, galleries — in search of my story. It was very odd to be made to sit at a special table in order to read a "pornographic" book, one that the catalogue could label as homosexual. It was very peculiar not to go out at night, to give up all that standing around and watching and random noise, and instead work alone, at night. And even when I was alone, when I got home from the library, I still felt watched, I still had to account for what I was doing. It became very difficult using certain words, the most ordinary of words, because I wanted to give them meanings which this city doesn't normally allow. When I write "we" for instance, I mean we gay men. I flinch and want to explain. This word would make perfect sense in a bar, but here I am using it in a book, and I have no way of knowing if the reader is gay, or a man, or has any investment in or commitment to understanding this language.

This is no ordinary lack of confidence. I have to fight the feeling that this effort to recover my own past is ridiculous, and I have to do so for very particular reasons. Anyone whose work can be labelled gay is told that they should produce real work, work in a larger culture, not mere footnotes. And I'm aware that the gay men's culture of this city, with its easily purchased signs of pleasure, vigour and sex, has little time or need to worry over its history, especially a part of its history apparently locked away in the hateful British closets of Literature and The Upper Class. This is a busy city. There isn't much time to stop and think, or look twice.

(He lights another cigarette, and begins to speak more loudly.)

Nonetheless, I think that we do have to speak to one another, in our own language. It matters that the patterns of my life were set by men who came before me. It matters that much of the sexual geography of this city was established a hundred years ago, not five years ago when I moved here. Every boy is looking to find his way around, looking for someone, because you arrive knowing nothing. You fall in love with people you never even talk to; that's a common experience. Men you never really touch or understand can lead you into a different part of the city. So, I've "fallen in love" with men I could never actually meet. I'm not embarrassed to say it, to say that I've fallen in love with some of those men from the past. I've even noticed the cut of their hair...

"What kind of man was he?"

1.
HISTORY

There are three ways of putting together a man's story. Each way of telling it is a sort of detective story, and it is also a fairy story, because it has a happy ending. Or, at least it has an ending, which in itself makes us happy. This is odd, because we ought to know that our story is not yet finished.

The first way of telling the story is the commonest, the one at which we have all had most practice. You yourself have told this story, though you may not have committed it to writing. Perhaps you have told it to a good friend, holding his hand; you may have experimented with several versions of it late at night, your head on a stranger's pillow. It is the coming-out story, the one in which you or I tell of a long personal struggle, which ends with the statement, "I am gay." It's alright, relax. We knew it all along. With practice, we have learnt to read the signs correctly.

The second way is usually undertaken in instalments, since it assumes that the story being told is a very, very long one. The hero now is not "I" but "we", and the story is the history of "homosexuality". After all the characteristic difficulties of infancy, childhood and adolescence (leading, in the late nineteenth century, to a meeting with the police and a gruelling but formative session with a doctor or analyst), this narrative finally shows us coming out, collectively, as the "adult gay men" of the late twentieth century. This second way of telling the story is closely based on the first.

The third way combines the historical methods of the second with the individual subject of the first. The hero in this case is a single, usually "great" homosexual. His fame rests in part on being hidden (either through his own efforts or through those of others), on being in need of revelation. His life and times are scrutinized, and reveal to the reader the secret of his story; that his homosexuality was in some way basic to his life and work. Layers of clues, suggestions and distortions (letters, works of art, symptoms) are stripped away until we arrive at the truth.

The first telling of the story ends with the "I" assuming a coherent contemporary identity; the second with "we" arriving at a coherent contemporary culture; the third with "him" truly deciphered, and enshrined as a major or minor character in the second story and patron saint or role model for the first. All three of these stories are biographies.

Biographies are best written when their subject is dead. Are you dead, that is, has your life stopped changing? Are we dead, that is, have we arrived in a city whose gay culture we now have only to buy and enjoy? Is your favourite hero "dead", that is, has his role as a source of information, inspiration and wardrobe suggestions been exhausted yet — or will you look at that familiar picture differently in a year's time?

There is another way of putting the story together. Well, not a story, exactly. Somewhere in the house, flat or room of each of my lovers and friends there is a draft of a book like this one. He's never shown me his manuscript, but I know that he has a record collection, a drawer of photographs, a wall of pictures, a mantelpiece of postcards, a bookshelf, a wardrobe of clothes. If you or he can "read" this collection of words and images, with all its attendant justifications, juxtapositions and cross references, you will have a gay story, a history. Some connections between things will be obvious — no one need explain to you why they have a picture of the young Brando on their wall. Some will become clear if you get him to explain — that wedding photo is precious because it includes a gay uncle, the one he never

Who *was* that Man?

met, the one his mother says was the only other gay man she
ever knew, the only other one in the family.

There will be some passages of narrative: a photo of a child
next to a photo of the man, or a sequence of ex-lovers indicating
moves from place to place. Other things will not indicate a
narrative at all. Next time you see him or talk to him, his
collection will have changed. There will be additions, or re-
arrangements, or he could have moved into a new room or into
another part of the city.

The place I started looking for my story was not the city, but
the library.

If a stranger asked you to name a homosexual, would you give
your own name in reply? Or if you asked someone else, your
sister, for instance, or your father, to name a homosexual, what
would their response be? There is one, just one, whose name
everyone knows. In fact he is famous above all else for being a
homosexual. And since his name alone can conjure my past, it
was his name I started with, the first entry I looked up in the
catalogue. His words began to ghost my writing. They measured
out precisely how the London I inhabit is so different from his
city. They also haunt us with their suggestions that our culture
is not as original as it seems, not as unique as we may believe.

Gay history is usually hard to come by, but as he is not only "a
homosexual" but also "Literature", it is quite easy to obtain *The
Complete Works of Oscar Wilde*. This is a single, fat volume,
containing all of Wilde's public writings. Since 1966 the collected
works of Oscar Wilde have been genuinely complete. Even the
controversial text of *De Profundis* (controversial because it is a
letter to the man he loved, the only honestly and explicitly
homosexual text he produced) has been released from the British
Museum, restored, corrected and printed in full.

But just when you think you've read everything, *The Complete
Works*, the plays, poems, essays and stories, and have the whole

picture, the full story, the book ends with two rather disturbing pages. They list a selection of books about Oscar Wilde published betwee 1905 and 1969 — sixty-two in all. Do I have to read all these books as well, just to make sure that nothing has been left out? I go back to the beginning and start to read again, and I notice that the introduction, by Oscar Wilde's son, although it says that he loved his wife, does not say that he loved Lord Alfred Douglas. Either that part of his life is considered to be common knowledge, and not worth mentioning, or to be embarrassing, and unmentionable. Clearly, as far as I'm concerned, *The Complete Works* are not complete.

So, to get a fuller picture, I went on to read Oscar's letters (also fully available, since 1962). And I've read the accounts of his trials, which record both what he said and what people (policemen, judges, journalists, lawyers and rentboys) said to him and of him. I read *Oscar Wilde: Three Times Tried* (Anon., 1912), which the Times Book Club refused to circulate among its subscribers. I read the introduction to the 1948 Penguin edition of the trial transcripts, which gave me a picture of how Oscar was viewed in 1948, when people still spoke of *the problem of Oscar Wilde's sexual inversion* and were surprised that *even from the witness box he attempted to justify his feelings*. In a second-hand bookshop I paid ten pence for a copy of *Oscar Wilde: Was he a Genius or just a Pervert?*, published by Four Square Books in 1960 as a tie-in to the Twentieth Century Fox film which cast Robert Morley and John Neville as the star-crossed losers. Its first page is at pains to take an up-to-date attitude: *These days the homosexual is tolerated and pitied, and accepted in most spheres. Conscious of his condition, he seeks the help of his psychiatrist.* Later the book tells me that Oscar's moral decay was evident in his conspicuously terrible skin, that he was as wide-hipped as the mother who made him homosexual by dominating him, and that his letters to Alfred Douglas are *absurd and revolting*. Mistrusting this version of events, I tried to get a less prejudiced account, and so I read a lot of newspapers, newspapers from 1894 and 1895, before and after the trial. To make sure I was getting the authentic picture, I read his *Salomé* in French (the language he originally wrote it in) with a dictionary open on my desk. To make sure nothing was being hidden from me, I compared the three- and four-act versions of *The Importance of Being Earnest*, and the two editions of *The Picture of Dorian Gray*. I pursued texts with the dogged energy I usually reserve for cruising; I became excited by the smallest hints; I scrutinized every gesture for significance; sometimes I simply stood close and waited for a response. I went to the most unlikely places. I even tried to find the *literal and unexpurgated* Paris version of "*Dorian Gray*", offered for sale by a pornographer (Carrington, 13 Faubourg Montmartre) in 1902. I got a ticket for the library at the British Museum, did as I was told, and sat at the special desk reserved for the reading of books kept under lock and key. There I was allowed to read *Teleny*, a pornographic novel dated 1893. It isn't listed in *The Complete Works of Oscar Wilde*, and in fact it seems to have been written by several different men, but it was sold (for five pounds, in 1903) via a catalogue which claimed that *the writer is stated on good authority to be none other than Oscar Wilde. This becomes the more convincing when we compare the style of his famous* Dorian Gray *with the present brilliant but* awfully lewd book.

The catalogue has a point; there are passages so close to Wilde that we cannot quite be sure whether they are by him or not, whether this is his voice or that of an expert and devoted mimic. What matters now is that whoever the author was, he wanted such a novel to be included in *The Complete Works of Oscar Wilde*, a novel by the "real" Oscar Wilde, a novel which would tell everything, which would confess our secret.

I've watched plays and films based on Oscar Wilde's work, and I've seen plays and films about his life, in the theatre and on television.

Someone offered to take me out to dinner, and I suggested that we go to Kettner's, still in Romilly Street, just as it was then. I saw that they no longer have the pink lampshades that Oscar and his boys enjoyed. I saw the river by night at Limehouse, just like Dorian Gray did. I staggered through Covent Garden at dawn — I hunted out the places where my explorations of London might still coincide with Oscar's.

But the picture wasn't complete. Bits were obviously and intriguingly missing. Some characters had been painted out, or rather had never been painted in. I found out, for instance, that Oscar knew both aristocrats and rentboys. But when his fiction leaves the grand parties, the houses of Belgravia, and goes in search of shadier entertainments, it never describes the bodies or gives them names. We never get to see the faces, and of course it is the faces that I want to see. How did the boys wear their hair in Soho a hundred years ago? Did they have the same lines around their mouths and eyes as they have now? One or two names are mentioned in the letters, so I looked them up in the transcripts of the trials. The trial records bring the boys themselves into the dock for questioning, to tell their stories — but then they disappear. To get a picture of Oscar, surely I have to include those men sitting either side of him at the table in the Solferino restaurant in Rupert Street in the spring of 1893. What are Parker and Taylor's stories? I can't find them. What did they do when it was all over?

As I pieced together more of the narrative, it became less, not more, clear. The shape of the story was unconvincing, even though it was familiar. Everything I knew focused too neatly on one central event, apparently reflecting our own contemporary situation, in which everything can be described as being before or after "coming out". Even the texts in the *Complete Works* seemed to be organized as either "before" or "after" the trials of 1895, when Oscar Wilde was proved guilty in law of being a homosexual, and so fell from grace. Before the trial everything hinted at homosexuality (the texts whispered of their guilty secret). After the trial everything struggled to explain or condemn it (the texts converted their passion into a set of symptoms or excuses). But if the trials were such a scandal, if the revelation of hitherto hidden aspects of a famous man's life was such a surprise to the newspaper-reading public of London, then why did Mr Justice Wills comment, in his summing up of the third trial: "I have tried many similar cases." What were those cases? Why were they so conveniently forgotten? So that the papers could sell their story as an exposé, the history of a unique monster?

I continued to wonder whether this reading of and about Mr Oscar Wilde wasn't making me more ignorant, rather than more informed. As clues proliferated, it seemed a mistake to focus my attention on a single subject. Why should I canonize only one man, anathemize him, record only one biography as "typical"? No one man can guide me around this city. Why can I find no books about a man named Simeon Solomon, also a fashionable success in his artistic career, and also tried and found guilty of associating with working-class homosexuals, in 1873? Unlike Mr Oscar Wilde, he seems not to have ever denied or concealed this part of his life. He kept on seeing his boys, stayed in London (supporting himself at one point by selling matches on the Mile End Road) and had the nerve to live on into our century, dying in 1905. How could I leave his story as just a note in my scrapbook? And never mind a picture of Dorian Gray, what about Vivian Gray, also known as Ernest Boulton, also known as Stella Clinton, a full-time homosexual transvestite whose society career as actress and mistress of Lord Arthur Clinton MP was only halted by another sensational arrest and trial in 1871? Why is it that whenever the famous are exposed or eulogized, when their pictures appear in the paper alongside a scandal or reappraisal of an illustrious career, I always want to turn away, to go back to the parts of the city we've forgotten, to get lost in the strange streets? I'd rather talk about some ordinary queen I know, I'd rather relate the story of some man I've met, describe the face of some dancer or beauty. A book which gives a picture of that part of my history which is called "Oscar Wilde" would have to include all these stories and others besides.

I subject the story of my own life as a gay man to constant scrutiny; we all do. We have to, because we're making it up as we go along.

I constantly re-read *The Complete Works of Oscar Wilde*.

▷

Do you remember Yvonne Fair singing "You Can't Judge a Book by its Cover"? (It was the B-side of "It Should Have Been Me",

Motown 1975.) You may find a certain man's body attractive, but that attraction will not guarantee you an understanding of the man; the erotic tension you feel standing outside the red-lit club doorway will teach you nothing about how to live with the men who go there twice a week; even when you have found a book from your own history, a book by a "homosexual", you have to learn how to read it.

How are we to read, for instance, "Oscar Wilde"? In 1894 the situation would have been clear; we would have been reading a commercially successful and fashionable playwright. In 1896 we would have been reading (probably discreetly) the testament of a banished pervert, a criminal (imagine Terence Rattigan suddenly becoming Jean Genet). In 1948 a literary classic, albeit one for whom it would have been suspect to show an excessive or an adolescent enthusiasm, especially if the text in question were one of the "minor" works. (I remember the tone of voice I used to try and tell my schoolteacher that I had enjoyed E.M. Forster's love story *Maurice*, enjoyed it more than *A Passage to India*, the book I was supposed to have been studying.) And now?

The first text, in my edition, is *The Picture of Dorian Gray*. It is a story of false appearances and fatal misunderstandings. Because people interpret or misinterpret the gorgeous face of its hero, their lives are wrecked. Although not Wilde's first work, it nonetheless opens this volume. Perhaps the editors placed it there so as to warn me of the seriousness of reading or misreading this book. The first page is a series of aphorisms, designed to alarm and instruct the reader. According to this page, which I always turn to when I take this heavy red and black book off my shelf, there are three ways to read this story.

Those who find ugly meanings in beautiful things are corrupt without being charming. This is a fault.

The first method of interpretation is one of attack. For instance, I can find "homosexuality" hidden in the most innocent or random of details, if my gaze is sufficiently obsessive or well-informed. All I need do is apply a characteristically gay skill —

the gaze that catches the dropped hint, the note of excess. I'll choose the most obviously innocent, the least sexual text; a story that could have been written for children. I read in Wilde's story *The Young King* that the king *had been seen pressing his warm lips to the marble brow of an antique statue that had been discovered in the bed of the river on the occasion of the building of a stone bridge and was inscribed with the name of the Bithynian slave of Hadrian.* I recognize the image, alerted by the suggestion of an attractive young man with passionate and dubious artistic tastes. My gaze is not deflected by the decorative prose. The young king appears to me as a homosexual adolescent in fancy dress, a young Londoner alone in his room reading a banned or borrowed book, a lonely young man practising his desires with the help of such fragments of ancient history as a nineteenth-century public school education in the classics has given him. I know this because I can supply the deliberately erased name on the statue. It must be that of Antinous, not only the slave but also the lover of the Emperor Hadrian, immortalized by imperial decree in a thousand second-rate classical statues after his early and suspect death from drowning in the Nile. The young king is embracing a history he can only dream of; his kiss is the kiss of a boy for a man, his first or imaginary man. On another occasion in the story he disappears, only to be found, sitting alone, gazing at a Greek gem carved with the figure of Adonis. I wonder if my hypothetical adolescent ever shook the rain from his coat when he entered the British Museum and then, as I did, hurried straight to the galleries full of classical marbles, walking there with eyes down past the other exhibits, then standing, silent, wondering whether he would ever be allowed to touch, whether these were images of real men, or of dead men, or of men he was going to meet, and dreaming of nothing more than spending a night alone in the gallery, with no one to watch him, looking and doing as he pleased. I place next to the story of the young king, and next to this memory of my own, the story of how the writer John Addington Symonds was found in the library by his father, gazing at a print of another statue, a cupid by Praxiteles, and how his father understood what this gaze meant, or could mean, and how he suggested that the boy look at another, female statue. We know there is only one true story. We all know, now, what Oscar was really trying to say, what he was hinting at but could not declare.

I would not myself consider this an ugly meaning to have traced in such an innocent text. I feel as unembarrassed doing this literary detective work as I do when shamelessly letting my eyes follow a handsome stranger down a crowded London pavement, just waiting to see whether I've guessed right, whether he'll turn at last and give a quick smile of recognition.

We often assume (rightly) that homosexuality must be hidden, that it has to be found. But what are we free to search for if the author's sexuality is common knowledge — as, in this case, it is — if the "homosexual meaning" of his texts is well-known, obvious, taken for granted, unconcealed? On the street, there is only ever time to wonder, "Is he gay?"; in the bar, where the answer is already known, you can begin to wonder, "What is that man's story?" The game of reading between the lines begins to have different consequences.

It is no longer the orthodox imagery of heterosexuality that is under scrutiny; but the new orthodoxy of Wilde as a gay pioneer and martyr. This may be scrutinized, challenged to reveal some truly ugly meanings. It is a commonplace to observe that "beneath" Wilde's charming exterior lay the night-life, the lurid Victoriana of nineteenth-century London (the brothel in a respectable street, the expensive gift making its way into the wrong class of pocket). But what if "beneath" the heavily lidded eyes of the sex criminal lay not the excitement of a life that dares to challenge and evade, every boy's dream of an escape into the darker streets, but merely the overweight cynical ease with which an economically privileged man can and does lead a homosexual life in London without having to pay more than money for it. My reading becomes bitter. Why does the young king always return to his palace in the morning? My image of Oscar in the dock loses its halo; he was no heroic victim, but a man lying and laughing his way out of acknowledging the realities of this city. He lied, and he lied at a crucial moment in our history, just when we were about to appear. If he had "told the truth", everything might have been different. Put down the book, and consider. If I read this story in a certain light, I begin to wonder, in what sense of the word was this most famous of homosexuals actually a homosexual? He was married. His best and most successful play, *The Importance of Being Earnest*, may be the most precious pearl of English camp, but it celebrates the triumph of marriage over all adversity, brings down its curtain on a trio of engagements, and was deliberately premiered on St Valentine's Day. What can it tell us, in any of the endless revivals, the endless resuscitations of its overdressed sentiments, except that the work of this man may bear no hint, no trace of his "true nature", may be a triumphant declaration of the ease with which we distort and ignore our own lives, preferring instead to engage in more general topics: love, mothers, fathers, property and its exchange. Nothing in the texts themselves demands that we read them otherwise; why should we, for instance, regard the love letters to Lord Alfred Douglas as more authentic or more important than the (lost) love letters to Constance Lloyd, Mrs Oscar Wilde? Why should the hints of slumming or possibly homosexual scandal in the story of Dorian Gray be so carefully traced, treated as more significant or more interesting than Gray's openly declared heterosexual interest in beautiful powerless women, actresses and farm labourers? *An Ideal Husband* ends with its hero not only reunited with a meekly loving wife, but elected to the Cabinet — a combination of ideals warmly and publicly applauded by the Prince of Wales on the opening night. So much for the radical gay author of *The Soul of Man Under Socialism*. So much for our lovingly constructed image of Wilde as martyr and hero. So much for the life that we imagine the handsome stranger may lead after dark. We were wrong to believe that a hidden meaning would necessarily be a subversive one, one that would help us to identify or liberate ourselves.

In 1911 a young man from Boston named C.M. Otis told his doctor: "Reading that case of Oskar (sic) Wilde, didn't help my case a bit." Exactly.

But excuse me, my reading is corrupt, and isn't charming.

Those who find beautiful meanings in beautiful things are the cultivated. For these there is hope.

The second method of interpretation appears to be a simple reverse of the first. Instead of criticizing the text (burrowing into it, attacking it, pursuing its obscure connections), I celebrate it. I don't dwell unnecessarily on the contradictions of Oscar's social position, or on the peculiarity of my choice of him as father and guide to the city. I am sure he knew what he was doing when he bought those boys dinner. He said he knew what he was doing. Surely I should extract as much pleasure as possible from such fragments of our past as I can recover. As I sit in the library, Wilde's books can make my face break into a ridiculous smile. I look round to see if anyone notices. I will read anything that is "about us", anything that makes me smile as I see myself, even a small part of myself, a half-seen gesture at night — but I am always slightly embarrassed by this naive hunger for images, this peculiarly gay vanity. I read in order to discover my solidarity with my gay peers — just as I go out to drink in order to forget my differences with the other men in the bar and to enjoy the simple fact of our shared experience, to enjoy the pleasure of crossing eyes in a mirror, the great pleasure to be found in the way we look standing side by side. Why devote any ingenuity to prove the difficulty of enjoying our culture, past or present? I read that Basil Hallward (my favourite butch-but-sensitive character in gay fiction) confesses to feeling the first time that he sees Dorian Gray: "I have always been my own master; had at least always been so, till..." I experience the commonest of gay pleasures: recognition. I recognize in this old book my own feelings when I wake and turn and look at the face of the man sleeping next to me. I discover the heart, the meaning locked in a text which cannot, for historical reasons, declare itself. I sympathize. I understand; I am one of them too.

But note, to read in this way, I have to be cultivated. Does this mean that I have to be well informed (well educated?) — or does it suggest that I have to belong to a certain class, or to a certain society, or to an identifiable minority, or to subscribe to certain defined tastes or ways of spending money?

They are the elect to whom beautiful things mean only Beauty.

The third method of reading obliterates even the possibility that I might find ugly, as well as beautiful, meanings in my past, my culture. Indeed, it elegantly does away with any complex or changeable "meaning" at all. It does not require the studied interpretation of signs; it does not need to be learnt or purchased. It is without difficulty. It presupposes that gay men recognize, enjoy and feel at home with gay things just as rich people recognize and enjoy the signs of wealth. Other meanings (gay signals operate in a straight world; wealth lives alongside poverty) are forgotten, just as we forget the hours in the gym and see only the natural beauty and health radiating from a well-muscled body. The works of Oscar Wilde, for instance, were written for us and for us alone, and only we can truly understand them. We belong together, don't you think?

Because the meanings we seek and need are usually hidden, or at least infrequent, we decipher small declarations; just one look over the shoulder, or a detail of dress, can make us sure or unsure of getting what we want. We remember messages on walls, the meeting of two athletes (any detail or gesture which can give us an erection or a pain in the heart), the history of an obscurely murdered king. Sometimes we collect our evidence in order to answer just the simple questions: *Is he? Is he available?* Sometimes we have other questions.
  Does this make sense?

If other people are involved in this story, if I join other men when I enter this history, if I am not the first man on these streets, tell me, does being gay help make sense of all this? These anecdotes, all the contradictions and excitements I have found trying to make sense of a single face, a single name, where does it get me?

Does it actually make this city any easier to live in?

Those who read the symbol do so at their peril.

2.
FLOWERS

I dreamed I stood upon a little hill, and at my feet there lay a ground that seemed like a waste garden, flowering at its will with buds and blossoms.

Every city needs a guide book — especially one as strange as Victorian London, always filmed in fog, always obscured by the padding and over-decoration of a costume drama. In order to make sense of the city, to make it into a real city, with streets and people, you have first to search for its characteristic details. Do not expect the city to give itself away easily.

Salomé, the seductress (the untrustworthy guide) has inspired many interpretations since she was reincarnated by Wilde in 1891.

She is always eager to please, this woman; curiously malleable for one reputedly so voracious. Lord Alfred Douglas was the first to interpret her, modify her costume and inflect her voice; in translating his lover's French original he turned her into the English heroine of a fashionable, even pretentious pseudo-symbolist drama. Beardsley, illustrating the same text, dragged the Princess screaming from Paris to London SW3, picturing her as a modern society woman on whose bookshelf festered unread copies of Apuleius, Baudelaire and de Sade. *The Times* (23 February 1893) found her *morbid, bizarre, repulsive and offensive*, while

Strauss (in 1905) elevated her into the respectable European repertoire by making her excesses musical rather than blatantly sexual. The libretto for his opera adapted the text by removing with curious discretion the only, tiny suggestion of explicit homosexuality, the lament of a page boy for his suicidal beloved. In 1923 Alla Nazimova responded by ruthlessly purging every taint of heterosexuality from the Princess, enshrining her in a Hollywood movie reputedly cast entirely from among the director's homosexual lovers and friends, swathing her in robes designed by Natacha Rambova, lesbian wife of Valentino. Kate Millet, in 1970, noted in passing her *stunning virtuosity*, while accurately dissecting her anti-feminist *Sexual Politics*. Salomé, Millet noted, had no right to the alibi of adolescence, even ignorance; she doomed herself to her fatal "feminine" desires two years after Ibsen's Nora had slammed the door on that doll's house, the London theatre, and walked away to a New Woman's life. Throughout all these variations, the Princess herself remained unperturbed; like all great performers she is rendered untouchable by her combination of sincerity and vulgarity. She never reveals her sex, and so remains sex itself. Now, her text looks like nothing so much as the most ludicrous, the most melodramatic of Wilde's comedies, with a dinner-jacketed Herod as the most harassed and most powerful of anxious upper-class husbands, struggling to control his rebellious wife and her vicious daughter. The daughter has become the ideal subject for a "problem drama", an idealistic, "modern" woman who threatens to dissolve the household. The Princess Salomé smiles, and it is her I follow.

Why should I follow her? Amid all these interpretations, whatever its meaning, surely nothing could be further from the life of a contemporary gay man than Wilde's Salomé. Haven't we outgrown the idea that opera and doomed heroines are our inevitable accessories? Even culture, a shelf of literary enthusiasms, is now an irrelevance. If I am looking for a guide, why hunt in such an obscure place?

Any gay tourist, even a casual visitor, in a new city will know how to find the park or pub where our secret resides. The reader

Say it with flowers.

has similar skills. Underneath its glass dome, I reinvented the library. It became a hothouse, a conservatory; the catalogue entries became botanical labels which for the connoisseur can indicate a perfume, a peculiarly perverse method of reproduction, a special texture of foliage in a dry Latin name. The locked bookcase became a garden of flowers in the centre of the snow-covered city. Remember, we are expert at finding our pleasure in the most unlikely of places.

She is like the shadow of a white rose in a mirror of silver... You must not look at her. Effeminate, religiose, guilty, the product of the artistic obsessions of a tiny minority, this text protects itself from anything remotely realistic, like the Princess clutching her famous seven veils. It makes the hundred years since it was written seem unbridgeable. But at any moment, in a single image, the text can come alarmingly alive. Out of all the gorgeous details that encrust and weigh it down, stiff like a flowered brocade — the jewels, the white peacocks, the stained ivory and the white — I'll choose just one to begin my argument.

Salomé, out of sight of her father, is seized with a desire to see the handsome body of John the Baptist. Not for nothing does he call her a *daughter of Sodom*; as she approaches his shining white torso, his burning dark hair, I feel sure she is about to reveal herself for what she really is. Her anxious desire is suddenly that of an adolescent boy; she is the fourteen-year-old I once was, the boy waiting for someone to take away the guilt of his desire by seducing him. If she is to get what she wants, she must persuade the young Syrian captain of the guard to bring the Baptist forth from the darkness of his prison. This enticement is easy, since the Syrian is obsessed with Salomé, breathless with love; he is about to die, asphyxiated by jealousy as he witnesses her approach to another man. I notice at once that he is accompanied everywhere by that doting page boy, but that he spurns him in favour of another, more dangerous love. The scenario seems familiar. Salomé turns to him as a snake turns to a bird, or as one man turns to another, and smiles at him, and she is sure that he will do what she wants. (I think it is this moment

Strange flowers... or the face of one's friend.

44

which originally made me read and re-read this text; beneath all the strangeness, all the costumes, here is a moment I recognize; my stomach turns cold, because a man turns and smiles and I know he is going to get what he wants and there is nothing to be said.) What she offers in return for this worship is not of course her love, but a cryptic token of her/his sex.

You will do this thing for me... and to-morrow when I pass in my litter beneath the gateway of the idol-sellers, I will let fall for you a little flower, a little green flower.

With all her great wealth, what the princess offers him, the morning after, is a little green flower.

After the theatres had closed, Wilde was to imagine his London as an oriental, a foreign city, with a white dome in the moonlight, a night sky like a jewel and the scent of jasmine. In the darkness of this oriental night I notice the detail that I have been looking for. Why does she specify that the flower must be green? Why so precise a detail in such a lurid spectacle, promising everything and delivering nothing? And why do flowers occur again and again in this book of Wilde's, and in the books that I select and arrange around it as my research continues?

I look along the bookshelf; Lady Windermere (*He should be here. Why is he not here to wake by passionate words some fire within me?*) arranges her roses in a blue bowl; so does Dorian Gray. Forty-two years later (1933) Mr Dulcimer, villain of a West End play called *The Green Bay Tree*, announces his queerness by calmly arranging roses as the curtain rises. Des Esseintes, hero of *À Rebours* (1884) by Joris-Karl Huysmans, whose book I place next to Oscar's *Works* because it was his story that was rewritten and resold as *The Picture of Dorian Gray*, devotes his life and income to the collection of the most monstrous and expensive flowers that the florists of Paris can provide. Jaques Silvert, fatally pretty eponym of *Monsieur Venus* (1884), is first seen in a garret of silk flowers, engaged in his profession of *fleuriste*. I immediately suspect him, having read in *Études de Pathologie Sociale* (1889) that floristry, along with hatmaking and hairdressing, was one of the professions that Mr F. Carlier, *Chef de Préfecture*, has identified as characteristic of the queens that he sought to rout out from the boulevards and pissoirs of Paris. My suspicions of Jaques's *en fleurs* are confirmed later when I am shown him posing against an antique carved panel depicting Henri III distributing flowers to the royal boyfriends, his profile matched by that of an adjacent bust of Antinous (of course), crowned with pampas grass, *his enamelled eyes lustrous with desire*. Teleny and his lover Camille des Grieux first express their passion by exchanging buttonholes of white heliotrope. Their kisses seem like *a rain of rose leaves falling from a full blown flower*, and when their passion is consummated rose petals fall from the ceiling onto giant vases which support the floral tributes of India, China and America. Later, in 1921, Marcel Proust imagined his Charlus waiting for a lover like an anxious, coquettish and infertile orchid. All the dandies, real or imagined, have rose-red lips and experience rose-red joys. They are inspired in their choice of buttonholes. They are at ease in the conservatoires of country houses. They perfect their décor with flowers.

The Princess promises to let fall a little green flower.

For me... flowers are part of desire.

Flowers are a sign of the natural. They bloom miraculously; they spring up. In Rome in 1900, almost dead, Oscar imagined that his walking stick, his rod and staff, would burst into flower when he caught sight of Pope Leo XIII on Easter Day. In prison, in 1896, he dreamed of the lilac and laburnum that would blossom in suburban gardens to herald his release. When he described, tears springing from his eyes, the death of a fellow prisoner in *The Ballad of Reading Gaol*, it was only flowers that could express his grief.

Out of his mouth a red, red rose!
Out of his heart a white!

But this library of *fin-de-siècle* flowers is a collection of very particular blooms. They are cut, they wither. They are a luxury that must always be reordered from the gardener or florist. They die and cease to give pleasure, just as surely as the head of John the Baptist will cease to satisfy Salomé once she has picked it and held it in her hand. They can be immortalized only in the flat floridity of Beardsley's pictures, or in the leather binding of a limited edition, tooled with marguerites or pomegranates.

The flowers that Beardsley drew for the Princess were never drawn from life, and indeed the flower that she promises her soldier, the flower she promises me, is a little green flower; it is the most unnatural flower possible. It is an artist's flower; luxurious, fantastic, beautiful. It is a work of art. It will never come to fruition. *The successful result of a plan, idea not able to produce babies*

It is superbly sterile, and the note of its pleasure is sterility. A work of art is useless as a flower is useless. A flower blossoms for its own joy.

In inventing homosexual characters who are all our Ladies of the Flowers, the artists who invented Dulcie, Des Esseintes, Dorian, Jaques Silvert, Teleny, Charlus and the Princess of Judea gave shape and colour to a phenomenon that had only just been given a name — *homosexuality*. Beneath the corrupt glamour of the orchids, beneath the strange perfume of the Parma violets which Dorian wears in his collar, we can see a new mythology taking root. A homosexual, like a hothouse flower, declares his superiority to the merely natural. He is unnatural, and as monstrous as he is necessarily beautiful. He is the result of laborious cultivation; if not an artist, then at least a work of art. He costs money. A homosexual, like a flower, is beautiful only when young, and useless when old. *Remember too how soon Beauty forsakes itself. Its action is no stronger than a flower, and like a flower it lives and dies.* Homosexuality, like an interest in flowers, is a sign of effeminacy. Homosexuals, like flowers, have no reason to exist; they delight only themselves. Homosexuals are sterile; they do not, like other people, have children. They blossom in the form of works of art. (Oscar himself, father of two sons, agreed when Bacon, with Plato and Marlowe in mind, said that

Flowers glass-hid from frosts and snows,
For whom an alien heart makes festival.

*the best works and of greatest merit for the public have proceeded from
the unmarried and childless men.*)

> Because our world has music, and we dance;
> Because our world has colour, and they gaze;
> Because our speech is tuned, and schooled our glance,
> And we have roseleaf nights and roseleaf days,
> And we have leisure, work to do and rest;
> Because they see us laughing when we meet,
> And hear our words and voices, see us dressed
> With skill, and pass us and our flowers smell sweet —
> They think that we know friendship, passion, love!
> Our peacock, Pride, and Art our nightingale!
> And Pleasure's hand upon our dogskin glove!
> And if they see our faces burn or pale,
> It is the sunlight, think they, or the gas.
> — Our lives are wired like our gardenias.
>
> Marc-André Raffalovich, "The World Well
> Lost IV", from *In Fancy Dress*, 1886.

Perhaps the poem refers only to the poet and his beloved (John Gray); but perhaps, just perhaps, it refers to *us*, men like us, the desired or imagined community of men. If so, then Raffalovich's poem is moving because it asserts, even before we were named, that homosexuals exist as *we*; that we have a set of shared characteristics, of differences from *them*. Of course we are wearing flowers; but more than that, we are sharing what is felt to be a characteristic life; a life forced into exquisiteness, the result of careful choices, discreetly on display, indicating a certain superiority of class or sensitivity, fragile and unnatural. Our lives are wired, like a flower worn as a buttonhole.

The Princess reveals, when she promises her young man a little green flower, that she is part of an elaborate imagery and system of beliefs associated with homosexuality. If the connection seems preposterous, consider the wealth of meaning attributable to a seemingly tiny detail from your own culture. Consider the length of explanation you would have to go to if you were showing a stranger around London in 1982, and he asked you why you were smoking Marlboro cigarettes. You would have to explain how a whole ideology and a whole poetry — America, the Marlboro man, single, rugged, masculine, addicted to nicotine yet indestructibly healthy and virile — were condensed in a single gesture. Consider, also, how the apparently archaic system of attributes of "the homosexual" to which the Princess alludes is still part of your own life. Keep measuring the distance between 1891 and the year of your own reading. Is this nineteenth-century set of references one you recognize, or is everything different now? Talking to a friend on the phone, I said, *You never can tell, Princess*. When I put the phone down I remembered that that's a line from *Salomé*, one that must have stuck in my mind. What else is there? I can't quite accept that in 1886, a hundred years ago, a poet could write, *Our lives are wired like our gardenias*, as if he knew then how I feel now, and could he really have meant *our* a hundred years ago? If that much is constant, how much of his thinking is still current? I certainly think of myself as necessarily sterile, childless by nature not from choice. I still rationalize the extraordinariness of our lives, their deformation under pressure, by reference to the notion of exquisiteness, the careful cultivation of certain skills and graces in a hostile atmosphere, a hothouse. I know that the gay culture of a big city is based on consumption; is expensive. All our pleasures are costly. I certainly collude in a culture which ascribes an overwhelming importance to beauty and youth. We are still flowery; in 1985, when an actor prepared to portray Oscar Wilde on television, he said: *Oscar was very bulky, physically strong and tough. He wasn't the flower everyone thinks of.*

I am not claiming that we have always seen ourselves like this; we are no longer nineteenth-century creatures. The suggestions of effeminacy and aristocracy, for instance, so central to the homosexual imagery of 1889, are clearly marginal to the image of a London leather bar in 1985. Few of us now spend time choosing buttonholes before we venture out. What I am claiming, though, is that some of my most basic ideas about myself as a homosexual man were invented for me by other men, in another time, in another city.

There is a moment in the life of that city which brings the image of the Princess and her green flower into even sharper focus. Raffalovich's image for the 1880s was a white, wired gardenia. The man who actually wore a green flower (it was a green carnation, and he first wore it sometime in the early 1890s) was Oscar Wilde. Some anecdotes claim that he invented and popularized the flower, but it seems more likely that he stole the fashion from Paris, where, it is said, the flower was the insignia of homosexual men. I have never been able to find any proof of that story; but it is certain that Wilde and his supporters wore the flower at the first night of *Lady Windermere's Fan*, 20 February 1892. The *Ladies' Pictorial* for March of that year denounced the green carnation as suggestively *unmanly*, but *The Artist*, in its April issue, announced the literal and unenigmatic details of this curious bloom's creation. It told you how to make your own: *The green carnation to which we have referred is a white carnation, dyed by plunging the stem in an aqueous solution of the aniline dye called malachite green. The dye ascends the petals by capillary attraction, and at the end of twelve hours they are well tinged. A longer immersion deepens the tint.*

With just such unnatural care are our signs perfected. The little green flower is evidence of far more than apocryphal sartorial outrage. Its perfume lingers; by wearing it Wilde ceased to be an individual homosexual with a flair for creating his own public image, and subscribed to a homosexual fashion. He declared himself to be one of an anonymous group of men for whom the wearing of the green carnation *meant* homosexuality.

He slipped a green carnation into his evening coat, fixed it in its place with a pin, and looked at himself in the glass, the long glass that stood near the window of his London bedroom. The summer evening was so bright that he could see his double clearly, even though it was just upon seven o'clock. There he stood in his favourite and most characteristic attitude, with his left knee slightly bent, and his arms hanging at his side, gazing, as a woman gazes at herself before she starts for a party.

They are unhealthy and bring with them the heavy
odours of the hothouse.

The aromatic odours of the south
breathe from the half-shut lotus of thy mouth.

But do you really object to the Green Carnation?
That depends. Is it a badge?
How do you mean?
I only saw a dozen in the Opera House tonight, and all the men who wore them looked the same. They had the same walk, or rather wiggle, the same coyly conscious expression, the same wary movement of the head. When they spoke to each other, they called each other by Christian names. Is it a badge of some club or society?

What if, for a moment, Salomé is offering her infatuated young man a green carnation. If she is, then at this moment she is no longer the Princess of Judea, encased in an outlandish costume by Charles Ricketts, but an opera queen in ordinary evening dress, marked only by his buttonhole, catching the startled eye of another man on the staircase at Covent Garden in the second interval. The little green flower is not simply a decorative flourish, or a subtle hint of perversity. It is a sign. A promise. The two men understand each other's intentions, and they share a desire. Salomé offers the Syrian a little green flower, and then smiles at him (*Look at me*) and knows that he will do what she wants.

The two men to whom I am transferring this moment of drama will also get what they want. Someone passing them on the stair may wonder why they are staring at each other like that, may see the green flower as a clue to their odd and antisocial behaviour, a sign of mystery. For the men who wear it, it is quite definite. Not only does it have a suggestive aura, a perfume; it has a specific meaning, for those who speak the language. Because it implies the possibility of recognition in public, it also implies a distinct way of talking, of declaring allegiance, of living together. This shift from suggestion to sign is a difficult one to trace, but it is one that we all make. Consider the difference (in your relation to other gay men, and to the straight world) between the times when you question another man through furtive eye contact, and the times when you casually, immediately acknowledge another gay man because you are both wearing identifiably gay items of dress. At the moment at which this man — he is a fantasy, so imagine him as handsome as you want, a Whistler portrait or perhaps a period photograph, the stiff collar and clipped hair setting off a square jaw, knees apart — at the moment when he slides the green flower into his buttonhole, takes one step back from the mirror, smiles and turns to pick up his dogskin glove, at that moment he is very close to us. Although neither of the words *homosexual* or *gay* can really be applied to him, since this is the summer of 1891, the summer of *Salomé*, this man has changed himself from a man with homosexual desires into a gay man. We recognize him, and not simply because he catches our eye; we recognize the most basic pattern of his life in the city. Although his London is a very different place, as strange as a green carnation, his life there, like ours, is written in code. Following a very specific set of signs, he lives in a city within a city, hidden and organized.

At what point in your history, at what point in the course of your day, do you stop modestly trying to look attractive to other men, and start dressing in a specifically gay style so as to score, to belong? When do you stop hunting for clues, and start to recognize the signs of a code — code in the sense of a system of signs that no one but us is fully qualified to understand. These codes are not an alternative to, but exist within, the imagery of our "ordinary" lives, just as our "ghetto" is hidden within, but co-existent with, the rest of London. Some of our codes are as peculiar and decorative as the green carnation itself; the notorious (and invaluable) coding of handkerchiefs and keys, in which a careful detail can imply frank and specific need and possibility. Not all are outlandish; quite ordinary clothes which carry no particular impact on the street become, at the moment of entry into a pub or club, signs to indicate your status or taste to a very particular audience; men wearing the same kind of clothes as you. Some are not worn as badges, final touches, or put on as temporary uniforms but are displayed in the body itself: consider the wealth of meaning implied in the transition from a limp wrist to the stern musculature of a well worked-out forearm. The secret signs of urban life are all unstable, subject to fashion. The green carnation is now meaningless. No one now (alas) flashes the details of their desire across a crowded bar in the eighteenth-century language of fans. Presumably we will eventually forget

that it once mattered whether you wore a blue or a black handkerchief in the pubs of London, and in which pocket. But if the
signs themselves are transient, the excitement and importance
of collaborating in their secrecy is not. It remains a step in the
formation of our self-identity. When a statement of identity
becomes as definable as this, even when signalled in a language
as fragile, temporary and exotic as that of flowers or as erotic as
that of fetishized clothing — we sense that it is made on our
terms, not on those of the culture around us.

Three Quotations for the Instruction of the Uneducated.

1890. Narcissus... not one blossom of his loveliness would ever fade.

Dorian Gray gazes into the mirror and christens himself. His
chosen floral synonym hints at his flower-like nature and all that
might imply to a well-read homosexual audience in 1890. (It
does not, incidentally, imply the narcissism which is supposed
to be our psychological hallmark, since that theory had not yet
been invented.) The name shadows his white-tie elegance with
a (potentially) homoerotic image from classical mythology: the
loveliest young man in the world, naked as a Greek. But this
meaning is not necessarily clear to anyone; the text is cautious,
conscious here of its novel-reading public.

*1892. Bobby; Bosie has insisted on stopping here for sandwiches. He
is quite like a narcissus — so white and gold. I will either come
Wednesday or Thursday night to your rooms. Send me a line. Bosie
is so tired; he lies like a hyacinth on the sofa, and I worship him.*

In the privacy of a letter from one man to another, the names
of flowers can become charged with a very particular set of romantic and erotic associations. Oscar wrote this letter during the
(brief) sexual period of his relationship with Lord Alfred Douglas,
and can assume that the other man will understand; that they
talk the same language of innuendo, in which *worship* carries a

Red rosebuds open to maturity.
But none can match this lithe boy's witchery,
Or blooms more innocently indiscreet.

His hand an orchid gave, was strange and rare
And caught my sense in beauteous stare,
Till sunlight for the furnace I forsook,
My heart grew drowsy with a sweet disease;
And fluttered in a cage of fantasy.

sexual meaning, and in which it is recognized that a man is only white and gold when naked.

1894. *It is only the gods who taste of death. Apollo has passed away, but Hyacinth, whom men say he slew, lives on. Nero and Narcissus are always with us.*

Wilde's aphorism was printed in *The Chameleon*, an Oxford undergraduate magazine which came as close to being explicitly homosexual as any publication of the 1890s. This language is spoken in public; but it is given an entirely new meaning by its context. Men here are no longer simply like flowers; the use of their proper names makes clear their identities, their natures. Hyacinthus was the lover of Apollo, killed over an affair with another jealous (male) divinity; Narcissus spurned all the women attracted by his fabulous beauty, and lived only for his own image, the eternal dandy in front of the mirror. The young man in the play called *The Blackmailers*, produced by the lovers John Gray and Marc-André Raffalovich in 1894, is called Hyacinth, In a letter to the pornographer Leonard Smithers on 24 May 1895, Oscar said, *for Narcissus and Hyacinth the Law Inns are best*, referring to the address and tastes of the famously paederastic Reggie Turner. He referred to both Maurice Gilbert (who was later to photograph his corpse) and Charles Hickey, two of Reggie's boys, as *flowers of the narcissus kind*. The word isn't just a euphemism; it denotes an attractive younger man. In 1986 likewise; the phrases *I met a beautiful boy*, and *tonight I am going out with my sisters* indicate not just any gay man but two very special and desirable species. These names of flowers have been written so as to be understood by homosexual readers. This is a set of signs which can be used in public (in a publication) but whose full meaning is clear only to some of us.

This is not a code I would normally understand. The little green flower, the narcissus and the hyacinth would have no perfume, no significance for me if I had not read my way through the library as determinedly as someone cutting and arranging a bouquet of out-of-season flowers. The details of my story have become very particular; I had supposed that this history would

be more ordinary, would reveal ordinary men, that is, men like
us. I didn't imagine that it would be written in this language of
cryptic allusion. How could something as obvious as love or sex
flourish in such a hothouse? How is it that we load so much
meaning into such delicate signs? Does any of this (1890-94)
mean anything to me, now (1981-88)? But I remember that the
signs can't have been easy for Oscar either. They didn't come
naturally. Like me, he didn't always live in London. He moved
there in 1879, and then he too had to learn how to live here,
he had to learn the signs. So it's the same story.

Perhaps I'll wear a green flower tonight.

In my collection, the most beautiful image of a Princess among
flowers is not a fictional one. It is not one that I've had to read
between the lines to savour. Because it is true, a document from
a real and ordinary life, it is as extraordinary and unlikely as any
image from Wilde.

Sometime in the 1860s an exiled Parisian by the name of
Zerline wrote a letter to her friend Javotte. Zerline had been
driven out of Paris by police harassment, The subject of her letter
was another queen, L'Homme Battu, so-called because her jésus
(affair) beat her up so often. Bruised but successful, she earnt
her living as a madam, and earnt enough (her brothel was staffed
exclusively by soldiers) finally to marry her man and carry him
off on honeymoon. At this moment of glory, her sisters crowned
her with a new name. They called her La Princesse Salomé.

> Ma Bichette Cherie,
>   All that you ask me about Saturday's fête is quite
> exaggerated; the guest list was very modest. We were only
> sixteen altogether, very intimate, no strangers. In fact it
> turned out to be more of a family affair than a party; still,
> we managed to dance until two in the morning, when we
> were served with an *exquisite* supper.
>   You know how long La Princesse Salomé has been
> pressing her attentions on this boy — without success. Well,

after a little mature consideration he finally decided to let her... *court* him; with such success that they're now together. It's about time; the princess was going crazy. It was to celebrate the marriage that we all got together on Saturday.

She was wearing a green Metternich robe, with white muslin trimmings and rose pompoms, the whole outfit was ravishing. As for *him*, it was a magnificent dress of white antique silk, done up with *real* camellias. Over a long black hairdo went a full-length veil of *broderie anglaise*, held on with a crown of orange blossom and a diamond aigrette. A great fat solitaire on his right hand... I tell you, in that costume he made me want to bite him, he'd bring the dead back to life.

The princess has fixed everything beautifully. She's promised him 15,000 francs a month.

Anyway, ma bonne Bichette, write soon, because I'm bored and boredom, girl, you know what it does to me.

I'm kissing you on both your big fat cheeks,
yours, Zerline.

The Princess with her promise of flowers seems here to take her real form. The flowery history becomes as hard as it is real, with financial and physical details, not the fantasies of an opera house or bookshelf. La Princesse, though she obviously understood the importance of flowers on such an occasion, no longer needed them to suggest or deviously indicate her desires. Her culture, like ours, included actions as well as hints and allusions. She didn't just promise her man a flower, the morning after, hoping he'd understand. She promised him 15,000 francs; she sent him a message he couldn't fail to understand.

▷

There is a flower that I have not been able to include in this chapter.

In the late 1830s a soldier was arrested with his breeches unbuttoned at ten o'clock at night in a public lavatory in

Westminster. He was with another man. Other circumstances transpired, *inducing a belief that a criminal connection had taken place.*

I have not been able to trace this soldier, to follow up the clues given by the newspaper report. The incident was only reported in the first place because the other man (the princess) was Mr William John Bankes, a Dorset MP. I could probably trace his story — the Duke of Wellington, the Earl of Ripon and the Master of Harrow stood as character witnesses at his trial, he raised £3,000 bail and was acquitted, and he appears in the *Dictionary of National Biography.* Anyone so well-connected must have left records of his life. Besides, he was arrested again for the same offence in 1841.

Again and again it is only the contributions of the privileged to the formation of our lives, and the mythology of those lives, that are recorded. As it happens, the silence surrounding this soldier may be accidental — the British Museum's copy of the newspaper which carried the full details of his arrest has been destroyed or lost. I could find only a transcription of a few details. Anyway, whether this soldier did, like the princesses Salomé, speak a gay language, I'll never know. Even as we discover the most obscure and outrageous fragments of our history, the more obvious and ordinary sources of information are lost. The codes of the past become unintelligible. I have a friend who is fifty-five, but I have never asked him to tell me what beliefs, enthusiasms, heroes or slang were current in London when he was my age. Our history is continually lost.

I want to know. I want to know what actually happened. The soldier was arrested in a cottage just around the corner from the House of Commons. Did his MP hire him regularly? Or did they meet by chance on the bridge over the river, one heading south, the other north? I once met a lover that way.

I want to see a strong white chest in an unbuttoned scarlet jacket. I want to see a photograph of his face. Was he as beautiful as his name?

Private Flower.

3.

FACES

Look at your past face to face. Sit down quietly and consider it.

I was never content with just words on a page, old books. What I always wanted to see was their faces. When I was a boy, I always wanted to know what other men looked like, what men looked like. First we look in mirrors. Later we use each other.

Here then is a collection of the men I've met, a gallery of faces. Place them side by side. Do any of them look "typical"? Do they belong together? The question then, as now, is: *How can you recognize one?* Then as now we were supposed to betray ourselves, give ourselves away. We exhibited symptoms of our condition. But the indications shift. Reading Wilde, I might pick the following biographical items as signs of our shared disease: he passed through rather than stayed within marriage, but still loved his sons (a familiar story); he was cynical almost to the point of political awareness, alienated; he was tainted with distinctive artistic and philosophical enthusiasms; he was violently if occasionally misogynistic, since all the women of his texts are losers, at a loss when faced by virile men, sentimentally happy to submit; he is in love with the Ideal Woman, ignorant of her struggles but eager to wear her frocks. Twenty-two years after Wilde's death, Marcel Proust described a different set of classic symptoms for his Baron de Charlus: it is his female gestures, his talent for interior decoration and the shrill voice in which he

Watch that man.

declares his preference for strawberry juice that gives him away, despite all his efforts to conceal his archangelic homosexuality beneath a brisk, frock-coated maleness. Sixty-three years later, in 1985 (Thursday 3 October), the *Daily Mirror* described another "great homosexual" thus: *There he was, all six-foot five of him, complete with an inch-deep tan, a vast smile and shoulders the width of a lorry. It was Rock Hudson — and he was doing his embroidery. "Don't you think this is pretty,"* he growled *in his bassoon voice.* The same article also noted that he had a mincing walk, drank gin, was square-jawed, had a *long-time friend* and went into agonies of indecision as to whether to eat avocado or melon for lunch. How can such dissimilar sets of signs be symptoms of the same disease?

The hunt is continual, a continual detective story, because the clues change. A sign can be extraordinarily devious; from what does it derive its meaning? Even the most ordinary of contemporary images can assume the fickle potency of extravagant historical costume. Dressed in jeans, leather jacket and a moustache I may walk down a London street feeling entirely confident; at the same time as being a recognizably gay man to those who matter, I also pass as straight. Walking into a bar I look as identifiably gay as if I had made my entrance in a Hartnell gown and tiara. Wearing the same outfit to make a train journey, leaving London for a small town, I simply look like an ordinary man.

So is there anything at all in these pictures that can tell you that they are homosexuals? Perhaps you have to know the names, the histories, the details.

The captions which accompany the faces are taken from A Categoric Personal Analysis for the Reader by Dr Magnus Hirschfeld, first published in Leipzig in 1899, translated and adapted by Xavier Mayne in 1908 or 1909. Are they strange or familiar questions? Do they create a picture of a homosexual, that is, of us? In 1889, the reader could return his or her questionnaire completed, and receive from the doctor an answer to the question, Am I At All An Uranian? What questions do we now address to these faces? Do we question them as ancestors, peers? Do we see ourselves in them, our own bones now revealed beneath these prehistoric features? Do we for instance recognize anything of the homosexual or the gay man in these portraits of The Uranian? The Uranian was one of the prime exhibits of the Victorian bestiary in the period before the invention and categorization of more modern versions of our lives. It was a creature whose soul was trapped in a body of inappropriate sex. It looked, of course, quite unlike our modern selves; I find these portraits old-fashioned, unrecognizable, until I look at the faces again. And pause. And remember that I too often require of myself and my partners a female nature — sexually available, domestic, a surprisingly good cook and at all times attractively dressed — inhabiting a male exterior — sexually aggressive, potent, financially successful, socially acceptable.

But the picture. What was he to say to that? It held the secret of his life, and told his story. It had taught him to love his own beauty.

high social class

Major General Hector MacDonald, D.S.O.
Have you any idea whether before your birth,
or after it, your sex was not quite acceptable
to your father or mother; especially to your
mother? (*It has been said that Lady Wilde had
longed for a girl and, when her second child turned
out to be a boy, she insisted on dressing him in
girls' clothes. This incident will be examined in
considering the problem of Oscar Wilde's sexual
inversion.*)

Simeon Solomon, the young artist. Were you
petted more than most children?

John Addington Symonds. Were you truthful,
industrious, strictly honest in action, and so
forth? (*What do you think of that face*, he said,
is it truthful?)

Phillip and Gerald. Was your sexual desire distinctively influenced by others? Or mostly spontaneous in origin or growth?

Mr Tuke. Would you like children of your own? Would you enjoy caring for them?

The Duchess. Is your wrist flat or round?

Anon. What is the general type of your build — heavy or slight, muscular or not robust, fat or thin, tall or short (for your sex) in stature?

The Duke. Is there much hair on your body?

Mrs Fanny Graham. Are your shoulders bony or muscular? Or round and soft — is there a decided femininity of line to be traced between the base of the neck and the fall of the shoulder?

Frederick William Park. Is your skin soft and fine, or rough and thick?

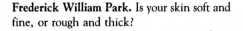

Stella Clinton (The Star of the Strand). Do you whistle well, and naturally like to do so?

Ernest Boulton. Have you ever remarked in yourself a tendency to make a sort of "coquettish" play with your eyes — to "show them off", etc — especially if in conversation with masculine interlocutors?

Is your look and glance from your eyes a quiet, direct, strong one? (Then as now the best way to spot a homosexual was to watch for an effeminate queen. This is not a foolproof method. This portrait of Kitchener hangs opposite that of Burnaby in the National Portrait Gallery. Kitchener is reputed to have fallen heavily in love with Captain Oswald FitzGerald of the 18th Bengal Lancers.)

In grasping anything, as also handshaking and so on, is your grasp vigorous or relatively weak? (Then as now the best way to spot a homosexual was to watch for an effeminate queen. This is not a foolproof method. This portrait, by Tissot, now looks like the height of effeminacy in both subject and style; an elegant, over-dressed, beautiful young man languishing in scarlet on a couch, the paintwork teased and prettified by a fashionable painter. It is a portrait of Captain James Burnaby, who was 6'4" tall, and reputed to be the strongest man in the army. He was not, so far as I know, a homosexual.)

Hugh Mundell. Did you ever suffer from nervousness, including some minor signs of it, such as nail-biting, movements of the eyes, and involuntary gestures and muscular movements? If so, have they passed away now?

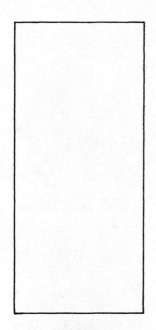

The Pederats [sic].

Mr Gibbings. Do you like to dance, and do you take pleasure in athletics? (The introduction to the Penguin *Trial* can't resist mentioning that Oscar Wilde didn't like games as a schoolboy.)

Mr Hammond. Would you say your face, considered as a whole, was more virile or feminine, if closely considered as to effect? (If this picture was dated 1984, we might reasonably assume that this man had made himself a clone — had adopted a distinctly gay image. But in 1889 short hair and a moustache indicated nothing. Outside of a tiny urban subculture, with its recognizably effeminate queens, there was no image to adopt. Whether in 1984 or 1889, however, this face was constructed for a reason: *I want to look like a man.*)

Walt Whitman. Do you take great care in your personal appearance and dress? Do you care decidedly for ornaments, jewels and jewellery; for bright colours, for what is pretty rather than handsome? (*He... appeared at a costume ball as Anne de Joyeuse, Admiral of France, in a dress covered in five hundred and sixty pearls.*)

Marc-André Raffalovich. Do you incline to any little eccentricities of manner, and to affectations? (*'E'll 'ave 'is 'air cut regular now!*; reputed to have been shouted by a prostitute at Bow Street when the verdict against Wilde was announced.)

Edward Hamblar. Do you feel at ease in the dress of the opposite sex? When so clad, do you easily and naturally pass for a person of that other sex?

Lord Arthur Clinton, MP. Does the theatre deeply interest and affect you? If so, what sort of drama do you prefer? (*I do not say you are it, but you look it, and you pose it, which is just as bad.*)

Anon. Are you particularly fond of Wagner? (*He would sit in his box at the Opera, either alone or with Lord Henry, listening in rapt pleasure to 'Tannhäuser' and seeing in the prelude to that great work of art a presentation of the tragedy of his own soul.*)

That Man. Have you any talent for acting yourself? If so, in what vein?

Anon. Would you say that sexually you are "haunted" and "drawn to one special type of person"?

Anon. How is the normal sexual act performed, if ever that occurs?

A Jewish Wedding, by Simeon Solomon, the young artist, 1866. In *ordinary* social life do you mix most agreeably with your own sex? (Do you want to be with men, or with gay men, or do you wish there was a "third sex" we could belong to?)

Anon. Are you happier in the passion that you receive or that which you feel and vent?

Sir Richard Burton. Have you ever been conscious of betraying or guessing, by a mere look, a brief exchange of glances (quite instantaneous often) that you or another person are homosexuals? This is absolutely apart from any gesture or incident that any third person would understand as hinting as simisexualism. (Are the signs voluntary or involuntary? Of course we know that our sexuality can be placed or replaced like a costume; you can be a leatherman or a lawyer depending on whether you are in the bar or in the office. But there are other less drastic costumes, and they also have their effects. What of the habits of childhood, that long and lasting epoch of concealment and profound good manners, when control of the eyes [don't look at him] and the body [don't touch him] was such a permanent effort that now, perhaps, we have to learn all over again how to give ourselves away.)

Anon. Have you ever seemed to yourself suspected of such a nature, though you have kept it concealed all your life? (*Sin is a thing which writes itself across a man's face... People talk sometimes of secret vices. There are no such things. If a wretched man has a vice, it shows itself in the lines of his mouth, the droop of his eyelids.* Is there something in the eyes? What is my alliance with these men — with any row of beauties, with the man you watch for five seconds on the tube, the stranger, these dead men? I don't, for the record, know anyone who thinks you can tell just by looking, But if you do recognize me, what form does that recognition take? As you step off the train, relieved to be back in the city, and that shock of seeing one, three other gay men just there, walking past, is repeated, are you pleased to be back in the comfortable company of men who happen to dress like you, or do you see brothers, a lover, a lost twin, comrades, a man you would defend?)

Simeon Solomon, the aging homosexual. Are you given to loving where you do not respect? Does such feeling last? Has such a person recurrent power over you?

Him. Do you, all things or most things considered, "feel satisfied" with life, and think that you have, or have had, your fair share of this world's happiness and peace? Or the contrary opinion?

NONE OF US MEN DO LOOK WHAT WE REALLY ARE.

DEMMED GOOD THING, TOO.

4.
WORDS

Mere words! Was anything so real as words!

I have no words for how I love you.

The letter L section of the *New English Dictionary*, the first self-proclaimed "complete" English Dictionary, and which was later to be the *Oxford English Dictionary*, was written from 1901 to 1903. This is the recognized authority on the words from which Wilde and the others contrived their language. It is the guide I am supposed to turn to. It devotes three and a half pages to the definition of the word love. This is a dictionary without peer, and so I read it carefully when it tells me that Love is *that feeling of attachment which is based upon difference of sex; the affection which subsists between lover and sweetheart and is the normal basis of marriage. Love: used specifically with reference to love between the sexes. Love: to have a passionate attachment to a person of the opposite sex.* I have no place in these pages, although I wonder if the editor knew what he was doing when he cited a quotation from A.E. Housman (A *Shropshire Lad* XVIII, 1896) as one of his authorities on the subject: *Oh when I was in love with you, then I was clean and brave.* At the end of the nineteenth century we had no name, even if we had the daring to speak. Under "H" (written between 1897-99) there is no entry for **Homosexual** (although one was included in the 1972 Supplement); there are entries for **Effeminate** (1888-93), **Invert** (1899-1901) and **Pervert** (1904-09), but I looked them up and none of them refer to us. We do appear at considerable length as **Sodomites** and **Buggers**, but these words are used of us, not by us.

According to the *Dictionary*, we had no voice of our own. Don't you believe it. In a different part of the city, our language was spoken, if not recorded. Our history is not a gallery of mute faces. We were using then the words we are using now, the words...

Oh! The shame of it, the shame of it. To tell it is to live through it all again. Actions are the first tragedy in life, words are the second. Words are perhaps the worst. Words are merciless... Oh!

The Dictionary is not a record of speech. Its tone is studiously academic. Among all the books of the library, the most precious and the hardest to find are those which record a man speaking for himself.

> *I met them in Soho Square. He took his hat off respectfully. "Go ahead, and I'll follow," said I... (We) crossed Oxford Street, to a long street, out of which turning up a paved court, he opened with a latch key a door, and up we all went to a first floor over a shop, and into a well-furnished sittingroom, and a bedroom.*
>
> *"Are you fond of a bit of brown" — he asked — I did not understand and he explained. — "We always say a bit of brown among ourselves" — he questioned me — had I been up a man. — "No" — There was no pleasure like it. — "Shall I suck it?" — "You?" — "Yes? — "Do you do so?" — "Lord yes, I have had it so thick in my mouth, that I've had to pick it out of my mouth with a toothpick." ... "Do let me sod you" said he all at once quite affectionately; "I should so like to do it to you and take your virginity."*
>
> A pick-up in the 1870s; from *My Secret Life*, Volume 6 pp 131-4.

A text such as this is moving, one hundred years on, not because of anything that is said, but because of the language that is used to say it. I suddenly realize that I recognize the words, that words I use have been used by others. I wasn't the first to talk like this, or to be attracted to someone because they do. Even if my phrasing sometimes seems forced, tentative, there is always this language, these ridiculous and lovable and necessary words that for a hundred years have been springing from the mouths of those men, the others. I recognize the voice because it is *ours*. In the enforced silence of the library, which is no more a still or quiet silence than the frantic rustling of a busy cottage, there is a moment of intimacy. I understand what this Soho queen of the 1870s is saying. This fragment of her voice, small as it is, tells me that there was a different world (how sweet is that *among ourselves*), a different experience of sex (of course being fucked is a pleasure) and, best of all, a different language (*I did not understand* — the tables are turned for once, it is he who is baffled by our words).

When we speak in our own language, we destroy the notion that talking about a gay experience is even worse than doing it. The best thing about talking dirty is that it makes both the act and the description clean; expressible, visible, imaginable. This technique of deliberate utterance becomes even more powerful when transferred from sex to other areas of our lives. To speak of sex is an abomination so widely acknowledged and broken as to be only a token taboo; *sod* was a common word then, and *fuck* is a common word now. But what if the Soho queen had talked of love? Imagine whispering to another man: *I want you to take care of me.*

Even these whisperings have a history. In the years between Wilde's London and mine the silences of the *Dictionary* were gradually filled in, by more or less hostile languages, languages that spoke of us, named us: medical, legal, "scientific", journalistic languages. Meanwhile, we were speaking for and of ourselves. We were speaking in the first person, rather than being talked about. The voices of confession and allusion, the documentary voice of the case study or the witness stand were not the only voices we used. It is not true that we were speechless or nameless. Our declarations of love were not always as tongue-tied as Basil Hallward's for Dorian Gray, or as Wilde's for Bosie (*You are the divine thing I want... but I don't know how to do it)*. We talked among ourselves.

The position of a young man so tormented is really that of a man buried alive and conscious, but deprived of speech.
Edmund Gosse to J.A. Symonds, 5 March 1890.

The need to talk among ourselves has made our language elaborate. Not for us the literary "realism" and simplicity of expression that is meant to characterize a confession or autobiography. At times we have talked in languages that no one else could understand. Wilde delighted in the language of imported poets and novelists — the strange ones — Mallarmé, the Flaubert of *St Antoine*, Verlaine, Baudelaire, Huysmans — those in whose hands words again became obscure, precious, horrid with new meanings. His delight was not just "literary". On the worst evening of Dorian Gray's life, the evening when he must dispose of the body of a man he has murdered (since such handsome, bloody evidence will surely give away his terrible secret, reveal him for what he really is), on that very evening Wilde has Gray elegantly pick up his copy of the 1881 Charpentier-Jacquemart edition of the poems of Théophile Gautier. He knows that a few obscure words in a foreign language have the power to transport him to another country, another city. He is safe again. Dorian, like his creator, understands the real Importance of Speaking Differently. Only a hundred pages into the novel, we recognize this devotion to *that curious jewelled style, vivid and obscure at once, full of argot and archaisms, of technical expressions and of elaborate phrases.* He could be describing Symbolist literature, or gay street talk, or talking dirty. The obscurity (*Keep your horrible secrets to yourself*) allows the man who writes or talks like this to distance himself from polite language. He can speak more or less in code, create areas of meaning that are open only to the initiate. He can speak to those he wishes to address. In Wilde's exotic, allusive vocabulary, high literature aspires to the status of slang.

This style was to bear its deadliest fruit in the works of Genet, where the thief (the connoisseur) was to litter his texts with *expressions banales, vidés, creusés, invisibles* (banal, empty, worn-out, unnoticed). A true queen, he too hoarded words that no one else fancied, words that no one else loved or could understand, just as Dorian furnished his house with what others would find revolting or incomprehensible. Genet's Divine Divine chooses to frock herself in other, uncherished colours on the day when the whole of France wears the red, white and blue; I hoard all these ridiculous words, the ones my straight friends don't understand, and I write them here. Genet created his style (in a prison cell, just like Wilde) because, he said, he was *"reprenant ma vie"*, keeping hold of his own life, talking to and for himself, keeping hold of his own experience, refusing to let it be taken over, spoken, rephrased in the language of the majority. I remember reading Genet for the first time, when I was a boy in a small town and had no one else to tell me stories, barely understanding a word (since I had no idea that the city was a real place, that one day my friends would be queens, that I too would walk home at dawn in the tatters of my drag, singing and drunk and in love), but sensing that these words were somehow meant for our ears only. And I remember that there are passages in Dorian Gray's story that sound as though they should only be whispered, late at night, by one man to another.

The *Dictionary* does not record a comprehensive gay slang in use in the nineteenth century. But the fragments I've been able to re-collect can be strung together; we had invented at least the idea of another, a different language. Remnants, single words, remain in our contemporary speech. Later, in the forties and fifties, our city was decorated with a gay slang of which whole sentences survive. *Polari* epitomizes the pleasures of being incomprehensible. It was designed to be used, if necessary, within earshot of the naffs; a true code. Now we use it only for pleasure; its expressions, however gorgeous, are now archaic, because we sense that speaking or living entirely in code is no longer a historical necessity. We are in the luxurious position of being able, sometimes and if we choose, to speak plainly for ourselves. We don't have to speak apart from the world. But the words are still there, however, should we need or want them, lying like spare jewellery in the bottom of the drawer. Some of them are replaceable — *hair, face, look, man* and *woman* will do for *riah, eek, varda, omi* and *polone* — if you don't mind the rest of the bus understanding you when you shriek your disapproval of an especially unfortunate haircut. Some are still used from necessity, because there is no precise equivalent. There is no word as accurate as *bona*, unless you are comfortable with the American *hot* as a commendation of an especially striking stranger; *cruise* doesn't capture the tackiness of *troll*; and anyway, who wants to *discuss* rather than *dish* a friend? Mostly the words are dusted off and brought out when we wish to *zhoosh* up the conversation, to announce a particular delight in our queenly style. This style is sometimes talked of as if it was extinct, an anthropologist's relic from *those days*. The *omi-polones* who created the language have changed into other creatures, but our past is not silenced. Gay men whose attitudes and self image are unrestrained by debts to the past can still use the words when they choose; one of the distinctive pleasures of our society is that our past is still with us, the words and the styles of the 1890s, or 1950s, are still being reused and rephrased, played with. Consider the pages of our dictionary again. Do you recognize any of the words there from your own lexicon of gossip, seduction or obscenity? Perhaps you also use the words *queen, trade* or *drag*. Does it follow that you would then be able to talk to, understand, even flirt with those men from ninety years ago, if on some extraordinary drugged evening we could all meet? It would be like costume night at the pub; such strangely different styles and voices, but no one a stranger. Since so much of our verbal finery is handed down, we would recognize some of the words and phrases. Would they still describe the same experiences? Would there be enough for us all to talk to one another?

The city changes. As we no longer speak only in private, or only in slang, or only in books, how do we, now, a hundred years on, talk about our lives? Our style must still always be various, chameleon, our speech adaptable, since we speak in such different locations, public and private (the bus, the bar, the bedroom, the living room); it must also accommodate itself to the fact that not everyone speaks the same language at the same time. East still meets West End; a butch queen can't be butch all the time; and a sixteen-year-old must talk to a sixty-year-old. A particular sentence must have a different meaning for a man who is still waiting to come out, a man who is rarely in a room filled with other gay men, and for a man who goes to a gay pub at least three times a week, who has a lover and has been on the scene for six years. A pub in Soho does not speak the same language as a pub in Wimbledon. An opera queen may want to confess to the crudest desire.

And our speech must constantly acknowledge and play with the fact that there is and cannot be a language that is ours alone. Our words are not entirely under our own control. The city of 1895 which I'd set out to explore only rarely had places that belonged entirely to us (the bedrooms, as always; some cruising grounds that were relatively undisturbed; some private houses). We think of our city as different, as having a relative wealth of spaces that are ours. But the language we use is still partly the language of the city that surrounds us. We use the same words. I would defend the right of any queen to go looking for a "real man"; but hidden in that phrase are straight ideas and straight desires waiting to surprise even those of us who really thought we knew what we were doing. Even those books which are for our eyes only (gay porn) continually phrase themselves in terms of a masculinity, a maleness which is hardly under our control. *Teleny*, published in 1893 and London's first gay porn novel, is full of gay characters and incidents, and certainly included gay men among its authors. It seems to relate our story, in our language, because it seems that this text — hidden for so long and part of our dark, private world, speaking a pornographic language which seems hardly to have changed at all — this text speaks of how close to our history I am, of how we created our own lives and own desires even then. But just at the moment when my reading of it becomes tense and excited, the text will, without pausing for breath, without changing its identity, lapse into vitriolically misogynist, heterosexual phrasings when it wants to eulogize the sole object of its devotion, a man's cock. The idea that this is in any sense a "gay language" evaporates. There is no separate stream of language, a gutter of arcane gossip, that we can claim as ours. Our language has always been part of the other languages which the *Dictionary* assembles. We should not be misled by the fact that a new word, "homosexual", had to be invented to describe us. All the other words we use to articulate our lives come to us loaded with existing meanings, and as we try to use them in new, appropriate ways we must be careful. We must remember that even the simplest words, the word "man" for instance, have a history. They have a life of their own.

▷

All the time, I needed to find our own words, even if I spoke the same language as other men. I knew from experience that this speech would be marred and decorated by resistance and confusion. We have very different things to express. This requires the invention of different mannerisms and inflections to alter the meaning of our city's language. I listened to my peers, to the continuous gay chatter of the past hundred years, and I learnt how to do it.

Our first experience of talking *as* gay men (which is always different from talking *of* gay men) is the experience of lying. I overhear lies again and again in the London of a hundred years ago. How else could Oscar Wilde have possibly spoken to Constance, what would have made any sense to her at all, since a married woman living in Chelsea could never have learnt the language of Lisle Street, or Leicester Square, or the Alhambra. We all still grow up as liars. At a certain point we become expert in describing our experiences falsely, as in "I am going to London for the weekend." Certain words become especially false: "I went out with a *friend*" (although a lover or a man you've just slept with is not a friend) or "I went to the pub" (a gay pub is not just the pub). Wilde was familiar with this mode, the testing of lies. When he tried to explain to Bosie's mother what had happened, he said, *I went as far as I could possibly go.* He took a deep breath and calmly said that he had first met Bosie when he was in *very serious trouble of a very particular character.* One of his characters notes that: *A short primer,* When to Lie and How, *if brought out in an attractive and not too expensive a form, would no doubt command a large sale.* Wilde himself later completed such a text, but it is not short, and is entitled *The Complete Works of Oscar Wilde.*

After this education, we have our revenge. Forced to deny the real meaning of some words, we invest others with senses that the other world would rather keep them pure of. Our revenge on the myth that we are without family, that we lead lives of thoughtless promiscuity, is to redistribute the conventional endearments of family, love and marriage with gay abandon: on our lips, *dear, darling, sister, daddy, boy, baby, mother, girl* are all free to fly from friend to lover to colleague to stranger. Striking even deeper, we describe one another, and those who listen to and watch us as *him* or *her* exactly as and when it suits us. The small phrase *look at her*, as applied to a straight man by a queen holding court with her sisters, redraws the perspectives of the city. It undermines the authority of the dictionary in its function of guide book to our culture's sights and monuments.

Creative abuse, now as then, is not enough. It makes our descriptions of the world seem forever provisional (perhaps that is their, and our, greatest strength). Consider our descriptions of our relationships. Our life is not the life of August 1894, but I always enjoy asking a friend, in all drunken seriousness, *how's the wife?* We both know that there is no useful comparison between heterosexual marriage and the relationship being referred to. But in using the word, I recall the house at 46 Fitzroy Street, WC1, where on 12 August 1894 Alfred Taylor and Charles Mason were arrested with sixteen other men, including one Arthur Marling, taken away in a frock of black and gold lace. Was it in that house that Taylor "married" Mason? What did they wear? If there was a ceremony, at least a gathering of other gay men, then it may have been staged as serious or riotous; but whatever the tone of the evening, it announced their participation in a tradition of gay London (and Paris; remember the Princess Salomé) which reaches back at least to the early eighteenth century. Then queens in frocks were called *mollies*; they refered to sex as *marriage*, to the private room in the pub where they met as the *chapel*, and they staged their own frocked-up ceremonies, behind closed doors, in their own world, on their

own terms. They insolently affirmed the status of a gay relationship by dressing it up in full finery; and their parody expressed
all the real and lovely bitterness we feel that our loves are not
solemnized or publicly celebrated. Oscar wrote to Alfred and
Charles to wish them well in their marriage, and in *The Portrait
of Mr W.H.* in 1889 he wished that Shakespeare might have
pleaded with his boy, *This great friendship of ours is indeed a
marriage.* And so we are right still to use the word (the word still
fits) because we have been using it for so long, because in using
it we invite those men from Fitzroy Street to be our witnesses,
because the word acknowledges how precious and how ludicrous
such love truly is. Of course we continue to use the word; how
could we not? We grew up knowing that "love", "security", "sex"
and "property" should all find their home within "marriage", and
we know that our desire for (some of) these things is as real as
anyone else's. Of course the word is fragile; its complexities of
meaning must be handled deftly. The joke can wear thin; I would
despair if anyone were actually to treat me as his wife, make me
stand behind his shoulder.

And often I wish that I had a word for the kind of couple we
are. I still wish sometimes that I could leave London, that there
was a new language for us, another dictionary entirely. The
existing words can become inadequate, painful. And *I love you*
still seems much harder to say than, *I want you to fuck me.* We
know that declarations of love between men are different, the
words cannot have (we do not wish them to have) the same
weight or meanings that they had for our parents. That is why
I hunt through the *fin-de-siècle* queen's vocabulary for inspiration
and reassurance; that is why I listen carefully when an older man
dusts off the phrases of forty years ago. That is why we love to
chatter, to bitch, to talk in slang, to talk dirty, to learn the
different languages peculiar to our version of the city, to rephrase
ourselves continually. We want the pleasure of saying what we
mean.

▷

Can you say what you mean to him (not just *him*, but any chosen man, anyone to whom you are giving or from whom you are taking any of the pleasures we choose to describe as love)? That is, do you have words for your love, a hundred years after we dared not speak our name, a hundred years after Oscar was speechless with love? (I could hardly continue reading the letters the night I read, *I have no words for how I love you*, in the same letter of July 1894 as he wrote, *I can't live without you*. That he should say that, the man who spent his whole life talking, writing words, the man who everybody said could talk so brilliantly, that he of all men could be silent, at a loss for words.) I've tried calling him *darling*. I've described him as my lover, my boyfriend (but only in joke), my friend, mate, fuck, trick, man (*That's my man*). He is master, husband, wife, affair, love, himself (*Where's himself tonight*), the other half, the number one. Words fail me.

▷

Why do you seem so afraid to say what you mean? *he replied with a most meaning look.*

I'm not at all delicate; but I wish to keep myself out of trouble. Who can tell who hears you out in the streets? *I said.*

Bugger 1) 1882-88 *New Eng. Dict:* In decent use only as a legal term. 2) Now obs. as a gay word, but perennially popular as a term of abuse among heterosexuals. **1870 (?)** ANON. *Secret Life:* We groped together. 'One at a time,' said she. I withdrew my hand, and I knocked against his prick, I laid hold of it, and I believe to this day that the sailor thought it was the girl who was feeling it. I clutched it, and a strange delight crept through me as I drew my hand softly up and down his stiff stander, which seemed larger than mine, 'Hold hard you bugger,' said he.   Also **'Buggers' Charter'**, sl. ref. to 1957 *Wolfenden Report.*

Camp Actions and gestures of exaggerated emphasis. Probably from the French. Used chiefly by persons of exceptional want of character. **1909** WARE *Passing English:* How very camp he is.   Used by gay men in London in 1869 (see ch. 6 Forgery), but first listed in *OED* (Suppl.), 1972.

Cottage Public toilet; public facility used by gay men for recreational sex, e.g. **1909** WARE *Passing English.* Etym. obscure. Said to be derived from the published particulars of an eccentrically worded will in which the testator left a large fortune to be laid out in building 'cottages' of convenience. Gay men have been cottaging and being entrapped by the police at least since the eighteenth century. **1742** *Select Trials*, London: In a little time the prisoner passes by and looks hard at me, and, at a small distance from me, stands up against the wall, as if he was going to make water. Then by degrees he fiddles nearer and nearer to where I stood, 'till at last he came close to — 'Tis a very fine night says he, etc. You know the rest.

Drag 1) Fancy dress; worn occasionally or habitually. **1909** WARE *Passing English:* Theatrical petticoat or skirt used by actors when playing female parts. Also given to feminine clothing to eccentric youths when dressing up in skirts.   **late 1860s** ANON. *Letter* : I am sorry to hear you are going about in drag so much — partly for selfish reasons. I know the moustache has no chance while this sort of thing is going on.   Also 2) Clothing worn to indicate any artificially assumed identity, in **1986** sl. leather drag, butch drag. **1980** BOWIE 'Teenage Wildlife': Same old thing in brand new drag. 3) Clothing worn by full-time or part-time drag queen. Specifically frocks.

Gay 1) **1897-1900** *New. Eng. Dict*: Addicted to social pleasures and dissipations. Often euphemistically: of loose or immoral life. Hence in slang use of a woman leading an immoral life, living by prostitution. **1885** *Hull and Linc. Times*, Dec. 26: She was leading a gay life.   **1870** (?) ANON. *Secret Life*: I ain't gay, said she astonished. Yes you are. No I ain't. You let men fuck you don't you? Yes, but I ain't gay. What do you call gay? Why the girls who come out regular of a night, and gets their living by it.   2) Members of a specific underworld, involving both gay men and gay women, casual and professional prostitutes. **1889** JOHN (JACK) SAUL, *DPP file 1/95/4/2*: I am still a professional *Maryanne*. I have lost my character and cannot get on otherwise. I occasionally do jobs for different gay people.   3) Homosexual, re. homosexuality adopted as an identity. **1986** sl: I am gay.   No evidence this word assumed this specific meaning during c.19. If it had, not even Oscar Wilde would have dared to write (*An Ideal Husband*, Act Two, **1894**): *Mrs Chievely* (languidly): I have never read a Blue Book. I prefer books… in yellow covers. *Lady Markby* (genially unconscious): Yellow is a gayer colour, is it not?

Hung Blessed. **1881** ANON. *Sins of the Cities*: Beautifully formed and well hung.

Married 1) **1903** *New Eng. Dict*: United to another in wedlock; living in matrimonial state.   2) **1861** *New Eng. Dict*: Cards in bezique, etc, the declaration of a king and queen of the same suit.   3) United in a long-term, publicly ackowledged gay relationship, not necessarily monogamous. **1894** WILDE *Letter*: Let me know, if you have time, what Alfred intends doing after next Monday is over, and how you yourself are going on in your married life.   4) Indicative of sexual role played in any gay sexual contact. **1986** sl: She's a married woman.   **1881** ANON. *Sins of the Cities*: I was perfectly agreeable to be his wife or husband, which ever he preferred.   5) Indicative of economically passive role in a sexual relationship. **1895** EDWARD SHELLEY *Wilde Trial*: They called me Mrs Wilde.

Maryanne A queen. **1909** WARE *Passing English*: An effeminate man. **1881** *Sins of the Cities*: That was what the low girls of his neighbourhood called him if they wished to insult him.   **1983** HODGES *The Enigma* (quoting usage in 1951): He was conscious of being called a 'Mary Anne' for intelligence and sensitivity.   **1986** sl: You're just a great mary.

Nancy A queen, but not quite as bad as a queen. 1909.WARE *Passing English*: Effeminate in a slight degree.   1908 MAYNE *Imre*: Lady nancyish rich young men.

Poof 1904-09 *New Eng. Dict*: A kind of elaborate female head-dress fashionable in the late eighteenth century.   2) Heterosexual synonym for sodomite. c.1850 H. SMITH *Yokel's Preceptor*: Margeries, Poofs, Sods. 3) Fashionable offensive gay self-description. **1986** sl: I'm a poof, pouf, pooftah, poofter etc.

Queen One of us. 1889 BARRÈRE *Argot and Slang Dict.* gives **queen** as translation of Fr. *tante*, passive sodomist. Also as proper name, ref. to quean, prostitute. 1870 ANON. *Secret Life* (of women): Brighton Bessie and one or two of my other queens.   1700 ANON. *Characters of Gentlemen*, London: A Dutch merchant of the Italian Humour, known as the Queen of Sheba, frightened over to Germany upon Capt. Rigby's fate, put in forty shillings just before his departure, and what benefits arise are to be spent in drinking his health amongst all the handsome Prentices that frequent Pauls on a Sunday afternoon.   1881 *Sins of the Cities*: Queen Anne, used as name of male prostitute.   1888 WILDE *Letter to R. Ross*: The volunteers played 'God Save the Queen' in my honour. — Can now be applied with infinite variety to anyone whom age cannot wither. **1986** sl: Boot queen, rice queen, Queen Sado-Machisma, self-destruct queen, South-of-the-River queen etc.

Renter A male prostitute. 1893 WILDE *Letter to Douglas*: I cannot listen to your curled lips saying hideous things to me. I would sooner be blackmailed by every renter in London...   1898 WILDE *Letter* (describing Alfred Jarry, author of *Ubu Roi*; not one of Oscar's most perceptive pieces of literary criticism): In person he is most attractive. He looks just like a very nice renter.   Now abbr. to **Rent, Rentboy. 1986** sl: Looks like rent to me.

Rough Gorgeous but (because) dangerous; working-class. May be used to patronize or sincerely to admire. 1900 WILDE *Letter to R. Ross*: Half Rough, half Hylas. **1986** sl: Rough diamonds are a girl's best friend — I just fancy a bit of rough.   See also **trade**.

Sod 1) The only term with which the nineteenth-century dictionary is really happy to describe us, since it makes its opinion of us so clear. 1865 R. MORRIS *Gen. and Ex.* 31, marg: The Wicked Sodomites beset Lot's home.   Also **sodomite, sodamyte, sodomit, sodomighte, soda-**

mite, **sodemyte**. 2) A man who gets fucked and is therefore considered to be a member of a particular species. **1870** ANON. *Secret Life:* He's in the bedroom — such a nice young man, and quite good looking. A young man out of work, wanting bread, and not a sodomite!   Also **sodomish, sodomical, sodomitic**: characteristic of sodomites. 3) As verb, to fuck. 4) Now abbr. as term of abuse. **1986** sl: Dirty sod.

Trade 1) **1909-15** *New Eng. Dict:* Anything practised for a livelihood, or intr. with a sinister implication; to drive a trade in something which should not be bought or sold.   2) Sex: the exchange of sexual commodities. **1869** BOULTON *Letter to Lord A. Pelham Clinton:* I am not going to apologize for being too solicitous today. I will confess I give you reason to think that I care for nothing but trade, and I think you care too little for it, as far as I am concerned. I will try not to talk so much about it when we next meet but I cannot help being excited can I?   3) Sexually available man or men, to be purchased or picked up rather than courted. **1986** sl: I see you've picked up a bit of trade then. Compare: I picked up some shopping on the way home.

5.

EVIDENCE

It is very painful for me to be forced to speak the truth.

Do you ever catch the eye of another man, and he looks *scared*?

When I started all this, I thought Wilde was a comic writer, but now I know better. All of his characters are in terror of being discovered. Their elegance of diction is only a front; anything rather than speak the truth. They sweat, they talk with revealing hysteria about the *secret of life*. The very titles of their stories tell us all we ever need to know about them — *The **Picture** of Dorian Gray, The **Portrait** of Mr W.H., Lord Arthur Savile's **Crime**, The Importance of Being **Earnest*** — for each one contains a secret, a clue, an object, a name, which if it is ever revealed in its true meaning will be either their salvation or their damnation. The stories themselves may give spurious fictional shape to the source of their terror — a poisonous philosophy or prophesy, a professional or marital scandal, a concealed parentage — but we all know now that the dominant theme of this fiction is the necessity of concealment and the fear of revelation. A single word would be enough to call them out of hiding. We detect its presence in *The Complete Works* not so much by the encoded hints of what is lurking beneath the text as by the single, obvious sign of its absence. Dorian Gray announces the significance of his portrait by hiding it, locking it away in his childhood schoolroom. In the course of his evil career he is proved guilty of adultery, debauchery, luxury, greed, vanity, murder and opium addiction. Only one of his vices is hidden, only one sin cannot be named.

Every word that Oscar Wilde wrote is about *it*.

> Could it be that written on his hand, in characters he could not read himself, but that another could decipher, was some fearful secret of sin, some blood red sign of crime?

> It is perfectly monstrous the way people go about, nowadays, saying things against one behind one's back that are absolutely and entirely true.

The crime or sin of homosexuality must never be named. It must be kept a dirty secret, even if it is a widely shared one. This imperative can produce the strangest concealments of the awful truth. In July 1890 the Tory Charles Whibley reviewed *The Picture of Dorian Gray* for *The Scots Observer*. He suggested, cryptically, that it was intended to be read by "outlawed noblemen and perverted telegraph boys". It took me three months of research to find out what he meant, namely that the book was written about and for homosexual men. This is hard to believe, because I thought that in 1890 we were invisible, that our invisibility was a fact; but Whibley's innuendo makes sense only if its references were easily and widely understood, if it refers to a previous occasion on which we had become scandalously and memorably visible. In July 1886 one Henry Newlove, a Post Office clerk, was caught seducing seventeen-year-old telegraph delivery boys (I wonder whether any of them later heard of or read Wilde's novel?). He would make love to them in the office, and then recommend them to a gay brothel at 19 Cleveland Street, W1, where they could earn themselves four shillings commission on a one pound trick. The clients at Cleveland Street included Lord Arthur Somerset (a member of the Marlborough Club and an associate of the Prince of Wales) who fled, when the press got hold of the story, to a happy expatriate life among the homosexuals of Monaco and later Florence. Hence "outlawed noblemen and perverted telegraph boys". Mr Charles Whibley was making himself quite clear; he must have been sure that his readers remembered the headlines of four years earlier, that his allusions would be comprehensible. But he cannot bring himself to say the *word*. All that is permitted is a suggestion, an ominous possibility, a threat, something to be guessed at or detected. Homosexuality cannot be spoken.

More precisely, homosexuality cannot be allowed to speak for itself. In 1895, the year Oscar was found guilty, it was threatening to do just that. Homosexual men were not only talking to one another in private, elaborating images and fantasies and constructing their own enclosed culture, they were also "doing it in public".

Consider the following calendar. It might be read as a summary of the evidence, as evidence against us, or as evidence of our existence. Against each date is a scrap of print, fragments from twenty years in the life of London, the twenty years to 1895. Studies, translations, histories, case histories, poems, novels, foreign novels, children's books, classics, newspapers from *The Star* to *The Times*, police reports, playscripts, reviews, magazines, porn magazines, official proclamations, militant declarations, obscure suggestions, but all in print. Anyone could have read them — constant borrowings and allusions, networks of reference, hints dropped, dedications, quotations, parodies, eulogies, theories, euphemisms, explorations, exhortations, accusations, confessions, anatomies, geographies, vulgarities, obscenities, statements, statements made in support of one another, coherent arguments; a set of contradictions, a mass of details, a babble of voices, references to send me back to the library again and again, arguments which we still have not resolved, recognized and unrecognized faces; evidence still disputed. In each item, sometimes obviously, sometimes discreetly, homosexuality is spoken of and discussed in public. Each item must be tested against a list of invisible questions. We must try to understand whether a text could be understood as referring to us, our lives, only by one of us; or could it be understood by, say, a judge and jury, an ordinary educated reader of novels, a working-class reader of a working-class newspaper, a member of the public. Do these fragments provide evidence of concealment of our lives, or are they declarations; if you speak in code, obliquely, are you really trying to reveal something, or to conceal something? Which language is being spoken? Are all these fragments evidence of a single phenomenon, or do they trace many lives? As evidence, are they "convincing"? Convincing of what?

I started my collection by copying quotations out of old books and pinning them to a wall. I started to collect them for an obvious reason; I thought there was nothing, and so wanted to hoard what I found. Only later did any patterns emerge; only later did I confine myself to collecting things only from these particular twenty years. This erratic labour of love had a very particular inspiration. In 1982 I read the British Museum's copy of a "pornographic" poem, anonymous, dated 1866. The poem is *Don Leon* — the poet wrapped himself in the cloak of Byron in order to say what he wanted. In the back of this old book there is an appendix, a kind of scrapbook or commonplace book, "evidence" assembled in the 1830s and 1850s. The scrapbook mostly comprises newspaper reports of legal prosecutions involving gay men. I know it isn't strictly accurate to refer to *gay* or even *homosexual* men in the 1830s, but what else am I to call a man who had such a sense of his own identity that he could collect, preserve and inter-connect all this disparate information about other men for whom he felt such an obvious sympathy? His cuttings are mixed in with scraps of erotica and quotations, literary exotica, quotes from Ovid, Petronius, Horace, Castiglione, Pepys. On my wall a handsome face is pasted up next to a fragment from a novel, next to the latest report of an arrest or persecution. The smallest items of information can be surprising, Did you know that in 1833 a man could be so angry with the current intellectual and medical "theories" about his life that he would make a point of noting, after quoting some especially inflammatory pronouncement, that *it does not follow as a natural consequence that paederasts are misogynists*. That, even then, we were already refuting that version of our lives. Sometimes you have to stop and re-read and think why this magpie has included a particular text. One of the strangest police reports is quoted as follows:

> Bow Street — Inspector Reason and Sergeant Hunt, officers appointed to enforce the regulations of the Common Lodging-House Act, attended before Mr Jardine to prefer complaints against several of the occupiers of rooms in Wyld Court, Drury Lane — one of the worst localities within the jurisdiction of the court... The usual caution was given the defendants, but when Hunt visited Carthy's rooms, in which four persons only were allowed by the regulations, he found two dirty beds on the floor, the first of which contained the defendant, his wife, a girl of sixteen, and two boys aged fifteen and ten; the second a man and his wife, a girl of thirteen, and two boys (fifteen and thirteen)... There were no partitions of any kind to separate the sexes. The total number of persons in this room was twenty, but seven only were allowed. Mr Jardine, after commenting with indignation upon the swinish manner in which these people huddled together, without a sense of decency or morality, fined Sullivan £5, and committed him for two months in default.

Taken in context (all the other cases included in the scrapbook deal with sex between men) this extract suggests that although the judge saw overcrowding among the poor only as a sign of their indiscriminate and criminal indecency, the compiler of the appendix to *Don Leon* saw it as evidence of something to do with his own life, evidence that the overcrowded bedrooms of central London were the site of frequent and casual homosexual contact. With this single quote, arbitrarily rescued in an unlikely place, the history of gay London is altered. If we can trust this author, then we can assume that his scrapbook here records a part of our city about which we know almost nothing. We know little of "ordinary" lives in this period, lives lived in stinking and over-crowded rather than public or fashionably furnished rooms. This odd detail stuck in the back of a book makes us think again.

Another entry alters our perception of the evidence of our past in a different way. It suddenly makes this history seem as immediate as a phone call from a distressed friend, short of change in a call box. The entry in question records the death of Mr Stanley Stokes, in Brighton in May 1836. The report seems originally to have been written by someone who didn't care very much, but its whole meaning is transformed by the way it has been preserved. Sitting in the library and reading this text was one of the strangest experiences of my research. I suddenly found myself trying to cry quietly so that I wouldn't disturb the other people working at the same desk.

> In the *Ledger* newspaper we read the following account of a gentleman who cut his own throat, driven to desperation by the most dastardly and ignoble treatment of a brutal mob at Brighton: "An inquest was held at Brighton on Tuesday on the body of Mr Stanley Stokes, a proctor, of Doctor's Commons, who cut his throat in East Street in that town on Saturday night. Saunders, the landlord of the New Ship Hotel, on Saturday night had laid plans to interrupt him, and accompanied by a crowd of fellows, after charging him with an indecent assault on a boy's person, they simultaneously mobbed him, smeared his face with tar, gave him severe blows to the head with fists, sticks etc., until he fell down. While undergoing the persecution, the unhappy man, in the open street, drew a penknife from his pocket, and inflicted a severe wound in his throat."

He died two days later. Also in 1836, James Stanhope, friend of the Oxford MP Richard Herbert, was exposed as a homosexual in a libel suit, and hanged himself. A Mr Bennett, accused in the *Age* newspaper of "improper intimacy" with a valet from Brussels named Valle, killed himself on 16 June 1836. I copied these three entries and carefully placed them side by side on my wall.

These scrapbooks draw no conclusions. They only bear witness to the need to collect and keep and compare notes. They amass evidence, reminding us that it is never true that we are silent, or safe, or that our speech is safe from those who would silence or forget us. The scrapbook is the true form of our history, since it records what we remember, and embodies in its omissions both how we remember and how we forget our lives. We are always held between ignorance and exposure.

My contemporary collection is as eclectic as its model. I simply moved from book to book, following clues, reading anything and keeping everything. The wall was soon covered in paper. Looking to my history, I am generous. I am fascinated by everyone. I suppose I treat past lives with this curious and indiscriminate respect because I want to know everyone's story. This behaviour is in marked contrast to that determined by our current tastes. Observing our contemporaries, we choose to know nothing of other people's lives, to remember little of other people's stories. This city is, after all, big enough and divided enough for us to live happily ignorant. We don't want to know.

Alongside the quotations in my collection (assembled over four years) there is another text, equally personal, which is not printed here. It is a list of names and addresses recorded in the diary of the first four years of my life here (the diary we all kept). In this diary, encounters with men, details of sex and of infatuations, books read and fashions imitated are all listed with equal and equally sincere enthusiasm, as if by writing it down I could make sense of it all. The ridiculous stream of events (ridiculous events) is carefully divided into days, nights, years. Each historical fragment could be paired with a contemporary detail, the name of the man I thought of as I read that, the name of the one who loaned me the book, the one who distracted me from that anger. Both collections are somewhat random; neither is a summary, the result of a systematic search. In the twenty years from 1875 to 1895 Oscar Wilde changed from the student at Oxford to the married man in Chelsea who lived too many lives and appeared too much in public. And from 1982 to 1986 I changed, and the city changed. It now looks, as I re-read, as if the quotations somehow lead to the crucial events of 1895. They become more explicit, the voices louder and clearer and more impudent, as if demanding that the crisis occur. In the final five years especially there is a new stridency and articulation in the voices, a sense that the silence is being challenged. In a similar way, my diary entries for the past few years seem to lead up to the man I am now.. But in neither case can there have been any intention. A diary lies if it gives too neat a pattern to its furiously assembled history, if it never surprises you with its events and choices. So why do we keep diaries? So we can look them up later and see what happened, and maybe then say what it meant, and for whom.

The next time some man asks me what it feels like, I'll bind all these fragments together and lend them to him for a night, and then ask him if he felt the same way reading them as I did. All I can do is lay them out, preserve them as a witness. I always thought that we were invisible, that our invisibility was a fact; now I lay down my pieces of evidence one by one, in defiance of all those who are ignorant of our culture. I will inscribe above them a quotation from the beginning of Wilde's own summary of the evidence of his career, the composition made from memory in the cell at Reading, *De Profundis:*

I went as far as I could possibly go.

I went as far as I could possibly go.

1875. Sodomy was practised by the nations of Cueba, Careta and other places... some of the head men kept harems of youths who, as soon as destined to the unclean office, were dressed as women, did women's work about the house, and were exempt from war and its fatigues. They went by the name of "camoyas".
>Hubert H. Bancroft, *The Native Races of the Pacific States of South America.*

Mr Bancroft claimed to have read 1,200 books while preparing this five-volume monument to scholarly homophobia. They are filled with such details of how other societies, far from London, honoured or persecuted homosexuals in the mid-nineteenth century. For whom was this information intended?

1877. That his affinity with hellenism was not merely intellectual, that the subtler threads of temperament were inwoven in it, is proved by his romantic, fervid friendships with young men. He has known, he says, many young men more beautiful than Guido's archangel...

> Walter Pater (on the letters of Winckelmann to Friedrich von Berg), *Studies in the History of the Renaissance* (second edition).

This is the volume which Wilde was to remember in Reading as *that book which has had such a strange influence over my life.* Edward Carpenter, in 1894, wrote in *Homogenic Love* that he was especially inspired by this text. Three translations of explicitly homosexual sonnets by Michelangelo were cut; but the meditation on the "troubled colouring" of Winckelmann's letters was expanded.

1878. Therefore because I cannot shun the blow
I rather seek, say who must rule my breast,
Gliding between her gladness and her woe?
If only chains and bonds can make me blest,
No marvel if alone and bare I go,
An armed Knight's captive and a slave confessed.

> J.A. Symonds, *Sonnets of Michael Angelo Buonarroti and Tommaso Campanella.* One of Michelangelo's love poems dedicated to Tommaso Cavalieri.

1879. There are moods and phases of passion which do not lie within the domain of art.

> *The Westminster Review.*

Symonds had changed the sex of the beloved in the poems entitled "Stella Maris" from male to female before publishing them; but still the critics noticed that something was wrong, and tried to silence him.

June 1879. There was an old person of Sark
Who buggered a pig in the dark
The swine, in surprise,
Murmured; God blast your eyes,
Do you take me for Boulton or Park?

The Pearl, Vol. 1.

Eight years after the event, a "facetious" straight pornographic
magazine pays tribute to two famous London transvestites arrested
in 1871. While Oxford academics argued about hellenism and
the classical tradition, up in the West End of London we were
famous.

October 1879. Opening his trousers and letting out his beautiful
red-headed cock... the sight was too exciting for me to restrain
myself, the cigarette dropped from my lips, and going on my
knees in front of him...

The Pearl, "Sport among the She-noodles".

Casual sex between adolescent boys provides a little light relief
(also another opportunity to discuss how big, manly and vigorous
the boys are) in a catalogue of heterosexual rapes and "seductions". Is this part of our history?

1881. We all do it my dear. It's the commonest thing possible in
the army. Of course we all do it for the money, but we also do
it because we really like it. So far as I can see, all the best
gentlemen in London are running after soldiers. One gentleman,
a nobleman, had me in his own house, in the room next to his
wife's boudoir. I heard her laughing, or playing the piano, while
her husband was on his knees, sucking my prick. I know two
men in the Blues who are regularly kept by gentlemen, and one
has an allowance of two hundred a year.

Private Fred Jones in *Sins of the Cities of
the Plain or, Confessions of a Maryanne*.

The 1934 Paris translation of *Teleny* claims that in 1899 Wilde
bought a copy of this from a bookshop in Coventry Street, Leicester Square, which is two streets from Lisle Street, the home of

Jack Saul, the famous (real) gay prostitute whose memoirs these claimed to be. Jack's sex life begins at the age of ten, when he plays with the other boys at school (as in every other gay biography, we want to know if he was "always like that"). Working in London as a delivery boy, he is introduced to aristocratic gay society by a Mr Ferdinand, who employs him as a prostitute. He gets a job at a private club in Portland Place under the drag name of Miss Eveline, and meets men who can afford the hundred guinea membership fee. He meets and has sex with Boulton and Park at a drag ball at Haxell's Hotel on the Strand. (*I would rather have had Boulton than anyone. His make-up was so sweetly pretty that I longed to have him, and him to have me.*) After the ball they take him home for a little mild bondage and birching. (*Ha, now we have her, the rude little slut!* exclaimed Laura.) His story includes frequent violent assaults on women. He claims to have been sucked off in the shrubbery at a garden party hosted by the Prince of Wales, which he attended, dressed as a sailor, with Lord Arthur Pelham Clinton. He attends an orgy in Grosvenor Square, and describes the Star and Garter in Richmond as a pub frequented by men like himself. The opening sequence of the book includes a realistic description of the rarest of all events in pornography: a long, expert and mutually enjoyed fuck between two men. In 1884 Saul was to be a witness in the Dublin Castle affair, and in 1889 he was questioned by the police about his life at Cleveland Street, his nocturnal trolling with his colleagues Lively Poll and Queen Anne. The Attorney General refused to prosecute him, since his evidence was too filthy to be made public in court. Is it too filthy for us too?

1881. A glimpse through an interstice caught
Of a crowd of workmen and drivers in a bar-room around the
    stove late of a winter night, and I unremark'd seated in a corner,
Of a youth who loves me and whom I love, silently approaching
    and seating himself near, that he may hold me by the hand,
A long while amid the noises of coming and going, of drinking
    and oath and smutty jest,
There we two, content, happy in being together, speaking a
    little, perhaps not a word.
                                        Walt Whitman, *Leaves of Grass.*

A glimpse of gay Manhattan as real as Jack Saul's London — included in the "Calamus" section of the Tubner and Co. London edition of Whitman's poem.

9 July 1881. SERIOUS CHARGE. John Cameron alias Sutherland, a corporal in the 2nd Battalion of the Scots Guards, was charged with one Count Guido zu Lynar, Secretary to the German Embassy, with the commission of an atrocious offence, at a coffee-house situated in Lower Sloane Street, Chelsea, where the two accused were apprehended.

Daily Telegraph.

The Cadogan Hotel, where Wilde was arrested, is close by, on Sloane Street.

1883. Spreaders of health (better than any doctor) to individuals,
    to the diseased prostrate nations, sustainers of ridicule, clearers
    of the ground laden with the accumulated wreck and rubbish
    of centuries,
Lovers of all handicrafts and of labour in the open air, confessed
Passionate lovers of your own sex,
Arise!
Heroes of the enfranchisement of the body (latest and best gift
long-concealed from men),
Arise!
    Anon. (in fact, Edward Carpenter), *Towards Democracy.*

Published by John Heywood (Manchester and London), who had also published an account of the lives and trials of Boulton and Park in 1871. Did he have an axe to grind?

1883. The true Hellenic manifestation of the *paederastic* passion [is distinct from] the effeminacies, brutalities and gross sensualities which can be noticed alike in imperfectly civilized and in luxuriously corrupt communities.
    J.A. Symonds, *A Problem in Greek Ethics.*
    ("Ten copies printed for the Author's use.")

1884. Jack was near enough for me
Not to seem to and to see,
Handsome, sulky, fair and nice,
Hard as iron, cool as ice.

> Marc-André Raffalovich, "A Story in Four Songs", from
> *Cyril and Lionel, A Volume of Sentimental Studies.*

Most of the poems leave the gender of the significant other significantly vague; in this poem Raffalovich puts himself in drag in order to make his description of Jack at least seem decorous.

3 July 1884. A thick veil must be cast over its more objectionable features, and the respectable portion of the public will be satisfied to await only the result.

> *The Times.*

The Times deprives its readers of the juicy details of one of the year's most scandalous lawcases, The Dublin Castle Affair. A headline takes away our history... Gustavus Cornwall (aka "The Duchess"), Secretary General of the Post Office, Dublin, sued William O'Brien MP for libel after he had suggested that Cornwall was a bugger. The libel was upheld and Cornwall arrested for buggery. The scandal made public the gay life of Dublin; the characters included Malcolm Johnstone (The Maid of Athens), Martin Kirwan (Captain of the Royal Dublin Fusiliers, aka Lizzie), George Tyler (who claimed he'd had sex in one of the hothouses in Dublin's Botanic Gardens on Boxing Day 1881), our friend Jack Saul and a host of gay friends, lovers and prostitutes.

1884. Like the Ephebe of antiquity, he makes his bed at the feet of Luxury.

> Rachilde and Talman, *Monsieur Venus* ("Roman Matérialiste").

Published in Brussels, but imported and read by both Symonds and Wilde. A society lady named Raoule (*the Christopher Columbus of modern Romance*) and le Baron (*an ex-officer of the Hussar, a brave duellist, but terrified nonetheless*) fight to the death for possession of the body and soul of the mysterious, gorgeous, androgynous, blonde and sexually passive Jaques Silvert, Monsieur Venus himself, (*he exists my friend, and he's not a hermaphrodite, and he's not impotent, but a handsome twenty-one-year-old man in whose body a soul of female instincts has taken residence*), hashish addict, transvestite and florist. Raoule, in butch drag, makes Jaques her wife; but he runs off in a frock to le Baron, who then beats him to a bloody pulp as he lies naked on satin sheets. In the final duel, Jaques is shot by le Baron. His immortal dying words, gasped as the lovesick Baron kisses him for the last time are, *No, leave me alone, your moustache is tickling me.*

1885. I know a lad with sun-illumined eyes,
whose constant heaven is fleckless of a cloud;
He treads the earth with heavy steps and proud,
As if the gods had given him for a prize
Its beauty and strength.
Rev. E.C. Lefroy, Echoes from Theocritus.

1885. France, Iberia, Italy, Greece, North Africa, Asia Minor, Mesopotamia, Chalaea, Afghanistan, The Punjab, Kashmir, China, Japan, Turkistan, the South Sea Islands and The New World...
Sir Richard Burton, the "Terminal Essay"
from The Arabian Nights.

A history and geography of a promised Land in which *the Vice is endemic and popular.* This is the Victorian gentleman-scholar at his maddest, proposing the existence of a *Sotadic Zone*, making the occurence of homosexuality a climatic phenomenon, possible only within a map *bordered westwards by the Northern shores of the Mediterranean (N. Lat. 43°) and by the Southern (N. Lat. 30°)...*

1886. Who often walked lonesome hills, thinking of his dear
    friends, his lovers,
Who pensive, away from one he loved, often lay sleepless and
    dissatisfied at night,
Who knew too well the sick, sick dread lest the one he loved
    might secretly be indifferent to him,

Whose happiest days were far away, through fields, in woods,
  on hills, he and another, wandering hand in hand, they twain,
  apart from other men,
Who oft, as he sauntered the streets, curved with his arm the
  shoulder of his friend — while the arm of his friend rested
  upon him also.
Whitman, Poems, London edition,
edited by W.M. Rossetti.

The preface announces the removal of "every poem which could
with any tolerable fairness be deemed offensive to the feeling or
morals or propriety in this peculiarly nervous age."

1887. He remarked how spare and muscular were the stranger's
legs and arms.
Edward Irenaeus Stevenson, White Cockades.

Andrew Boyd, a motherless sixteen-year-old only son with blonde
hair and well-developed legs of his own, catches his first glimpse
of Bonnie Prince Charlie in an adventure story for boys with a
twist. It concludes by noting: "History, which seldom has space
for such trifles, does not state that ever after at the Prince's side,
upon sea or land, there was a Highland lad..." Stevenson was
an American journalist, theatre critic and novelist who also wrote
under the name Xavier Mayne.

1887. Probably his unorthodox views had as much to do with
accusation of "vices sent from hell"... it is certain that he had
friends amongst the finest-natured men of his time.
Havelock Ellis, appendix to Christopher Marlowe,
Plays, edited by J.A.Symonds.

Ellis also reprinted and approved of two of Marlowe's tastiest
witticisms: "St John the Evangelist was bedfellow to Christe",
and "All thei that love not tobacco and boys are fooles."

1887. He hesitated with a sweet, half-timid smile. "Well, I must
explain — I don't know how to address you." Such titles as

108

captain, dear captain, etc, would certainly no longer meet our case. What was it to be? I made answer: "Oh, it is perfectly simple..." (and I racked my brains fruitlessly for what was so simple). "It is quite simple. You have only to put Dear Brother, which will be quite true, and a correct commencement to your letter."

Pierre Loti, *My Brother Yves*, translated by Mary P. Fletcher. (Published, like Symonds's *Marlowe*, by Viztelly and Co.)

The story is of the love between "Captain Pierre" and the Breton sailor Yves Kermadec, "tall and spare like an antique statue," tattooed on the left breast with an anchor and on the right wrist with a bracelet and a fish.

1888. I have not wronged thee, by these tears I have not,
But still am honest, true, and hope, too, valiant;
My mind still full of thee; therefore still noble.
Let not thy eyes then shun me, nor thy heart
detest me utterly; oh look upon me,
Look back and see my sad sincere submission!
How my heart swells, as even 'twould burst my bosom.
Fond of its gaol, and labouring to be at thee!
What shall I do, what say to make thee hear me?
                    Jaffier to Pierre in Otway, *Venice Preserv'd*, 1682.

Noel Roden, who shocked J.A. Symonds by openly and happily gratifying his taste for the Household Cavalry, was appropriately employed by Ellis to write the preface to the Mermaid edition of Otway. He attributed to the passionate friendship of Pierre and Jaffier the characteristic role play of a nineteenth-century affair between a "masculine" and an "effeminate" invert; Jaffier is *luxuriantly feminine in his sensibility* while *his dearest friend* Pierre is *a man of sterner fibre.* He also tried to trim the shadowy figure of Otway himself to our history, noting that *the ardour and constancy of Otway's personal attachments are very notable.*

1888. An overdevelopment of the intellect, combined with an exaggerated appreciation of the physical, disappointments in love

— these, we think, are the usual causes...
Paul Verlaine, preface to Henry d'Argis, *Sodome.*

Verlaine's preface excuses this biography of a homosexual by describing it as a case study, an investigation into the causes of a disease. It ends with the hero-victim dying in an insane asylum screaming "Sodome! Sodome!" Wilde read it and in a letter to the home secretary requesting early release from Reading Gaol (2 July 1896) ascribed his fall from grace and suffering to a form of "erotomania" identical to that described here.

December 1888. He would sometimes be accompanied by the slim, fair-haired Court pages, with their floating mantles, and gay fluttering ribands; but more often he would be alone.
Oscar Wilde, *The Young King.*

An image of Oscar and his boys slipped innocently into the Christmas issue of *The Lady's Pictorial.*

1889. Open this book where these letters stand
And write again in a bold, round hand:-
"He loved boys and thieves and sailors..."
Charles E. Sayle, Untitled, in *Erotidia,*
published by George E. Over, Rugby.

Some bitter moments in a crowded place
And then I know that I shall see, instead
Of many faces, only one tired face,
Your darkened eyes and lips carnation-red.
Marc-André Raffalovich, from
It Is Thyself (Scott, London).

A hundred and forty-six pages of chaste, fierce, original, intimate love poems from one man to another. I still keep this pinned over my desk.

July 1889. Hyacinth and Apollo, Narcissus, Plato and Agathon, Alectryon (a *boyfriend* of Mars), Tenes (a well-favoured and handsome lad), Iolas (the youthful favourite of Hercules), the Festival of Diana Orthia, which featured the whipping of Spartan youths. (The expression of a steady and determined endurance under pain in a young face would task the talent of an artist surely, as would the complex emotions of pride, compassion and love in that of the father, elder brother or lover who would be the lad's natural aid or attendant at the sacrifice.)

> *The Artist and Journal of Home Culture* (making its
> monthly suggestions for subjects for pictures).

This is, as far as I know, the first recorded instance of the word boyfriend used in a gay context.

26 October 1889. Edward Hamblar, sixty-one, respectably dressed and described as a ship's joiner, was charged with disorderly conduct and being dressed in female attire. Insp. Ferret, H. Division, stated that on Saturday night he saw a crowd of about six hundred persons in Bromley Street, Ratcliffe. He went up and found the prisoner detained by two men. He was dressed in woman's attire. He was wearing the hat and veil produced, also a black jacket, print dress, two flannel petticoats, and a large dress improver. Witness told Hamblar he should arrest him, and took him to the station. All the people around the prisoner imagined he was "Jack the Ripper", and the excitement was very great in consequence. Prisoner gave an explanation of his conduct. Prisoner said it was only a freak. Mr Saunders said the prisoner had been guilty of very foolish conduct. He did not make a handsome woman (laughter).

> *The Illustrated Police News.*

1890 (?). She shut the door and left me with him. He was not much like a working man, and looked exceedingly clean... no one could have imagined him as a man, so round, smooth, white and womanly was his entire backside and form... immediately I had an ineffable disgust at him — I could scarcely be in the room with him — he said, "you've made me bleed" — at that I nearly vomited.

> "Walter", *My Secret Life*, Vol. 8.

An exhaustive eleven-volume pornographic autobiography of a married man, detailing his sexual life from boyhood to middle age. It is at times nauseating and unbearably misogynistic (he says of one prostitute: "I could tell more of her history, but this is my life, not hers"). One of the text's main themes is "Walter's" growing obsession with other men's penises (for which he uses at least twenty-three different words) and with sodomy as a means of proving his virility. In volume 8 comes "the most daring fact of my secret life": he hires a male prostitute, locks the door and inexpertly buggers him.

28 February 1890. In the streets, in the music halls, you have these wretched creatures openly pursuing their avocation. They are known to the police, yet the police do nothing to stop this sort of thing... these poor and wretched creatures live to minister to the vices of those in a superior station. Is there any man who will not feel indignant that boys employed in one of our public offices should be tempted into indecencies more gross than were committed under Louis XV?

Henri Labouchère, in the House of Commons, accuses the government of covering up the scandals over the Parnell letter (1890) and the involvement of Lord Somerset in the Cleveland Street trials.

April 1890. Deep blue water as blue as can be,
Rocks rising high when the red clouds flare,
Boys of the colour of ivory,
Breasting the wavelets, and diving there,
White boys...

> F.W. Rolfe, aka Baron Corvo, in *Arts Review*
> (vol 1, 4), celebrating the finer things in life.

20 June 1890. Why is it, Dorian, that a man like the Duke of Berwick leaves the room of a club when you enter it? Why is it that so many gentlemen in London will neither go to your house nor invite you to theirs? You used to be a friend of Lord Stavely. I met him at dinner last week... Stavely curled his lip, and said

that you might have the most artistic tastes, but that you were
a man whom no pure-minded girl should be allowed to know,
and whom no chaste woman should sit in the same room with.
I reminded him that I was a friend of yours, and asked him what
he meant. He told me. He told me right out before everybody.
It was horrible! Why is your friendship so fatal to young men?
There was that wretched boy in the Guards who committed
suicide. You were his great friend. There was Sir Henry Ashton,
who had to leave England with a tarnished name.

> Oscar Wilde, *The Picture of Dorian Gray*.

The Cleveland Street scandal was only eight months old, and
that too featured boys in the Guards and a disgraced Lord who
had to leave England. The charges against Dorian are dangerously
topical and almost specific.

1891. Frank, try to see me as I am. I am as God made me, and
I cannot help it; I would have been different if I could...

> Louis Couperus, *Noodlot*, translated by Clara
> Bell, edited by Edmund Gosse.

Gosse's editorial choice had a distinct purpose; he says in the
preface that "much is freely discussed, even in the novels of
Holland and of Denmark, which our race is apt to treat with a
much more gingerly discretion."

In April 1891, *The Picture of Dorian Gray* was published in book
form by Ward, Lock and Co. The text was changed significantly
from the magazine version of 1890, and the changes indicate
that the reader may, if he so wishes, accuse Wilde of removing
the sodomitical taint from Dorian's story. For instance, a sentence
has been taken out of Basil Hallward's declaration of love to
Dorian: *It is quite true that I have worshipped you with far more
romance of feeling than a man usually gives a friend. Somehow, I
have never loved a woman.* The fact that Wilde felt obliged to
remove this sentence makes its meaning quite clear. Did anyone
notice?

1891. The young man wore a beige felt hat, perched far back on his head, soft, wide-brimmed and with an eagle feather stuck in the ribbon. The collar of his shirt, loose and low-cut, revealed a sinewy and soft-skinned neck.

> Gyp (Countess Sibylle Gabrielle Marie Antoinette de Martel de Janville), *Un Raté* ("A Failure").

J.A. Symonds noted at the time: "What a number of Urnings are being portrayed in novels now! *Un Raté, Monsieur Venus,* this *Footsteps of Fate* — I stumble on them casually and find the same note."

1891. If we cannot alter your laws, we will go on breaking them.

> J.A. Symonds, *A Problem in Modern Ethics*: (Fifty anonymous copies printed for his private use in 1891; one hundred public copies, "addressed especially to medical psychologists and jurists," 1896.)

October 1891. ...you leap and fling
Your weight against his passage like a wall,
Clutch him, and collar him and rudely cling
For one brief moment till he falls — you fall.

> Rev. E.C. Lefroy.

A paean to an adolescent goalkeeper, printed in *The Artist*, with a note suggesting that any reader wanting to know more of the connection between True Art and Bodily Culture should "read the *Calamus* of Walt Whitman".

1892. I recalled what the old man told me: that male-loving men were accustomed to meet on the E. Promenade. After a hard struggle, and with a beating heart, I went there, made the acquaintance of a blonde man, and allowed myself to be seduced.

> Krafft-Ebing, *Psychopathia Sexualis.*

Krafft-Ebing's concern is to create a categorization of sex, structured around the distinction between "Psycho-sexual hermaphrodites" (female men) and "Homo-sexual individuals or Urnings" (male homosexuals). His categories are illustrated by individual case studies:

> Case 86: Handkerchief fetishism in a case of Contrary Sexual Instinct.
> Case 94: I preferred young fellows, from sixteen to twenty-five years old, without beards, but they had to be handsome and clean. Young labourers dressed in trousers of Manchester cloth or English leather, particularly masons, especially excited me.
> Case 123: I do not smoke or drink, and can neither whistle, ride nor do gymnastic feats... Real men, in close-fitting uniforms, make the deepest impression on me.

1892. I don't know what it is, but there is something about him different from other people, I couldn't say precisely what...

Louis Couperus, *Ecstasy*, translated by A. Texeira de Mattos and John Gray.

1892. Yet he felt there was something wanting to tinge his life
   with joy —
He lived and spoke like a statesman, but felt and thought like
   a boy.
He dreamed he stood by a River that flowed through a flowery
   land,
And boys like himself were thronging its shores in a happy band.

John Gambril Nicholson, "Through the Gates of Sleep in Love" in *Ernest, A Sequence of Fifty Sonnets in the Second Person*, dedicated to his mother.

Reading the poems without knowing anything of Nicholson, what are the clues? The beloved is rarely given a sex, and is never female; the love seems always to be undeclared, repressed, nightmarish, threatened by scandal ("We have our hidden past, dear, you and I, / Where things unutterably precious lie."). The story becomes clearer when we find poems to a cricket captain ("Yours is young David's beauty debonair"), to boys dressed in white for their first communion, and the riddle of the volume's title solved: "'Tis Ernest sets my heart aflame."

April 1892. *The Artist* reaches new heights of obviousness; in printing the following delightful notice: "An interesting novelty at the Empire Theatre are the feats of strength of a troupe of Bedouin Arabs, who are not less noticeable for their handsome physique than for the grace with which they go through the performance."

1892. When, as it happened — and this was strangest of all —
quite suddenly, the most unexpected thing in the world,
To a casual little club, which once a week he was in the habit
of attending, there came one night a new member,
Of athletic strength and beauty, yet gentle in his manners,
And with a face like a star — so steadfastly clear and true that
he the sufferer felt renewed by merely looking on it.
But what was even more strange, the newcomer turning spoke
friendly to him, and soon seemed to understand,
And from that time forward came and companioned him and
nursed him, and stayed whole nights with him and loved him.
Edward Carpenter, "As It Happened", from the enlarged
Towards Democracy, T. Fisher (ed.).

4 March 1892. Mr Oscar Wilde and a suite of young gentlemen, all wearing the vivid dyed carnation.

The Star reports on the glittering audience at the first performance of John Gray's translation of Theodore de Banville's *The Kiss*, performed by The Independent Theatre at The Royalty.

1893. The lads... were asleep, Gerald with one hand under his yellow head and the other just touching Phillip's arm; as if he would have him mindful, even in dreams, that their existences now had ceased to be divorced.
Edward Irenaeus Stevenson, *The Ordeal of Phillip
and Gerald, or Left to Themselves.*

An adventure book for boys. The adventures of young Gerald ("Nice youngster that Master Gerald is! No extraordinary thing that strangers should take a fancy to him, eh? Pretty Boy!") and the slightly older Phillip, shipwrecked off the New England Coast. Stevenson ends with a flight of fancy which makes it clear that the story is imagining, not describing a life: "If one yields to the temptation to be among the prophets, and closes his eyes, there come, chiefly, pleasant thoughts of how good are friendship and love and loyal service between man and man in this rugged world of ours; and how probable it is that such things here have not their endings, since they have not their perfecting here, perfect as friendship and service sometimes seem. Therewith the inditer of this chronicle sees Phillip and Gerald walking forward, calmly and joyfully, and in an unlessened affection and clearer mutual understanding — into their endless lives."

1893. I love as I love no other;
Nearer thee than any brother;
I would cling to thee.
In innermost thought and motion
I could live with sweet emotion
And drink joy from thee.
                    James M. Brown, "To My Ideal", in *Verses*.

This edition, published by the Glasgow Labour Literature Society, includes a biographical note on the dead socialist poet: "He succeeded in quite a marvellous way in interesting men of all kinds in the movement; workmen and masters, students and artists, farmers and stable boys; and invariably the local physician and policeman."

1893. 1 January 1533; Without due consideration, Messer Tomao, my very dear lord, I was moved to write to your Lordship, not by way of answer to any letter received from you, but being myself the first to make advances, as though I felt bound to cross a little stream with dry feet, or a ford made manifest by a paucity of water. But now that I have left the shore, instead of the trifling water I expected, the ocean with its towering waves appears

before me, so that, if it were possible, in order to avoid drowning,
I would gladly retrace my steps to the dry land whence I started.
Still, as I am here, I will e'en make my heart a rock.

> Translated by J.A. Symonds in *Life of*
> *Michael Angelo Buonarroti.*

Michelangelo drafted his New Year's declaration of love to
Tommaso Cavalieri three times before daring to send it.

1893. Come home with me, said Teleny, in a low, nervous and
trembling voice. Come and sleep with me, he added, in the soft,
hushed and pleading tone of the lover who would fain be
understood without words.

I pressed his hand for all answer.
Will you come?
Yes, I whispered almost inaudibly.
And you will be mine, mine alone?
I was never any other man's, nor ever shall be.
You will love me for ever?
And ever.

I was in his hands like a slumbering child, or a man in a trance.
I seemed to be a man in front, a woman behind.
I am afraid I am hurting you.
You have made me feel like I have never felt before.
How I love you, my Camille!

> Anon., *Teleny*, published Leonard Smithers.

Fragments from the first love scene between Teleny and Camille
de Grieux. Other highlights include the central orgy scene ("Ah!"
said the Arab, quietly lighting a cigarette, "What pleasures can
be compared to those of the Cities of the Plain?") and this other,
more familiar scene:

> They seemed to be looking for somebody, for they either
> turned around, scanned the person they met, or stared at
> men seated on the benches that are along the quay. I noticed
> that a man, who had sprung up from somewhere, was

walking by my side. I grew nervous, for I fancied that he
not only tried to keep pace with me but tried to attract my
attention, for he hummed and whistled snatches of song,
coughed, cleared his throat and scraped his feet... finally I
looked at him. Though it was cold, he was but slightly
dressed. He wore a short, black velvet jacket and a pair of
light grey, closely fitting trousers marking the shape of his
thighs and buttocks like tights.

As I passed by another bench, someone again scraped
his feet and cleared his throat, evidently bent on making
my head turn. There was nothing more remarkable in him
than in the first man. Seeing me look at him he either
buttoned or unbuttoned his trousers. This person touched
me lightly as he passed by. He begged my pardon... his eyes
were painted with kohl, his cheeks were dabbed with rouge.
He was quite beardless. For a moment I doubted whether
he was a man or a woman...

He did not stare, but cast a sidelong glance at me as he
passed by. He was met by a workman — a strong and sturdy
fellow, either a butcher or a smith by trade... I could not
hear what they said, for though they were but a few steps
away they spoke in that peculiar hushed tone of lovers; but
I seemed to be the object of their talk, for the workman
turned and stared at me as I passed. They parted. I looked
at him. He was a brawny man, with massive features; clearly
a fine specimen of the male. As he passed me he clenched
his powerful fist.

With a few minor costume changes, this scene could be placed
unnoticed in several contemporary British cities.

17 February 1893. Now Corydon is gone, the Loves lament,
And with the Loves a troop of lovely boys,
For cruel laws have slain Love's sweet content,
And cruel men have mocked at gentle joys.
                    Percy Lancelot Osborn, in *The Spirit Lamp*,
                        edited by Lord Alfred Douglas.

22 February 1893. The young captain has slain himself! He has slain himself who was my friend! I gave him a little box of perfumes and ear-rings wrought in silver, and now he has killed himself!

> Wilde, *Salomé*, originally written in French; published in the English translation by Bosie in 1894 with pictures by Beardsley.

1 March 1893. It is a narrow room; walls high and straight
Enclose it; here the lights that counterchange
Pale midnight shadows scarce can penetrate
The fretwork of far rafters rough with gold...
Then I was ware how 'neath the gleaming rows of cressets
A fair ivory couch was spread;
Rich Tyrian silks and gauzes hyaline
Were bound with jewelled buckles to the bed;
Thereon I saw a naked form supine.
It was a fair youth from foot to forehead laid
In slumber. Very white, smooth and fine
Were all his limbs; and on his breast there played
The lambent smiles of lamplight.
But a pool of blood upon the pavement strayed...

> J.A. Symonds, "Midnight at Baiae", in *The Artist.*

Set free in a luxurious and erotic pseudo-archaeological fantasy, the Victorian homosexual can still only imagine his obscure object of desire as an artwork, or a corpse.

12 March 1893. ...charged on ten accounts with the commission of acts of gross indecency with five persons in Belfast in 1887 and three succeeding years... twelve months imprisonment with hard labour...

> *The Times* reports from Antrim Assizes, Belfast, on the sentencing of Edward de Cobain, ex MP for Belfast East.

1 April 1893. ...thy godlike shape
Is, to a woman's coarser curve,
As to the trod live-blood of the grape
Unto dull water.
>   Lord Alfred Douglas, "Hyacinthus", in *The Artist*.

1 May 1893. LET MEN BE LOVERS, AND TRUTH BE TRUTH.
>   *The Artist* prints its *In Memoriam* for
>   John Addington Symonds,
>   who had died on 19 April.

May 1893. Did we not, darling, you and I
Walk on earth like other men?
Did we not walk and wonder why they spat upon us so?
>   John Gray, "Poem XVII" from *Silverpoints*; the
>   edition paid for by Wilde and dedicated
>   to him, with poems to Verlaine,
>   Rimbaud and Löuys.

August 1893. I love thee sweet! Kiss me again, again!
>   Theodore Wratislaw, *To a Sicilian Boy*.

Prudently omitted from the public edition of his poems *Caprices*, but shamelessly published by *The Artist* in its August issue.

October 1893. ...I saw thee
In thy white tunic gowned from neck to knee,
And knew the honey of thy sugar lips.
...Oh! food to my starved eyes!
(That gaze unmoved on wanton charm of girls)
As fair as the lad on Latmian hills asleep.
>   Lord Alfred Douglas, "A Port on the Aegean", *The Artist*.

On 31 August 1893 Douglas wrote to Charles Kains Jackson, the editor who was responsible for making *The Artist* a forum for homosexual theories and practices, and told him that the genesis of the poem was in the phrase *sugar lips*, which he had picked up from one of the erotic translations of Richard Burton.

8 December 1893. Meaning! It is a piece of mu-sic, in which I have skilfully e-lu-ded ALL meaning!

John Todhunter's *The Black Cat*, produced by J.T. Grein at the Opéra Comique.

The play contains a character called Cyril Vane who delivers this account of one of his own poems, and is clearly a Wildean homosexual dandy, standing conspicuously apart from all the play's melodramatic "modern" heterosexual intrigues. There is another allusion to Dorian Gray: Vane causes an artist to slash his most treasured portrait to ribbons.

1894. It is hardly needful in these days when social questions loom so large upon us to emphasize the importance of a bond which by the most passionate and lasting compulsion may draw members of the different classes together.

Edward Carpenter, *Homogenic Love and its Place in a Free Society*, Manchester, the Labour Press Society Ltd. (for private circulation only).

1894. What shall I say Gellius, wherefore those lips erstwhile rosy-red, have become whiter than wintery snow, thou leaving home at noon and when the noontide hour arouses thee from soothing slumber to face the longsome day? I know not for sure! But is rumour gone astray with her whisper that thou devourest the well-grown tenseness of a man's middle?

Leonard Smithers in Richard Burton's *Catullus* (privately printed). Burton's notes are characteristically direct: *By the shamelessness of this passage, it would seem to be a quite usual thing amongst the youthful Roman aristocracy to possess a bedfellow of their own sex.*

February 21 1894. Ah, Horace: you find us in the middle of a game of romps: "*Ride a cock horse to Banbury Cross*" ... you know. Boys will be boys. Ha! Ha!

Arthur Law's *The New Boy*, a three-act farce (published by Samuel French in 1921).

The plot hinges on the fact that a man is mistaken by the staff of a public school for an adolescent boy. Here Mr Felix Roach (aged 40) dandles Mr Archibald Renwick on his knee. The idea is, presumably, that a boy on a man's knee is recognizably funny. *The Artist* wrote a review of the piece, stating that it found this travesty of paederasty extremely offensive.

17 June 1894. Hyacinth; What would you give for a secret? Only think of having to keep a watch over your face, your gestures, to be acting before one's nearest. Oh! that must be exciting, delightful, must be knowing that one lives...

Hyacinth Halford Dagmar, in *The Blackmailers*
by John Gray and Marc-André Raffalovich,
produced by J.T. Grein at the Prince
of Wales Theatre.

In Act 2, subtitled *Master and Pupil*, the lonely, licentious, bisexual Claud Price plays Vautrin to Hyacinth's Lucien de Rubempré, seducing the younger man into joining his own criminal profession, that of renting high society. He strokes his hair, and makes the following declaration of love (which has been cancelled in the Lord Chamberlain's copy of the typescript, submitted for official approval):

> *Price:* Hyacinth, don't think that my loneliness has weakened my judgement. I am not more tempted than I have ever been to share my wisdom and my gains and the excitement of my life with somebody else; but until I found you again I had not discovered anywhere in anyone else what I sought, what I wanted.
> *Hyacinth* (afraid and flattered): And you, so clever, so independent, so bold, have really found in me...
> *Claud:* My pupil, my comrade who is to be. Little Hyacinth Dagmar, you are getting the man you were meant to be. I read in you the light of your childhood. You are unfolding yourself, freeing yourself from all the trammels of stupidity. I believe in you.

Hyacinth: You make me almost believe in myself when you talk like this. There is something infectious in you...

At the end of the play, Hyacinth's family discover his infamy. He pours himself a glass of poison, but is saved by the arrival of the following note from Claud:

My dear Hyacinth,
I send this by someone who will know how to find you. You have the keys of my rooms, and of the top drawer of my desk. Go there at once, and you will find enough money to bring you to where you can meet me. Stop the night in Paris, in the house you have heard of. You are expected there, and you will be told how to find me. We are on the eve of success, of real success. But I don't want to triumph without you, my pupil, soon to be my equal. Come. We understand each other now, and the World.

September 1894. A human being who dares to be ridiculous.
Richard Hichens, *The Green Carnation.*

Oscar Wilde is blatantly caricatured under the name of Mr Esmée Amarinth. His "friend" is called Lord Reggie, combining the name of Reginald Turner with the features of Lord Alfred Douglas. In the novel, Esmée sends the telegram "What a funny little man you are", a line which in real life Bosie used against his father. Although there is endless debate about the relative merits of natural and unnatural relationships, the novel anatomizes the life of its queens in terms of manners rather than sexual identity; there is nothing in the book to suggest explicit homosexuality at all, and Wilde is not named. So why was it withdrawn from circulation when Wilde was found guilty?

December 1894. To think that we are all the same is impossible; our natures, our temperaments are utterly unlike. But this is what people will never see; they found all their opinions on a wrong basis. How can their deductions be just if their premises are

124

wrong? One law laid down by the majority, who happen to be
of one disposition, is only binding on the minority legally, not
morally. What right have you, or anyone, to tell me that
such-and-such a thing is sinful for me? Oh, why cannot I explain
to you and force you to see — and his grasp tightened on the
other's arm.

John Bloxham, "The Priest and the Acolyte",
in *The Chameleon* (100 copies).

In the same magazine, an anonymous queen contributes the
following comment on Cleveland Street, five years after the
event. Compare this allusion with that of Mr Charles Whibley;
a completely different language is being spoken, a different audience being addressed.

> I am sure we must all constantly feel that we are under the
> deepest obligation to certain companies, and, strangely
> enough, to the Government Officials connected with the
> Post Office, for filling our streets with the graceful, neatly
> uniformed figures of those that bear our messages and our
> telegrams.

3 January 1895. Nowadays, with our modern mania for morality,
everyone has to pose as a paragon of purity, incorruptibility, and
all the other seven deadly virtues — and what is the result? You
all go over like ninepins — one after the other. Not a year passes
in England without somebody disappearing. Scandals used to
lend charm, or at least interest to a man — now they crush him.
And yours is a very nasty scandal. You couldn't survive it.

Mrs Chievely (Oscar Wilde), *An Ideal Husband*.
Two months before the Fall.

14 February 1895. Once a man begins to neglect his domestic duties
he becomes painfully effeminate, does he not? And I don't like
that. It makes men so very attractive.

The Importance of Being Earnest.

At this point my calendar ends. A month later, the scrapbook begins to fill with newspaper cuttings, the first news of Wilde's arrest.

"It is quite true, Dorian," said Lord Henry, gravely. "It is in all the morning papers."

▷

It never is in all the papers. On the Bank Holiday weekend of spring 1984, I remember, I was on my own. I wasn't working, and it was the first good weather of the year. (I called a friend to check this story, he remembers it too; it was the first weekend when all the boys came out in their summer clothes. Every man in town was wearing a white vest that weekend.) I went and lay in the sun on Hampstead Heath, and flirted and talked seriously with a man I'd never seen before. At two in the afternoon, we sat and talked and watched the families and their dogs and the other gay men. Then I cycled, downhill for miles, to Earl's Court, and I talked to another stranger; he said that he'd seen me before; I don't think he was lying, but I didn't recognize him. At some point, I remember, I watched a man in white tie and tails sing "Beautiful Dreamer" in a club in Brixton; and the holiday weekend ended at two o'clock on the Tuesday morning in the East End. I found two dear friends trapped in the middle of a crowd at closing time. There we were, laughing and trapped and drunk, surrounded by beehives and stilettoes, chopsticks in the hair of the geisha girls. There were policemen everywhere that weekend, policemen on horseback on the Heath, in a van cruising the Brompton Cemetery, in a parked car in Hoxton. I wrote a letter to a man in Paris, listened to my lover crying on the phone, and then I left town, went home to visit my parents. Some parts of that story are simply personal and of no great account (I may have confused several different weekends — did I really cycle from the East to the West End, from North London to South, in one weekend? Why was my lover crying? Did I talk about the weekend when I got home to my parents, or remain silent?).

But other parts of the story will soon be history, exactly the kind of details of a life that we always want to know. What does it feel like? I've read newspapers for that weekend, both dailies and Sundays, and nothing of what I remember is mentioned. Nothing in my experience of that weekend merited a public record. There is no evidence of that weekend. If someone ever wants to re-member, to reinterpret that particular geography, to piece to-gether those details, to imagine what it must have been like (Which pub was where? With what pleasure or hysteria was gay London celebrating that holiday? Why, at the beginning of the summer of 1984, were we being so carefully watched by the police?) then they will need more than what survives in the newspapers to help them. What survives can never give a com-plete picture.

But the past can suddenly flare up in the dustiest corner of the library. When I returned to town after that weekend I went back to the books, went back to my search for the evidence. I found a book dated 1909, entitled *The Intersexes, a History of Simisexualism as a Problem in Social Life.* I was expecting another treatise on our disease, our pathological condition. That was all the entry in the catalogue led me to expect; a dissection, rather than a body. I found a book written in the first person, a book written by a homosexual man about his own life and times. At the end of the nineteenth century (there is nothing in the book to make the date more specific) these are the details which one man wanted to transcribe as evidence of his life. He knew a man who kept *a picture gallery of male subjects of all sorts — from criminals to classic marbles.* He owned and quotes from a huge library of homosexual texts, both historical and contemporary. In London, he knew gay men who talked in their own slang, and who referred to each other by drag names — a Henrietta who was also Henry, a Charles who became Charlotte. He knew that they considered themselves to be either *feminine* (sexually "passive", effeminate) or *masculine* (heterosexual in appearance, devoted to "real men"). He expresses violent contempt for his effeminate, queenly con-temporaries, preferring aristocratic, military and monogamous versions of homosexuality. His culture was polarized by divisions of class; all his stories and the stories given him by his informants, seem to be of masters and servants, clients and prostitutes, officers and soldiers, customers and waiters. He notes, evidently and proudly speaking from experience, that in Aldershot, Portsmouth, Woolwich or Hyde Park you could, for a fee of up to a sovereign, easily (if you could afford a sovereign) pick up *the fine flower of the British soldier-prostitute, dressed in his best uniform, clean-shaven, well-groomed and handsome with his Anglo-Saxon pulchritude and vigour — smilingly expectant.* The gay men he knew met and socialized in private clubs and in public baths. He knew gay street boys, soldiers, actors, models, clerks, aristocrats, businessmen, waiters and servants. He gives case histories of gay relationships in the army, on ships, in factories, in prison, in villages, in schools, in colleges, in theatres and among gypsies. He records with particular pride the words of a man who says: *He and I have lived together now for more than three years, just like a married pair. We have never had one quarrel. Rudolf is somewhat jealous, but is kindness and thoughtfulness itself.*

His gay world contains both happiness and pleasure. He fills thirty-five pages of his book with accounts of gay men and women whose lives were wrecked or damaged by blackmailers. He describes the organization of gay lives in the cities of Britain, North America, France and Germany, even listing which American cities have the best gay bathhouses. I think the most beautiful text in his book is an undated clipping from a London newspaper which gives us a moment from the life of a young man, working as a servant at the time, who was arrested in the Euston Road:

He wore an irreproachably-fitting black walking-costume of the newest fashion, made to order, a grey feather boa, and a coquettish sailor-hat of fine felt... He resisted the arrest, in great indignation, declaring to the officer, "You wretch! I am a lady!" As the officer did not regard this statement, the complainant gave him a violent blow in the face; and a fierce battle began at once, in which the "lady" bit the officer's finger. Only with the assistance of three other policemen could he be overpowered and brought, struggling, biting, scratching and spitting, to the police station.

What this accumulation of detail means, most simply, is that the gay culture of London was there. It was organized in a variety of forms, spoke both private and public languages, inhabited both private and public spaces, was both terrified and courageous. We can assert that it wasn't because it didn't exist that the homosexual culture of London was "invisible". A city is full of cultures that "don't exist".

This evidence places any insistence that our lives had to be "revealed", any pious declarations of innocence or ignorance, in a very particular light. The "discovery" of homosexuality in London in 1895 was a contrived spectacle. Then, as now, the fiction that we are hidden must first be constructed, so that when it is opportune or politically expedient to do so, we can be discovered.

The Wilde trial of 1895 wasn't the first "discovery".

> England... has invented and established Public Opinion, which is an attempt to organize the ignorance of the community: *The Case of the Queen vs Boulton and Others, London, 1871.*

I've transcribed the following documents at length because they're so hard to believe. The fiction of our invisibility remains influential. Most people, ourselves included, think that we are invisible, both in the contemporary life of the city (as in *I don't think I know any other gay people, only you,* or *Are there any gay pubs near here?*) and in the history of that city. Even after I moved here in 1981, moved right into a busy and complex gay scene, anything outside my immediate experience remained invisible. Never mind the nineteenth-century prehistory of the streets I was walking, I had no idea that my local library stocked popular novels with gay characters published in London thirty years ago, or that there were any gay clubs before the discos of the late seventies, or that the part of town I lived in was famous for its drag queens during the war. It was only when I started searching that I realized how much I'd missed. I tried to explain all this to another man, one of the older men whose story I'd missed — a middle-aged Irishman who lives alone in the block next to mine — and he got angry. He'd heard it all before. He stood up and looked out of the window, away from me, and said: *That's it; there's nothing new in it. You should watch those old queens sometimes, they had their own way of doing it, their own performance. A lot of those queens paved the way for you, that was my generation. You should watch us a bit, you boys, you young men, you might learn something.* I try to remember what he said when I'm copying out these stories. The fact that men like him are invisible, whether in the 1980s, the 1950s, or the 1870s, is incredible. When I find traces of his life, and of other lives, I'm not sure how to react, whether to celebrate, or turn away and look out of the window like he did, angry, angry that all these stories have been forgotten. This "evidence" raises important questions about our own attitude to our own history. Do we view it with dismay, since it is a record of sorrow, of powerlessness, a record of lives wrecked? Or is it possible to read even these texts, written as they were by journalists, policemen and court clerks, with delight, as precious traces of dangerous, pleasurable, complicated gay lives?

1870. Among the many extraordinary cases which are from time to time brought before the public, none have created more sensation, or a greater degree of dismay in the respectable portion of the community, than the astounding, and, we fear, too-well-founded charges against Boulton and Park, and the outrages of which they have been guilty; the social crime, for so it is, which they have openly perpetrated, cannot be too strongly condemned.

We speak firmly, and without the slightest hesitation, when we say that the proceedings of these misguided young men deserve the heaviest punishment which the law can possibly afford, for however their intention may be explained, we say at least there is one peculiar trait in the evidence which stands out in bold and audacious relief and too plainly shows the base and prurient natures which these misguided youths (for they are but little more) must possess. We refer to the entrance of Park into the retiring room which is set apart for ladies in the Strand Theatre, who had the unblushing impudence to apply to the female attendants to fasten up the gathers of his skirt, which he alleged had come unfastened.

This act, simple as it appears on paper, is sufficient in itself to arouse the just indignation of every true Englishman. We can now ask, and with just cause too, what protection have those who are dearest to our heart and hearth, those loved ones whom we recognize by the endearing titles of mother, sister, wife or daughter. Is it right, moral or just that their most sacred privacy should thus be ruthlessly violated?

Day after day, month after month and year after year we are startled out of our propriety by some fresh scandal, some fresh crime, the mere idea of which is more than sufficient to evoke the blush of shame upon the modest cheek. We are continually shocked and alarmed at the rapidly increasing follies and crimes of society, as they are laid before us in the columns of our newspapers.

And to those who are thinkers, it is, alas, too evident that the most revolting profligacies of the guilty cities of the plain, or the debauchery of Ancient Rome during the days of Messalina and Theodora, could not possibly outvie many of the atrocious phases of London life as they exist in the nineteenth century.

These young gentlemen (heaven save the mark!) rejoice in the respective cognomens of Ernest Boulton and Frederick William Park, their ages being twenty-two and twenty-three; the former describing himself as of no occupation, and the latter as that of a student of law. As we have no intention of endeavouring to screen these persons (for in our indignation we cannot apply a milder term) we copy from the newspaper reports the addresses which are, in all conscience, aristocratic enough; Boulton resided at Shirland Road, Westbourne Grove, and Park at Bruton Street, Berkeley Square — their present residency being at Her Majesty's House of Detention and for the present they are guests of a paternal Government.

It appears that on Thursday night, the 28th April, that no little excitement was caused in the Strand Theatre by the entrance of two very handsome women, accompanied by a young gentleman, into one of the private boxes. In fact the personal charm of these ladies was so great that they attracted considerable attention, and we have it on good authority that more than one bet of no inconsiderable amount was placed between some of the regular habitués of this place of amusement, with the object of deciding to which nation they belonged. The general opinion throughout the house was that they were two stars about to shine in the firmament of the demi-monde, and their beauty, their fascination and their paid-for smiles would, before the London season expired, cause many a poor dupe to curse the hour in which he had been born. These and numberless conjectures received their foundation from the nonchalant manner in which these ladies leaned over their box, twirled their handkerchiefs, and lasciviously ogled the male occupants of the stalls.

How few in that vast assemblage thought that these creatures were but men in masquerade. Lecherous leering and subtle fascinations, if displayed by women, are much to be condemned; but what words can paint the infamy of such hellish proceedings of men towards those of their own sex.

On Thursday night, 28 April 1870, Mr Frederick William Park, aka Mrs Fanny Winifred Park, aka Mr Vivien Gray, aka Miss Mabel Foster, aka Mrs Jane or Fanny Graham, but known as Fanny to all her friends, was wearing a blue silk dress, and a wedding ring. With Fanny was Mr Ernest Boulton, aka Lady Arthur Clinton, aka Stella, Star of the Strand. Stella was in low cut, very low cut scarlet satin with a white moiré antique trim and a white muslin shawl, a blonde chignon, bracelets, and a necklace and locket. White kid gloves, and a fan. Under the satin were white ladies boots, a very full padded bosom, stays, flannel and calico petticoats, but no drawers.

Fanny and Stella were being watched. They had been seen *giggling and chirruping* at each other. They had been observed touching each other under the chin and lighting their cigarettes with gestures of unnecessary flamboyance. It had been noted that *they did not swing their arms like men, but walked like women do.* As they left the theatre Fanny popped into the ladies' room to have her lace repinned.

"Was she dressed as a woman?"

"Dressed as a Lady. The Lady said, 'Have you a Ladies' Room,' and I said, 'Yes, madam, walk this way if you please.' I took them for gay Ladies."

Frocks adjusted, they stepped out onto the Strand, where the
police were waiting for them. They were arrested on the charge
of committing a "misdemeanour", of *being men and dressed in
female attire*, and carried off to Bow Street.

Fanny and Stella's appearance in the dock there the following
morning was by no means their first public appearance. The
frocks they wore on that occasion, for instance, were merely the
highlights of a much larger collection. The scale of their activities
can be judged by the splendour of their wardrobe. A selection
of their finery was later to be exhibited in court; a catalogue of
confiscated items was solemnly recited: *One mauve satin trimmed
with black lace. One corded white silk with white lace; one pink satin;
one white glacé trimmed blue satin with lace. Stays, silk stockings,
petticoats, twenty chignons and curls and plaits and all sorts of things.
Curling irons, boxes of Violet Powder and Bloom of Roses. Coloured
kid boots, white boots and shoes.* Nor had the Strand Theatre been
the only site of their infamy. Their behaviour there was not
exceptional, but typical. They had been seen in drag in Regent
Street, Brunswick Square, the Holborn Casino, the Haymarket,
Highbury Barn (scene of a *Bal d'Opéra*), Portland Place, the
Lyceum, the Alhambra (where, in March 1870, the ladies had
once again been thrown out of the ladies' room), Evans Restaurant (where one Mr Francis Cox, city businessman, had taken
Stella and her lover to a champagne dinner. Mr Cox's unsubtle
advances to Stella had caused the lover to leave in a fit of
jealousy, whereupon Mr Cox took the opportunity to kiss *him,
she or it, believing at the time that it was a woman.* When Stella
revealed her true gender, he had her thrown out of the restaurant), the Burlington Arcade (their favourite trolling ground both
in and out of drag, where they strolled *arm in arm with such an
effeminate walk. Stella was once seen to wink at a gentleman and
turn his head in a sly manner,* whereupon the Beadle asked them
to leave. They refused. He attempted to eject them physically.
Stella turned to him and she said, *I shall go where I like*), Chel-
tenham, the Boat Race, numerous minor country houses. This
is not a random geography. Out of town, Fanny and Stella only
appeared at the best places; they aspired to being treated not as

women but as Ladies. In town their sense of place, like their sense of dress, was impeccable. They stuck to places of entertainment or crowded streets or to private houses or fashionable districts where the appearance of wealth guaranteed their safety. They knew when to take cabs and when to walk. Moving carefully in and out of the West End, they seem to have known, like so many of us, just how far up, and just how far down, it is possible and advisable to go.

Although I'm sure that they looked less than dazzling after a night in the cells, during which they had been subjected to a forcible and illegal medical examination, Fanny and Stella attracted a large crowd to see them appear, exposed, in court.

It is important that we do not imagine Fanny and Stella as living only in public, indulging their taste for outrage in the peculiar anonymity of crowded streets or theatres until forced into visibility by the spotlight of police attention. They do not seem themselves to have conceived of their lives as "outrageous", necessarily public. They lived as queens off the street as well as on it. Stella lived with and was kept by none other than Lord Arthur Pelham Clinton, Member of Parliament. Though there is no record of Arthur taking Stella home to meet the family, Stella's mother was certainly delighted that her lower middle class son had a Lord and MP for a friend, especially when Arthur sent a case of champagne home for Ernest's twenty-first birthday party. The part of society mistress was played to the hilt. The housemaid at 36 Southampton Street, the Strand, who doubtless made the double bed in which the happy couple slept, and who heard Arthur calling Stella *darling* over breakfast, challenged her:

> I said to him, "I beg your pardon but I really think you are a man." He said he was Lady Arthur Clinton, he said, "I am Lady Clinton, Lord Arthur's wife."

And to prove her point Stella showed her the ring. She had monogrammed cards printed with the legend *Stella, Lady Clinton*. She had Arthur pay for a hairdresser who came to the apartment every day.

Worst of all, Fanny and Stella could not claim the alibi of originality. They could not appear in the dock as unique monsters,
individual aberrations. They were not the only ones. The Public
Record Office file from which these details are all taken contains
the calling cards of several homosexual prostitutes; illustrated
papers of the time carried pictures of a stereotyped, that is, widely
recognizable, effeminate male homosexual; evidence at the trial
described a circle of at least twenty young men who were in the
habit of cruising the West End together, either in drag or at least
in full slap. Some of the more effeminate witnesses even left the
stand to the sound of appreciative laughter. In other words Fanny
and Stella were recognized not as eccentrics, but as the visible
representatives of another world. Mr Thomas Gibbings, who had
hosted drag balls at Haxell's Hotel, and whose voice and manner
were decidedly effeminate, appeared to regard the modern pastime
of *going in drag* as perfectly harmless; and was applauded for saying
so.

It became clear in the course of their trial that they were not
simply drag queens. They could not be dismissed as theatrical
creations, men in private, women in public, alternately visible
and invisible. At the time of their arrest they were engaged in
what seems to have been their favourite joke: that of dressing
and passing (with, apparently, complete success) as ladies. They
had other habits, nastier, troubling — troubling because they
involved not a concealment but a proclamation of the wicked
ways (being a sodomite) which dressing in women's clothes only
implied. When not in drag, they adopted a fearlessly effeminate
style. Wearing tight trousers and low-necked shirts, opened very
wide at the front, their necks powdered and their cheeks painted,
they adopted the airs and gestures of prostitutes, looking over
their shoulders and glancing at men. That is, they adopted a
public style, a style which made public their sexual identity.
Worse still, these queens made their style more than a hobby;
they made it a career. They were actresses. In 1869 they had
played polite melodrama and one-act operettas (making the most
of Stella's wonderful soprano voice while it lasted) to full houses
in Scarborough, Brentwood, Chelmsford, Southend, Maldon,
Romford, Bishops Stortford, Gravesend, Billericay and Braintree.

Their performances were by all accounts as outrageous as they were successful. When Stella took the part of Mrs Chillinton, in a sentimental one-acter entitled *The Morning Call*, in which, according to the text, the said Mrs Chillinton never leaves the stage, she nevertheless contrived to change her costume twice, appearing first in black corded silk embroidered with flowers; then in a mauve moiré antique with white lace; then taking the curtain in a pink number decorated with black stars. That night she received fourteen bouquets after the show, and photographs of her in costume sold as fast as they could be printed in the seafront shops of Scarborough. The *Essex Journal* reported:

> Looking at him with both one's eyes open, listening to his extraordinary voice and criticizing however narrowly his wonderful feminine appearance and charm, it is really difficult for a moment to believe that he is not a charming girl.

That is, the audience knew what they were seeing: a drag queen. One wonders what they made of a playbill published in 1868, advertising another show, entitled *Love and Rain*, announcing that the part of Lady Jane Desmond, a young widow, would be taken by Mr Ernest Boulton Esq., while that of Captain Charles Lumley (the handsome soldier who wins the lady's hand) would be taken by Lord Arthur Clinton, MP. By what stratagems, or was it just ignorance, did the audience contrive to enjoy the spectacle of a drag queen and her lover enacting a heterosexual seduction? Who saw, and how, that these were two sodomites?

This is the question which the trial set itself the task of dramatizing. It focused on a single question. Were Fanny and Stella visible? As their glamorous triple lives, as queens, prostitutes and actresses, were revealed and scrutinized in court, the confused fury of the law was expressed again and again in a single accusation: Boulton and Park, Fanny and Stella, had *exhibited* themselves.

The Attorney General opened the trial by declaring:

> Well, Gentlemen, the general nature of the charge is this:

that the defendants... associated together, spoke and wrote to each other, in such a manner as to indicate that relations subsisted between them such as are only permitted between men and women; that by sometimes dressing in female costume, sometimes in male costume, with a studied air of effeminacy, powdering their necks, painting their faces, by amatory airs and gestures, they endeavoured to excite each other's passions, and to make themselves objects of desire to persons of their own class.

He continued:

Perhaps I am not going too far when I say that you and I and all of us will experience a sensation of relief if we could come to the conclusion that the popular apprehension was unfounded.

The actual charge was conspiracy to commit a felony. The Attorney General was arguing that the lives of Boulton and Park were to be read in their entirety as evidence of a single crime: that of sodomy, being a sodomite. At the same time he is announcing that he (the embodiment of the Law) wishes that such a thing as a sodomite did not exist. He suggests that the real purpose of the trial was to prove, somehow, that London was not the home of such a creature. The court is sitting not to punish, but to render the criminal non-existent.

The trial scrutinized three main sets of details in its hunt for evidence. Even though all three were in fact very different, they were treated as if they were the same; scandalous, disgusting details which only the stern legal process had the manly stomach to itemize and interpret. All the gorgeous details of queenly life had to be reduced to one thing — evidence.

The extensive medical evidence given in court (given first, because then as now the body could not tell a lie) centred round a single question of interpretation: could dilation of the anus be considered proof of sodomy? Here, at once, the process of the trial began to falter. The shocked tones of Mr James Paul, the police surgeon, "I have never seen anything like it before," failed to take effect. Precisely because he had never seen anything like it before, because he had no other cases with which to draw comparisons, his findings could not be interpreted. They were not "evidence" of any acknowledged or described phenomenon. They remained unsuggestive statements of fact.

Second, the court turned to the details of Fanny and Stella's external, public appearance. Their precious hoards of slap, frocks and jewels were displayed in court, as if they could give up the secret which the actual bodies had refused to betray. If it could be proven that the dresses had been worn to seduce men, if that was their meaning, then the defendants were definitely guilty. There was no question that they wore frocks; the question was, what did the frocks signify? The defence argued that they were merely signs of an adolescent sense of fun, of frivolity; the prosecution countered by observing, correctly, that "the adoption of these dresses was not an occasional frolic or escapade, but as far as we can make out it appears to have been made in a great degree the occupation and business of their lives."

The defence retaliated with the argument that their style of dress was indeed the sign of an occupation; it was the professional dress of actresses. Crucial evidence on this point was given by Miss Martha Stacey, who worked at 13 Wakefield Street, where Fanny and Stella kept their wardrobe and where they would drag up together. Martha was not sure if they shared a bed, but she was sure that they came dressed as men and left dressed as women. She knew that they took no trouble to conceal this from either her or their fellow lodgers, and she knew that their outfits were far from inconspicuous:

"I think it was very extreme."

"The dress was?"

"Yes."

Martha concluded that the dresses indicated that Fanny and Stella were regularly and frequently employed as theatricals. She could not let herself imagine that they meant anything else. I would read Martha's evidence differently. I would recognize that the frocks were the costumes of sodomites, and I would applaud the men who wore them in their determined efforts to use their frocks to create public space for themselves in London, in the separate but overlapping worlds of the actress, the prostitute and the demi-mondaine. Fanny and Stella themselves seem to have known exactly what they were doing. The nerve and precision of their performance is in marked contrast to the amateur criticism that the court subjected them to. They were well aware that they were playing precise games with their appearance, and that an exact understanding of the rules was a prerequisite of survival. They were always in danger, at the points where their codes of dress, which carried safe and assured meanings within their own culture, in their domestic lives, and in their work as actresses, collided with the ignorance and potential violence of London at large. One solution was to make their drag so effective that they could pass safely as women, making themselves visible as sodomites only when and to whom they chose. Another was to adopt sufficient tokens of masculine appearance so as to confuse any suspicious members of the public, to bury one set of signs under another. This attempt was not always successful. One of Stella's admirers wrote:

> I have told mother that you are coming. I thought it well
> to tell her that you are very effeminate, but I hope you will
> do your best to appear as manly as you can, at any rate in
> face. I therefore beg of you to let your moustache grow at
> once.

A photograph of Fanny was produced in court.

> Is that a likeness of Mr Park?
> Yes.
> Are you able to say whether this was a natural moustache?
> I believe it was a natural moustache.
> That is a male character in some performance?
> That I am not able to say. I do not know if Mr Park was
> in character at that time.
> You never saw Park in a green satin dress with a moustache?
> No.

Fanny did manage to grow both moustache and whiskers in time for the trial.

After ripping the costumes to shreds, the court scrutinized the script. The third area of evidence was the private letters of Fanny and Stella. The most "sensational" of these were read out in court by the prosecution in a final, convulsive fit of contorted, heterosexual logic. Explicit records of these men's lives were read out in public in an attempt to make them sound like cryptic messages of perversion, signs that could only reveal their meanings under cross-examination. The question was, who understood these letters; and how, and why, and on what terms.

> During the reading of the letters the audience in the body of the court appeared to be exceedingly amused, and the prisoners themselves smiled — the learned magistrates remarked that it certainly was no laughing matter.

Was the court laughing at or with the prisoners? Did it perceive as evident a set of meanings that the prosecution was attempting to depict as difficult, dangerous and dirty, even beyond belief?

> *Dec 4 1868*
> I am just off to Chelmsford with Fanny where I shall stay till Monday. We are going to a party tomorrow. Send me some money, you wretch.
> Stella Clinton

> *Undated*
> My dearest Arthur,
> You really must excuse me from interfering in matrimonial squabbles (for I am sure the present is no more than that) and though I am as you say Stella's confidante in most things, that which you wish to know she keeps locked up in her breast. My own opinion on the subject varies fifty times a day, when I see you together. Sometimes she may treat you brusquely, but on the other hand see how she stands up for your dignity and position. As to all the things she said to you the other night, she may have been tight, and did not know what she was saying, so that by the time

you get my answer you will both be laughing over the whole affair, as Stella and I did when we fought down here — don't you remember, when I slapped her face. Do not think me unkind dear, as I have told you all I know and have not an opinion worth having to offer you. Goodbye dear,

Ever yours, Fan.

P.S. Is the handle of my umbrella mended yet? If so I wish you would kindly send it to me as the weather has turned so showery that I can't go out without a dread of my back hair coming out of curl.

To Stella, undated:
My darling Ernie,
I had another cry on the train after leaving you, then lay back and managed to get some sleep. After all as you say in a few weeks time we shall meet again. I am consoling myself in your absence by getting screwed.

I had a cry on the train, said the Attorney General. A man crying at being parted from another man for a few weeks? Gentlemen, what language is that? Is it the language of friends? Or the language of love? It seems to me strange, very strange, he being a grown up man and not a mere boy, a man of at least twenty-six.

Indeed, what language is that? Who understands it? Who understands its slang? Who understands the significance of a Frederick signing a letter as Fan; who can judge whether the use of the phrase "matrimonial squabble" to describe a row between two men is literal, metaphorical or merely ironic; and on the basis of what experience do they make this judgement? The prosecution, without ever being able to bring itself to use the actual word sodomite, was quite clear in its understanding of whose language was being spoken here. It was not to be explained away as playful, metaphorical or theatrical. Its meaning was not to be blurred. Even though the letters contained no explicit admission of sexual relations, the Attorney General was quite right to say to the jury: *In such a case you do not expect mathematical proof, or proof at all approaching mathematical proof. You expect such proof as reasonable men ought to act on.* He continued: *Gentlemen, no stain is inflicted upon the honour of this country by such offences being committed by a comparatively few persons, for let us hope that they are few. But our national character might be stained if such offences, when detected and proved, were suffered to go unpunished.*

The fear of being stained, of being tainted, of being infected with a plague (all images that run through the prosecution's case) was intimately related to the question of Fanny and Stella's visibility as sodomites. For the jury to accuse them, to announce that it saw them as sodomites, the jury would have to admit that they understood the letters, that they recognized the significance of the frocks. Such admission would suggest a dangerous proximity to the object of their scrutiny. It would involve an admission that they lived in the same city as Fanny and Stella. It would involve the admission of the existence of a world only two of whose representatives were in the dock. The Attorney General had asked the jury by their verdict to *stay the plague,* but the defence had asked them to *perform a nobler and better function,* and to declare by their verdict that no such plague existed; that *England was happily free from it, and was not yet tainted by its foul infection.* You cannot legislate against a language simply by imprisoning two people who speak that language. Better to deny the existence of the language altogether. Fanny and Stella's defence brought the case to its conclusion by doing just that:

My friend used the expression that crimes of this kind are always committed with great precaution. True, gentlemen, from the very nature of the crime and its unnatural character of course it would be one which those who indulge in it, and who unsex themselves for the commission of such an outrage upon decency, Morality and upon Nature itself, would not be likely to bring public attention to their acts, but would try... to avoid exciting the suspicion of others... But here the very course which my friend has taken, by producing evidence of visits to Theatres, visits to Casinos — visits to Arcades and other places of public resort and amusement and other acts — improper and unjustifiable acts if you please — acts of Extravagance and Folly on the part of those persons to whom I refer, yet those very acts themselves, in place of showing that they were contemplating something over which the pall of darkness was to be drawn — the indulgence of some such horrible crime that men should shrink from suggesting even a trace or suspicion to those who might be suspicious of their intentions — I would say that the mere fact of all this publicity is of itself a strong argument... in favour of my clients.

Mr Digby Seymour, for the defence, is arguing that sodomy is shameful, furtive and ugly, and that therefore Fanny and Stella, whose public words and images were shameless, blatant and elegant, could not possibly be guilty of that crime. He is refusing the very possibility of a sodomite being visible on his own terms, of a sodomite speaking for himself.

After forty minutes of deliberation, the jury agreed with him.

Fanny and Stella were declared not guilty.

Fanny, bless her, fainted in the dock.

The verdict seems unbelievable. The evidence of Fanny and Stella's visibility was converted into proof that they didn't exist. The contortion of the law is testimony to how desperately it needed an appropriate verdict. Only by silencing, not punishing, the sodomites, could the court breathe a sigh of relief. When Boulton and Park were dismissed, declared improbable if not impossible, the existence of a homosexual culture in London was effectively denied. (I wonder what they did then? Did they leave the country, or just wait and then resume their metropolitan lives? Did Stella find a replacement for her lost Arthur — he killed himself when his name began to appear in the papers. Does anyone remember her? Perhaps someone kept her photograph.) The denial had to be actively maintained, however; it could not be a simple, single operation. The world of which Fanny and Stella were part was an extensive one. I was reading the *Illustrated London Police News* for 1889, and I turned to the wrong page as I was checking a detail of the Cleveland Street Scandal. And there I found a picture and a report of another

queen, arrested on the street, arrested in a frock. The case of
the Queen versus Boulton and Others was made sensational: we
do not always make the front page of *The Times*. But it was not
an isolated case.

The active denial of the existence of our culture in London in
the twenty years of my scrapbook, from Fanny and Stella to Bosie
and Oscar, can be traced in the form of a heavy silence. All
through these twenty years there was an intense scrutiny of the
"underworld" of London. The tactic of using the journalistic
"scandal" or exposé to boost the mass circulation of a newspaper
was invented in this period; and journalists were joined in the
lower depths by social reformers, who made their crusading inves-
tigations into precisely those parts of the city where we should
have been found. They left behind them a mass of texts, which
ought to be a gay historian's dream, full of detailed "eye-witness"
accounts and transcriptions of informant's voices. Mayhew, for
instance, in the course of his exhausting, exhaustive researches
into the lives of the poor, the unloved, the criminal and the
politically dangerous, produced (in Volume Four of *London Labour
and the London Poor*) a categorization and documentation of
twenty-five different kinds of prostitute then working in London.
He noted, first-hand, the lives of Sailors' Women, Soldiers'
Women, Thieves' Women, Park Women; but even though he
observed, met and talked to all these members of the profession
his book records no trace of homosexual prostitution. And yet
we know, from Jack Saul, that the "gay people" included both
men and women, who shared the same trolling grounds in the
West End, and sometimes even the same pimps and premises.
And Mayhew himself, even if his informants were to blame for
the silences in the accounts of their lives, must have *seen* the
"Piccadilly Vultures" amidst the crowds that worked Drury Lane
and Leicester Square, crowding the theatre side of the street from
Trafalgar Square as far as Temple Bar. In the wake of Mayhew,
novelists and journalists created a whole school of "documentary"
writing, which was licensed to be sensational and lurid precisely
because it was "honest" and "factual". They created a new and
dark geography for the city, searching out the "Byways of Modern

Babylon", "The Wilds of London", "The Bitter Cry of Outcast
London", "Odd People in Odd Places". These texts claimed to
expose the worst evils — journalists vied to locate the *worst*, not
the most typical slum. They revealed the existence of the unsuspected and the scandalous. And yet, never, not once, are we
included in these texts. I found just one possible veiled hint:
"No form of vice and sensuality causes surprise or attracts attention... the vilest practices are looked upon with the most matter
of fact indifference" — in "The Bitter Cry of Outcast London",
Pall Mall Gazette, 1883. But these writings existed to give concrete
details, statistics, proof, not suggestions. Child-prostitution,
murder and fatal diseases were all thoroughly investigated and
documented, but not us.

Wilde himself contributed to this documentary school in his
bestseller *Dorian Gray*, when Dorian goes to an opium den in
Dockland. Oscar was involved in the daily, ordinary reality of
"other" (homosexual and criminal) London in 1891, so for him
discovering the truth, the secret life of the city, was a pleasure
rather than a missionary or journalistic employment. His researches, though, were not made public; he kept his personal
account of the lower depths a secret until it was forced out of
him in 1895. In print all he did was to repeat the clichés of the
descent into London's underworld in one of its most hackneyed
locales. Perhaps the author hadn't even been there in person,
was the implication. Perhaps he wasn't writing up his notes at
all; perhaps he borrowed the details from another book. James
Greenwood, a prolific urban anthropologist of the 1880s, had
already described a very similar opium den for the *Daily Telegraph*
as part of his compassionate exposé of Tiger Bay, a famous con-
centration of leisure facilities on the edge of Dockland, where
Limehouse's Chinatown met Stepney East. Perhaps he took the
details from Richard Rowe's book *Found in the Streets* (1880) —
Rowe had described the very same den. It seems that the
documentary exposure of scandal, based as it was on the image
of a single explorer discovering and briefly illuminating the
darkest place, could easily and profitably be repeated. The
backstreets were easily and repeatedly located; their discovery
was not intended to provide information, but increase sales.

Dorian's visit provides us with no new characters or vices. He meets Adrian Singleton, another character with an unmentionable history. The reader leans forward at this point, eager to catch an incriminating word as they talk; the women sidle up and begin to chatter. Dorian turns his back on them, and says something in a low voice to Adrian Singleton. That's all there is. No evidence there.

The specific claim of all this writing is that it is *true*. Because the middle-class journalist, or working-class author, has been there, is reporting back, the details of his text have the status of evidence. Evidence of a life whose existence a shocked public is hard-pressed to acknowledge. Evidence is always of *another* life.

This insistence on "truth" in accounts of an underworld gave these texts a double edge. The fiction of documentary assures the reader that the problem being exposed is a distant one, so distant that only a novelist or journalist or policeman can cross the great social divide and return safely with the evidence. But the documentary is also troubling; it creates a picture of an uneasy London, a city in which poverty, vice and violence have a constant presence, in which they could at any moment cease to be simply scandals, reports in a newspaper, and could erupt onto the streets. All these texts, of course, were written about the East End, but intended to be read by those who imagined that the West End was their natural home, whether as residents or shoppers.

But this geography could not be maintained. If our absence is described as a silence, then we should remember that throughout the period of my scrapbook London was disturbed by noises, sudden outbursts. The streets were unquiet. Every night working-class women walked in hordes from the East End to the West End to work as prostitutes. In January 1879 the unemployed made the journey, roaming the streets in violent mobs. In February 1886 Trafalgar Square was taken over by rioters; the riots lasted for three days, until the crowd was finally dispersed by a specially drafted police force. In October 1887 the Square was so crowded with people sleeping rough that they spilled into St James's Park itself, almost within sight of the Palace. In South Audley Street, in Piccadilly and in the Pall Mall club you could hear the sound of breaking glass. In November three people died when the police cleared the Square again. In 1894 the West End heard the dim echoes of the Greenwich Park explosion, and everyone saw the gory pictures in the paper. Even the most beautiful and stupid people in Wilde's plays talk incessantly about scandal, about *days like these, these dreadful Socialistic days*. They worry about *the problem of the East End*. Lady Bracknell herself is informed enough to fear *acts of violence in Grosvenor Square*.

In a city like that, site of violent struggles between the powerful and the powerless, our voice was one that had to be strictly controlled. By 1895, the silence could hardly be maintained. Homosexual men were becoming evident. The likes of Fanny and Stella (the likes of us) could no longer plausibly be dismissed as improbable or impossible. Look back at the calendar of events again. Medicine and psychology are beginning to formulate a language to describe us. The law itself has named us and legislated against us as a distinct threat to law and order. But most of all we are beginning, however deviously, variously and inconspicuously, to find our own voice. The scrapbook for those twenty years contains much more than simply information *about* us. Many of those books, even if they were couched in the polite language of Literature, and were read by only a few people, come very close to speaking explicitly of their true subject. They are articulate in a way that would have been unthinkable fifty years earlier. All have the exploration and tentative definition of a homosexual experience as their more or less explicit theme; some (Symonds, Carpenter, Wilde's *The Portrait of Mr W.H.*) make extraordinarily bold and definite assertions about the structure, history and future of homosexual men's lives. And throughout the twenty years, as pornography (produced for the first time for a distinctly homosexual audience), confessions, newspapers and court reports inform us, the street life of the queens and the prostitutes and their men continued to flourish, as lurid and courageous as ever.

In May 1887, Jack Saul picked up Lord Euston and introduced him to the boys at 19 Cleveland Street — in Piccadilly, between Albany Courtyard and Sackville Street. *He laughed at me and I winked at him. He turned sharp into Sackville Street*, one street away from Burlington Arcade, Fanny and Stella's favourite cruising ground in 1869. Sackville Street also crosses Vigo Street, which is where Oscar Wilde met the clerk Edward Shelley before taking him to dinner at the Albemarle Hotel. To get to Cleveland Street Jack and his Lord (aka the Duke) might have passed Fitzroy Street; Simeon Solomon lived at number 12, and Taylor and Mason held their drag parties at number 46. The evidence begins to suggest a busy, crowded life in the city, constant activity, constant chatter and noise.

Oscar Wilde, in 1895, became the means by which the silence was re-imposed. There was a very particular reason why he presented such a threat to the status quo. Lord Alfred Douglas's brother, Viscount Drumlanrig, had been involved in a relationship with the prime minister, Rosebery. Rosebery had elevated him to the peerage, and had made him his private secretary so that he could keep him close by, in the Houses of Parliament. Then in October 1893 Drumlanrig had died in what could have been interpreted as either a shooting accident or a suicide. There was a pressing threat of scandalous rumours, revelation if Douglas's choice of companions was scrutinized too carefully. Thus the whole process of Wilde's trial, however it appears, was directed towards stifling rather than exposing Wilde and the men he was seen to represent.

However, it is true that Wilde, as he himself claimed, stood in symbolic relation to his own age. That is, he wasn't placed in the dock because of a particular conspiracy against an individual homosexual. He was *seen* to be symbolic. He was a successful playwright with a high public profile. He made a career, in his plays and in his journalism, out of advancing skilfully rephrased, fashionable versions of dangerous ideas — amoral aestheticism, socialism, nihilism, hedonism — which attacked the moral, political and artistic status quo. His ideas were not lethal — *The Soul of Man Under Socialism* makes tame reading compared to the works of Edward Carpenter, and *Dorian Gray* is tame compared to *Teleny*; but unlike those texts, Wilde's work in 1895 was public, controversial, in the London papers. *Teleny* had only an underground circulation; Carpenter was publishing pamphlets in Leeds, when *The Importance of Being Earnest* had its royal première. Wilde was not intolerable because he was a homosexual. He was intolerable because he was a public man who was a homosexual. It is worth asking what, since he had already gone so far in 1895, would he have written in 1896, if he had not been incarcerated in Reading, forced to make special requests for writing materials, writing an unpublishable confession on miserably thin paper, which on the day of his release was hurried to the safety of a discreet friend, and thence to the British Museum, where it was to remain for fifty years. Although, as we shall see, Wilde lived beyond the law after as well as before his trial, the silence was to be long, effective and bitter. What would our culture as gay men in this city have been like if Wilde had still been living and writing in London in the 1920s, if his career as a homosexual artist had been as long as, say, André Gide's. If his example to us was not of how a man can be swiftly and violently silenced, but of how his work can endure, not as evidence of a disaster, but as witness, seducer, guide?

> I know that there are men with horrible secrets in their lives — men who have done some shameful thing, and who in some critical moment have to pay for it, by doing some other act of shame. — oh! don't tell me you are such as they are!

Oscar was not, like Fanny and Stella twenty years earlier, acquitted. He was silenced by being found guilty. That is, instead of being publicly declared meaningless, the life of the defendant was found to be full of the worst meanings imaginable.

The verdict may have been different, but the process by which it was achieved was the same. In this city we can only ever be furtive or flamboyant, secretive or outrageously public, invisible or too visible. The two roles are complementary halves of the same identity. In either case, we are the scrutinized; the details of our lives can only ever be the details of a scandal. Within this bizarre structure, great energy was used to force a man to tell the truth. It is important to remember that Wilde, throughout his three trials, was lying all the time. He denied or distorted the significance of the texts, incidents and relationships described in evidence against him, knowing all the time what was their "true meaning". He *was* a sodomite. Likewise, the prosecution's pose of outraged, fascinated ignorance, its portrayal (amplified in the press) of homosexuality as something which had suddenly, shockingly appeared in the form of Oscar Wilde was precisely that — a pose. The court was not entirely ignorant of twenty years of London's culture and daily life; they read the papers. The court was certainly not ignorant of the implications of Rosebery's potential involvement in the case. Both the defendant and the prosecution conspired to maintain the "innocence" of Lord Douglas, although his complicity in Wilde's life was obvious to the judge, to the jury and presumably to the audience and to all the journalists in the courtroom. Mr Justice Wills specifically instructed the jury not to dwell on his involvement in the case. Mr Charlie Gill, who appeared for the prosecution, had appeared for the defence in the Cleveland Street trial six years earlier, so he well knew about the lives of "such men". A very particular version of "the truth" was being constructed.

What is remarkable, in the face of all the evidence, is that Wilde contested the case at all, or that the verdict was not announced on the first day. Why did the terrible "truth", which was evident from the beginning (even if no one dare even whisper such a suggestion), have to be dragged out at such length? What Wilde and the court were contesting was not the evidence, but who had the right to *interpret* that evidence. It is no accident that the line *the Love that dare not speak its name* haunted the trial, and has stayed with us ever since. It is not the love itself which was on trial, since even the law, even our parents acknowledge that some men do have sex with other men. What was on trial was the right to speak (invent and articulate) the name of that love. The question was, and is, who speaks, and when, and for whom, and why. As the perverse pantomime of the trial was enacted, the power of speech was taken away from us and given to our judges. Wilde never spoke out; he only answered questions. The evidence of our lives was placed under their control. They assigned its meanings.

Just explain to me what you really mean.
I think I had better not, Duchess. Nowadays to be intelligible is to be found out.

▷

I wrote a letter to my love / On my way I dropped it / Someone must have picked it up / And put it in his pocket. The first piece of evidence in the trial was not a confession from a witness, or a report by a policeman. It was not a person who was examined, but a letter. The question was: what does this letter mean?

Or rather: what is this letter evidence of? As I copy it out here, what can I make it mean?

> *January (?) 1893, Babbacombe Cliff.*
> My own Boy,
>   Your sonnet is quite lovely, and it is a marvel that those rose-red lips of yours should have been made no less for the music of song than for the madness of kisses. Your slim gilt soul walks between passion and poetry. I know Hyacinthus, whom Apollo loved so madly, was you in Greek days.
>   Why are you alone in London, and when do you go to Salisbury? Do go there to cool your hands in the grey twilight of Gothic things, and come here whenever you like. It is a lovely place — it only lacks you; but go to Salisbury first.
>
> > Always, with undying love,
> > Yours,
> > Oscar.

> *1896, HM Prison, Reading.*
> It was, let me say frankly, the sort of letter I would, in a happy if wilful moment, have written to any graceful young man from either University who had sent me a poem of his own making, certain that he would have sufficient wit or culture to interpret rightly its fantastic phrases. Look at the history of that letter! It passes from you into the hands of loathsome companions; from him to a gang of blackmailers;

copies of it are sent about London to my friends, and to
the manager of a theatre where my work is being performed:
every construction but the right one is put upon it; Society
is thrilled with the absurd rumours that I have had to pay
a huge sum of money for having written an infamous letter
to you; this forms the basis of your father's worst attack; I
produce the original letter myself in court to show what it
really is; it is denounced by your father's counsel as a
revolting and insidious attempt to corrupt innocence;
ultimately it forms part of a criminal charge. The Crown
takes it up; the Judge sums up on it with little learning and
much morality; I go to prison for it at last.

(That text, from *De Profundis*, must be one of the most extraordinary pieces of literary criticism that the nineteenth century
produced, more fantastic and with even darker implications than
Poe's *The Purloined Letter*. It may serve as a caution, reminding
us that the meaning of any text depends on who is reading it
and where.)

The Old Bailey, 24 May 1895: Mr Justice Wills.
...a letter from the prisoner, of which it is difficult for me
to speak with calmness, as addressed from one man to
another. It is for you, however, to consider whether or not
that letter is an indication of unclean sentiments and
unclean appetites on both sides. It is to my mind a letter
upon which ordinary people would be liable to put an
uncomfortable construction...

The History of That Letter (1)

*Hidden meanings have most unjustly been read into the poetical and
prose works of my client.* Sir Edward Clark.

The first attempt at interpretation of the letter was made when
the prosecution examined it by placing it alongside a series of
other texts. (I am not the first to explore the library in an effort
to understand Wilde's work.) The letter was not to be scrutinized

as an isolated utterance; the true test as to whether it was *an indication of unclean sentiments* was could it be proved to be a part of a larger, more dangerous language, the language of homosexual culture. The suggestion was that the letter bore a family likeness to certain other texts. (This is a literary variation on the theme *they are all the same*.) Two poems by Lord Alfred Douglas, including the line *the Love that dare not speak its name*, and John Bloxam's *The Priest and the Acolyte* had appeared in *The Chameleon* alongside a text by Wilde, entitled *Phrases and Philosophies for the Use of the Young*. Bloxam and Douglas had produced militant (if carefully phrased) homosexual texts; since Wilde had shared the pages of a magazine with them, then he shared the same language, one which had its origin in a sexual identity (*they shared the same bed*). And the prosecution went on to point out that J.K. Huysmans's *À Rebours* was the source of much of *Dorian Gray*; it stands in the same relation to Wilde's fiction as an older man to a boy. The prosecution's contention was that since Wilde's text was demonstrably an associate, an acquaintance of these other texts, then they must be engaged in a conversation, speaking in the same voice, formulating the same perverse language. Wilde countered the attack by denying even the possibility of a perverted text, of a text whose voice originated in a shared and unnatural vice. (*Do you consider that decent? — It was an attempt to write a prose poem in beautiful phraseology.*) He strenuously denied any intimacy between his writings and the others mentioned, as strenuously as a man ignoring an ex-lover, unfortunately encountered in a public place and by daylight. He heaped literary abuse on Bloxam's story. He defended Huysmans on the grounds that his artistry could never be reduced to mere evidence of perversion (*I don't know what you mean by a perverted novel*), knowing that the whole of *Dorian Gray* is an investigation of the perversion both of Dorian and the reader, an investigation of the possibility that a fiction can both be perverted and have the power to pervert or cleanse its reader. About Douglas's poems he simply lied. He said that in Douglas's *Shame*, the word referred only to "a quickened sense of modesty". He knew, however, that the word was homosexual literary slang, a specific euphemism for homosexual love among the poets of the 1890s. Douglas said of his symbolic boy, *his name is Shame*, and Raffalovich, in 1885, had already made Piers Gaveston a symbol of the other love by saying, *men call him Shame*. Wilde attempted, too late, to revive the contrived moral ignorance of the 1870s, the "ignorance" which had rescued Fanny and Stella. He tried to scrub his words clean of their "hidden meaning", to protect himself by concurring with the popular fiction that a text could never conceivably dare to be expressive of homosexuality. Such a thing is not only impossible, he suggested, but unthinkable, because there is no "homosexuality", or certainly no homosexual culture, to express. Homosexuality, by implication, is something that can only ever be read into a text.

The History of That Letter (2)

...(this) work was intended to be understood by the readers to describe the relations, intimacies and passions of certain persons guilty of unnatural practices. Queensberry's plea of justification at the first trial.

The second interpretation of the text was much more definite. The prosecution argued that the texts should be understood as not just being associated with perversion, seeming to *breathe an unholy passion*, but as being direct and intentional, even personal statements. Every text thus becomes a fragment of an autobiography, and intended to be understood as such.

In particular, Wilde was challenged over the passage where Basil Hallward confesses to the dangerous effects that Dorian Gray has had on his life and art. He tells him that he loves him: *It is quite true that I have worshipped you with far more romance of feeling than a man usually gives a friend. Somehow, I have never loved a woman. I suppose I never had time... Well, from the moment I met you, your personality had the most extraordinary influence over me. I quite admit that I adored you madly, extravagantly, absurdly. I wanted to have you all to myself. I was only happy when I was with you. When I was away from you, you were still present in my art.*

May I take it that you, as an artist, have never known the feeling described here?

I have never allowed any personality to dominate my art.

Then you have never known the feeling you described.

No. It is a work of fiction.

So far as you are concerned, you have no experience as to it being a natural feeling?

I think it is perfectly natural for any artist to admire intensely and love a young man. It is an incident in the life of almost any artist.

But let us go over it phrase by phrase. "I quite admit that I adored you madly." What do you say to that? Have you ever adored a young man madly?

No, not madly...

Then you have never had that feeling?

No. The whole idea was borrowed from Shakespeare. I regret to say — yes, from Shakespeare's sonnets.

I believe you have written an article to show that Shakespeare's sonnets were suggestive of unnatural vice?

At this moment, Wilde was able to return to safer ground. He began to talk about culture. He was able to say that the passage is not really about his personal experience of unnatural vice at all, but about the renaissance tradition of neo-platonism; it is a contemporary meditation on a Shakespearean theme. He picks up the same argument when he claims that the letter would have been understood "by a young man from either University" — that is, the language of the literary, the educated. The "true meaning" of the text remains locked in the world of culture, remote from either the crudity of sex, or the blatancy of autobiography, of "real life". The means of expression and interpretation no longer rest with anything so vulgar as direct speech. The code is placed in the hands of the responsible few. Having once let his argument roam the city, Wilde now tried to bring it back under control.

Oscar's argument is an influential one; much of our culture has been wrapped in the fog of "Culture". To remind myself of whose language is being used, and why, I looked up the passage which the prosecution selected for criticism, and then looked up the equivalent passage in *Teleny*, where the narrator of the novel confesses to his (male) beloved that he too loved him from the moment he saw him. He too says, *You must know that I do not care for a single girl in this world. I never did. I could never love a woman...* The word homosexual is never used in this text, any more than it is in *Dorian Gray*. The idea that this romance is an affair between and for sodomites or inverts is never baldly stated. And yet we are in no doubt about the meaning of this fragment of text. This is not because of the language, which is remarkably similar to that of *Dorian Gray*, but because we know that the text from which it is taken is not a piece of "Culture", but a piece of pornography. The definition of pornography is that we know exactly what the text is going to mean even before we open the book. We never doubt what pornography intends us to understand. You don't have to be cultured to get the message. You don't need educated ears to hear the voice.

The History of That Letter (3): *He Admitted He Had Given Him £2*

Finally, the prosecution was able to transform the letter into a text about whose meaning there could be no doubt at all. They introduced new evidence. They proved the letter to be the one for which Wilde had been blackmailed.

Wilde claimed that he had paid money for the return of his letter simply to show his contempt for the idea that it contained a definite homosexual meaning, that it could be used against him. He made final, desperate use of his favourite alibis, arguing first that the letter could not possibly be perverted, because he had passed it around London Society (he claimed to be unembarrassed that a copy had been shown to Beerbohm Tree, the distinguished director), that it could not possibly be perverted because it was Literature (he had authorized Pierre Löuys to translate it into a sonnet and publish it in a magazine). Then he admitted that he had paid a group of blackmailers for its return. One of them had said, *A very curious construction can be put on that letter.* The point is, however, that for a letter to be of any use to a blackmailer, or to a court, its meaning would have to be neither curious or in need of construction, but obvious. At this point in the trial, the letter ceased to be a text full of suggested or contested meanings. Its meanings become specific. It becomes evidence of one thing only.

To achieve this interpretation of the letter, the court reconstructed its entire history. It went through the perverse process of amassing a mountain of evidence in order to reduce all the details of that evidence to evidence of a single crime, allowing them to contain no suggestions or digressions, no spaces in which a life could be tasted or elaborated, but only one awful truth. The crime could not be silenced by an admission of guilt; it had to be silenced by being spoken, explicated, pronounced upon, proved, noted by clerks, reported in the papers. If Wilde had reduced the court to silence by simply announcing himself guilty on the first day, the trial would have failed in its purpose.

The actual history of the letter is as follows. Oscar Wilde wrote the letter to Lord Alfred Douglas. Lord Alfred Douglas knew a clerk named Alfred Wood. Wilde met Wood, who had the letter in his pocket (he had found it in an old suit of Douglas's) at the Florence in Rupert Street. Wood worked for the pimp and blackmailer Alfred Taylor. Wilde arranged to meet Taylor *to discuss it*. Clibborn and Allen, two of Taylor's *employees*, called round at Tite Street and tried to rent Wilde for £60. They failed. A copy of the letter made its way to Lord Alfred Douglas's father, and provoked him to insult Wilde publicly. Wilde was in turn successfully provoked into bringing an action for criminal libel against Queensberry, and so ended up in court accounting for his letter. The history does not stop there; it is not so neatly circular. Through this letter, Oscar had made the acquaintance of the men who frequented Alfred Taylor's rooms at 13 Little College Street; the letter proved to be a point of entry into a new world, one in which its language was commonly spoken and understood. From now on his life becomes decorated with the names of boys. Edward Shelley, the clerk; Alfonso Conway, whom Oscar took to Brighton and Worthing, dressed in a blue serge suit and a new hat, dressed him, that is, as a member of his own class. At Taylor's rooms, Wilde met Charles Parker

(Taylor's *little wife*). Charlie, who enjoyed being taken to Kettners because of the pink lampshades. And later he met Fred Atkins, the unemployed comedian, Maurice Schwabe, Ernest Scarfe, Sidney Mavor, Walter Grainger, Antonio Migge and "the waiter at the Boulevard des Capucines". At Little College Street, the court heard, he entered something like a gay family — a group of young men who worked (as blackmailers and prostitutes) from the same premises, slept together, sometimes for sex, sometimes perhaps because there was nowhere else, and sometimes lived together, casually supported one another. Mostly they were low paid or unemployed (servants, out of work valets). But they dressed in splendid drag, held parties, and when the money was there, they got themselves taken to the seaside, taken to the Savoy for chicken and champagne, they received silver cigarette cases and silver-topped canes, gold rings, and pawned them when they needed to. They offered Oscar a different city. He was asked in court if these were the sort of men with whom he chose to dine. The court rose up and demanded, in all its outraged glory as defender of sex, money and class, *Are they the sort of persons you would expect to find in the company of persons of education?* Oscar countered, in a rare moment of honesty, by speaking the truth. He enjoyed breaking the barriers of class, and he was quite aware that his money enabled him to do just as he pleased. He admitted that he belonged, and wanted to belong, to this world.

This extraordinary narrative, the true meaning of the infamous letter, was, of course, the evidence which finally made Wilde guilty. It didn't simply make him guilty of an individual crime (an error of literary taste, an incautiously obscene expression, an indecent act). It made him guilty of *being a criminal*, guilty of belonging to a particular world. At this point (*he came to the point at which admission must cease and confession must begin*) all rights of interpretation and expression were taken from him. The letter became part of the evidence; all his letters, stories, his novels, plays and poems now "meant" just one thing; they collapsed into a single, horrible text.

His plays were closed as soon as he was found guilty. His name was erased from the posters. His publisher had his windows smashed.

In tracing the full history of Wilde's letter, that is, in giving a full account of the lives of the men who used it to blackmail Oscar, the prosecution assembled one of the most extensive and glamorous collections of details about our life which those twenty years in the city have left us. (*What I want are details. Details are the only things that interest.*) In describing Taylor's rooms at 13 Little College Street, the witnesses in the dock documented a perfect image from our past. The windows of the rooms, the court was told, were kept permanently shuttered, covered with art muslins and dark curtains and lace curtains; the rooms were lit only by coloured lamps and candles and kept heavily perfumed. Dark rooms littered with discarded drag, a wig, and on the floor just a mattress, no bed, and through the door a constant supply of men, young men from sixteen to thirty... *there were frequent tea parties, meetings of friends, prostitutes and lovers. I am a boy once more in a tall hat and walking wearily among a crowd of well-dressed (hopelessly well-dressed) people, up and down a certain promenade. I enter the young prostitute's chamber, where he is arranging his photographs of fashionable beauties and favourite companions, and stay with him; we are at ease and understand each other.* The house is no longer there, but the street remains. It's worth the pilgrimage, and when you get there, turn round and look at the walls of the Houses of Parliament, from which it is only a few hundred yards, and wonder how it felt to wander through those rooms looking at your face in the mirrors, knowing that the government was within screaming distance, wondering if they'd hear those scandalous and barely muffled shrieks. When Oscar came down from the West End, he must have driven down Whitehall with a smile on his face, past the Palace of Westminster, knowing where he was going. And all of this can be traced from that single letter, read as traces from that single piece of paper.

But don't get excited. These records aren't meant for you. They are *evidence*. They aren't meant to inform us of anything; they are there to help form a verdict. They weren't written so that we could identify ourselves, imagine ourselves, remember ourselves, understand the contradictions or pleasures of Wilde's life — What was it like to be unemployed and in the gay world of 1895? How does a household of men function? What happened to the boys afterwards? Did they have children? What kind of frock was Taylor wearing? (What I want are details. Details are the only things of interest). By putting us in the dock, by making us speak the truth, they silenced us.

It is a terrible thing for a man to find out suddenly that all his life he has been speaking nothing but the truth.

Twenty years of culture were to be reduced to evidence of a crime. All the words to just one word, *guilty*. All of Oscar's life, its stratagems, its inventive, evasive work of expressing the life of men who loved men, was to be reduced to a single truth.

Henri Labouchère, who campaigned for the Labouchère amendment, the law which made men who have sex together officially guilty, ran a newspaper. It was called *Truth*.

It was his duty to confess, to suffer public shame, and to make public atonement.

The crime of which you have been convicted is so bad that one has to put stern restraint upon oneself to prevent oneself from describing, in language which I would rather not use, which must rise to the breast of every man of honour who has heard the details...

Gentlemen, have you agreed upon your verdict?

We have.

Do you find the prisoner at the bar guilty or not guilty of an act of gross indecency with Charles Parker at the Savoy Hotel on the night of his first introduction to him?

Guilty.

Do you find him guilty or not guilty of a similar offence a week later?

Guilty.

Do you find him guilty or not guilty of a similar offence at St James's Place?

Guilty.

Do you find him guilty or not guilty of an act of gross
indecency with male persons unknown in room 362 of the
Savoy Hotel?

Guilty.

And is that the verdict of all of you?

And I? May I say nothing, my Lord?

(Wilde's last words in the courtroom before being taken to Pen-
tonville.)

▷

Of course, Oscar Wilde did not *say nothing*. Neither are we silent.
We should not assume that gay London stopped, even temporar-
ily, after the trial. In prison, knowing that everything he wrote
would be scrutinized by the prison censors, Wilde tried to speak
again. In the images of a writer imprisoned he recognized a true
image of his condition. He wrote another letter, one which
contains the following phrase: *You must read this letter... right
through, though each word may become to you as the fire or knife of
the surgeon that makes the delicate flesh burn or bleed.* At the top
of the page he wrote *H.M. Prison, Reading,* and then he begins
the letter, as before, with *Dear Bosie.* This is no simple or hurried
note. It takes up eighty-four pages in the *Complete Works,* and
is an elaborate and obsessive attempt to say exactly what the
court had not wanted to hear: what had actually happened in
his life, his life with Douglas. It amasses the fondly and bitterly
remembered details of that life not as evidence for or against the
author, but in order to describe what happened. This letter
(which we now call *De Profundis*) abolishes the titillating drama
of revelation and indiscretion. Although we do not believe that
Wilde ever really told the truth, we recognize this impulse to
record the actual details of a career. We are moved and fascinated
because rarely, if ever, had so many consecutive pages been
devoted to describing this strange business of what two men do

when they are together. Wilde seems to have realized that an individual admission that a man is a homosexual, that he is guilty (*Are you gay then?*), does not conclude his history, but begins it. He seems to have realized that he could, now, attempt to "tell the truth":

> I remember when I was sitting in the dock on the occasion of my last trial listening to Lockwood's appalling denunciation of me — like a thing out of Tacitus, like a passage in Dante, like one of Savonarola's indictments of the Popes at Rome — and being sickened with horror at what I heard. Suddenly it occurred to me, *How splendid it would be, if I was saying all this about myself!* I saw then at once that what is said of a man is nothing, the point is, who says it.

▷

It was his duty to confess, to suffer public shame, and to make a public atonement.

Do you remember when you're fourteen or seventeen you spend a long time walking, walking around feeling so horny, just hoping that somebody will notice and take you home. And do you remember that feeling as you walked home from the first time (and even now, riding home on the tube after an especially passionate encounter), down the High Street, and you felt as though it was written all over your face? You're surprised that no one picks you up. You're surprised that no one can tell what you've been doing. You're surprised that no one picks you up and arrests you. They don't.

We know from experience that most of the time the city around us doesn't see the evidence right in front of its eyes. But when it chooses to, it can repeat the rituals of the law in the most intimate or casual forms. You are walking down the street, well-dressed, feeling in control, then a car slows down. A single word of abuse is shouted, and with that one word the whole night is taken away from you. Or: you are walking down the street, holding hands. It is daylight. You've just forgotten, that's all; you are not holding hands for anyone else's benefit, just for each other, demanding no public response at all. And then the laughter begins. This laughter converts you into a spectacle; the image you present is suddenly on their terms, not yours. They are forcing you to be public, to make a spectacle of yourself, to be guilty of public speech. By playing priest, they make you confess.

If one tells the truth, one is sure, sooner or later, to be found out.

6.
FORGERY

A forger of no mean or ordinary capability.

After 25 May 1895 ("Guilty") Wilde could no longer pass.
Everyone knew that Oscar was a forgery, a fake. He was not
what he had appeared to be. It was no defence that he himself
had never claimed to be anything other than both forger and
forgery. ("The first duty in life is to be as artificial as possible.")
He had modelled himself on the liars, the comedians, the critics
— "the fool, the fraud, the knave" — anyone who had signed
no contract with truth; the embroiderers and inventers of the
truth, the prostitutes. *He was entirely lacking in wholeness and
completeness of nature.* He wished, in fact, to be completely unnatural. He was a creator of copies, borrowing and reprocessing
fragments of his own and other people's works. He assiduously
composed his public life as father, husband, and moralist, and
he created a career for himself as a playwright whose plays are
littered with the wrecks of fathers, husbands, and moralists
struggling to prove that they are who and what they say they
are. His "private" homosexual life was an elaborate drama of
deception, lies and, most of all, inspired invention. He could
not, even in 1895, after concealment had failed, reveal his true
nature. There was no real Oscar Wilde, if by real we mean
homosexual. He did not, like us, have the alibi of "being like
that". London in 1895 had no conception of a man being "natur-

ally homosexual". A man who loved other men could only be described as an invert, an inversion of something else, a pervert, an exotic, a disease, a victim, a variation. Wilde was an artist as well. He was entirely uninterested in authenticity.

One can fancy an intense personality being created out of sin.

After his release from Reading Gaol, on 19 May 1896, Oscar Wilde ceased to exist. His place was taken by a Mr Sebastian Melmoth. Reggie Turner gave him a dressing case, stamped with the initials S.M. In 1897 mail was forwarded to the Hotel Sandwich, Dieppe (the first of many such hotels) c/o Monsieur Sebastian Melmoth. Carrington's 1905 Paris edition of Barbey D'Aurevilly's *What Never Dies* attributed the translation (falsely) to *Sebastian Melmoth (O.W.)*.

This was not the first transformation. Changes of costume were not just metaphors for these men; they were bone-deep. Oscar Fingal O'Flahertie Wills Wilde, a big, strong, heavy, virile Irishman, had become a London queen. In the 1890s, the "Oscar" of the back streets had changed back into "Mr Wilde" by the time the cab reached Chelsea. Some men spoke of a scarcely human character known as "The O'Flaherty". Boulton and Park had emerged from their dressing rooms at 13 Wakefield Street as Mrs Fanny Graham and Lady Clinton. Alfonso Conway had strolled along the seafront with Mr Wilde dressed up and no doubt feeling just like a gentleman's son, which, since he sold newspapers for a living, was not his natural state. Jack Saul, also from Dublin, had made the same change when he had left town after the persecution of 1884 and moved in with Hammond at 19 Cleveland Street. John Gray had ceased to be the eldest son of a family of nine children in Woolwich and was to become the consort of the wealthy Marc-André Raffalovich; that Canon Gray for whom Raffalovich built a church where, once a year, a mass was said for the repose of the soul of Paul Verlaine. Lord Alfred Douglas became, when his beloved wrote in despair from

Holloway on 3 May 1895, *Prince Fleur de Lys*, and was then to be just *Bosie*, a lord no longer, when he received *De Profundis*. Simeon Solomon had become a successful exhibitor at the Royal Academy, then a Bohemian, then finally a criminal, insane, alcoholic, perverted pavement artist. I've seen photographs of myself four years ago, and I hardly recognize myself.

When this man chose his new name, which could not be discarded at the end of an evening (I've met a Vera who is Steve by daytime, and I know a Blanche who is always Blanche, but he never appears in the daylight), he did so with care, undaunted by Lady Bracknell's warning that an adult baptism is both *grotesque and irreligious*. *Sebastian*, we may suppose, is from the saint of the same name, whose life is an appropriate blend of fact and homosexual fantasy. The title is fitting, since the subject was now sitting for his Portrait of the Artist as an Old Man; it was to be an altarpiece, with the offstage violence of British justice dignified by the suggestion that the criminal is a martyr. The body displayed in such pictures is always handsome, the martyrdom always more or less sexual, the arrows inflicting multiple, anonymous penetrations on the half-desiring flesh. *Melmoth* is from *Melmoth the Wanderer*, the Gothic horror novel by Charles Maturin, our hero's maternal great-uncle. The name maintains a tenuous link with the lost family, the lost country; but the hero of the novel is the antitype of the Celtic, Ossianic heroes whose names were borrowed by an idealistic, nationalistic mother for her son's first christening — Oscar, Fingal. For his second christening, the profligate son inverted the glamour of his heritage. He took the name of a hideous, heartless man, condemned to wander the earth, homeless for eternity, in penance for some hideous, unnamed, unnamable crime.

The choice of names indicates the bitterness and the care with which the new personality was to be forged. What had in fact been imposed (exile, loss of family, being a criminal) was made to appear chosen, a chosen role.

One name is as good as another, when one has no right to any name.

Mr Sebastian Melmoth travelled Europe supported by his friends until his death in 1900. He enjoyed and endured a combination of pleasures and miseries entirely appropriate to the role of exiled Queen, until he chose to announce his personal *fin de siècle*, unable to face the prospect of enduring into a new century. He was always on the make, making things up, wearing make-up. He wasn't destroyed, denuded or stripped down to his "real" personality. He was nothing if not inconsistent. He was reunited with his one True Love, the only man who could make sense of his life (*I feel that it is only with you that I can do anything at all*), the man to whom he addressed the thousands of terrible, agonized, sincere words of *De Profundis* — and he fell in love again, fell out of love, lived with him in a Neapolitan villa, left him several times.

Meanwhile he corresponded happily with English public schoolboys and a Harvard undergraduate. He fell madly in love (usually for three days or less) with all the boys of Rome, Naples, Paris and Genoa, and was quite unable or unwilling to distinguish between the services of prostitutes and lovers. (1 January 1899: *I am practically engaged to a fisherman of quite extraordinary beauty, aged eighteen.*) His letters, now that he had nothing to lose, blossom with boys, flowers, obscenities, wines, the small delights of European travel. He lived entirely for pleasure, but also found time to write two signed and serious letters to the *Daily Chronicle*, arguing with informed compassion for practical reforms in the English prison system. The first was written just nine days after his release. It is about the systematic maltreatment of children and the mentally disturbed in Reading Gaol. Surely these are not the writings for which "Oscar Wilde" is famous. And just three years after the première of *The Importance of Being Earnest* he published *The Ballad of Reading Gaol*, his hardest, darkest fiction, and not under his old name but as C33, his cell number in Reading, as if that conferred dignity enough on the text. (*He who lives more lives than one / More deaths than one must die*, he wrote.) On 9 September 1900 he was reading Edward Carpenter's *Civilization, Its Cause and Cure*, as if the author of *The Soul of Man Under Socialism* was finally taking himself seriously, now that he was experiencing real material and financial need for the

first time in his life. In April, knowing that he was the anti-Christ
of Europe, he had made a point of having himself blessed by the
Pope on Easter Day, occasioning religious sentiments of such
sincerity and ludicrousness as to make both Firbank and Rolfe
seem quite sane:

> I have again seen the Holy Father. Each time he dresses
> differently; it is most delightful. Today over his white and
> purple a velvet cape edged with ermine, and a huge scarlet
> and gold stole. I was deeply moved as usual... I have become
> very cruel to boys, and no longer let them kiss me in public.

He also attributed the Pope with the power of curing his food
poisoning, and of inspiring an appreciation of Bernini. Was he
serious? Were his religious affectations, after the pieties of the
cell in Reading, merely being sent up to Heaven in a final,
sacrificial pantomime? Who was the *real* Sebastian Melmoth?
What was his life like?

In four years he lived the lives of several men.

On 16 November 1897 he wrote: "My existence is a scandal."

Insincerity is simply a method by which we can multiply our personalities.

▷

A new life! That was what he wanted.

The characteristic name for the heroic life of things or people
which have no right to exist was invented, along with so many
other features of our lives, during the life and times of Mr Oscar
Wilde. It is a word that we still use. We still consider inventing
a new life to be an ordinary, even inevitable activity. If you can't
be authentic (and you can't), if this doesn't feel like real life
(and it doesn't), then you can be *camp*.

Mr Wilde himself never committed the word to writing, although the first traceable record we have of it used as part of a

gay language dates from his schooldays. On 21 November 1869, Frederick Park wrote to Lord Arthur Clinton:

> I should like to live to a green old age. Green did I say? Oh, *ciel!* The amount of paint that will be required to hide that very unbecoming tint. My campish undertakings are not at present meeting with the success they deserve. Whatever I do seems to get me into hot water somewhere. But *n'importe*. What's the odds so long as you're happy?
>
> Believe me,
> your affectionate sister-in-law,
> Fanny, Winifred, Park.

For Fanny the word does not indicate a decorative set of gestures or enthusiasms, but an *undertaking*, a serious activity. The 1972 Supplement to the *Oxford English Dictionary* assures us that the word is derived from the French *se camper*, and is invariably associated with "exceptional want of character", by which it presumably means publicly gay men, Harrap's *French/English Dictionary* notes that a painter may camp (pose) his subject, as may an author too: *Voilà votre homme campé en peu de mots"* — *there you have him in a nutshell. Bien campé* — well built, well set up. Rachilde's *Monsieur Venus* gives us another implicitly gay use of the word in 1884, when we see her hero Jaques, whose effeminate beauty is such that only his large hands give him away as a man (ah, how true!), sitting surrounded by flowers in the luxurious apartment bought for him by an admirer, *se campant vis-à-vis la glace qui lui renvoyait, multiplées, toutes les splendeurs de son paradis*. How am I to translate that? Either Jaques is *posing himself before the mirror which reflected and multiplied all the splendours of his paradise* — or he is *sitting in front of the mirror in his luxurious apartment and camping it up*. The pose of Mr Sebastian Melmoth is best described as camp. Remember that the initial charge had been that he had posed — *To Oscar Wilde, posing as a somdomite* [sic]. From 1894 to 1900 he was posing, camping not just to save his life, but to find out if any life at all was possible.

A new life! That was what he wanted.

To forge can mean two things. Forgery is "the making of a thing in fraudulent imitation of something". To forge is to make a copy, a fake which, when detected, alarmingly reveals that a fake has just as much life, as much validity as the real thing — until detected. It is then revealed as something that has no right to exist. It puts into question authenticity. It even has the power to damage, specifically and effectively, certain specific forms of authentication. Wilde, for instance, was married, and from the same class as his judges. But he invited Parker back to Tite Street while the children were asleep; he enjoyed sharing his money, body and conversation with working-class men. So what sense could the words "married" and "gentleman" retain when applied to Oscar Wilde? Wilde's plays bore all the hallmarks of successful comedies; but when, in the spring of 1895, they suddenly revealed an entirely unsuspected new set of meanings, they were hurriedly closed down. They all conclude with happy marriages, but they also catalogue the pains of innocent wives, husbands touched by horrible scandals, obscurely threatening, and unmarried, fashion-able men. One society lady idly remarks, *The secret of life is to appreciate the pleasure of being terribly, terribly deceived*, but the audience did not agree. Oscar Wilde was exposed as a forger. The scandal of his existence was not simply that he had lied, but that he had effectively debased the very values which he had appeared to endorse.

To forge can also mean to hammer out, to create in a forge, to create something new with fire and ingenuity and amidst flying sparks. The dazzling career was not interrupted by being exposed; Mr Sebastian Melmoth was to be the most brilliant forgery yet.

Something that is forged has no intrinsic value. Rather it has the value with which the forger himself manages to invest his creation. There is no intrinsic value to homosexuality. There is no "real" us, we can only ever have an unnatural identity, which is why we are all forgers. We create a life, not out of lies, but out of more of less conscious choices; adaptations, imitations and plain theft of styles, names, social and sexual roles, bodies. The high camp of Sebastian Melmoth's life is a true model for us, not because we are all devastated upper class queens, or want to be, but because we too must compose ourselves. We may not talk like him, but we still rephrase everything, we give new meanings to things, wear the wrong clothes in the wrong places, refuse to have any but the most provisional form of integrity. Could you possibly summarize the daily fluctuations in your physical appearance with a single name? Which is it to be — the casually dressed citizen, or the well-dressed nightclubber? Or will it be the naked lover, as "spontaneous", for once, as the half-remembered boy. Select a photograph to send me, to introduce yourself to a stranger. Choose something from the stuffed wardrobe, all those versions of yourself acquired since that moment when you reduced yourself to zero by announcing, "I am gay". Choose carefully, since it is only now that you realize that you are leading just one particular gay life among many. You have moved from the impossibility of that life in a small town to the possibilities of this city life. And now, what traces of authenticity, of the man you were supposed to "grow into" (as if the fitting had already been made), what traces remain, and where in your face or body can you find them, those remains of the heterosexual child they thought you were? Oscar Wilde was a queen, an invert, a pervert, a sodomite, an Uranian, a simisexual, a homosexual and a Maryanne. Each word describes a different creature. We can never say of any man that he was (or is) a homosexual, and leave it at that. Consider your own variety of poses over the last four years. Or make your own list of the extraordinarily various forms we've taken in the last forty years: since coming home from the war, we have been The Flaming Queen (Fitzrovia, 1959; *Bolts* or *Benjys* 1979), The Speed Queen (Soho, 1963; Leicester Square, 1986), Leather Boys (c. 1960 to the present day), the Macho Man (*Subway* ad infinitum), The Clone. Our reading has included "sensitive" novels, *Jeremy*, *Mister*, *Him* and *Gay News*; we have read in the papers about Alan Turing, Wildeblood, Wolfenden, Thorpe and Trestrail; there has been life before, during and "after" Gay Liberation; we've enjoyed True Love, Fucking Around, Boy George and Safe Sex. My summary of our identities might describe a procession of mannequins, a chronology of exhibits, a genealogical tree in whose privileged shade you stretch out. Or it may describe the transformations of a single, literal body, someone you know. We never arrive. There is no single story in this city, where your (his) narrative may be punctuated by, but never quite conclude with, friendship, or independence, with several loves, or few or none. Nobody I know cares to remain constant.

Who wants to be consistent? What kind of integrity is that?

We are all fakes, all inventions. We are making this all up as we go along.

To invent anything at all is an act of sheer genius, and, in a commercial age like ours, shows considerable physical courage.

7.

POSSESSIONS

A Bazaar of Dangerous and Smiling Chances, 1894

Time: The present. The room is artistically and luxuriously furnished.

I remember so well how, with a strange smile on his pale,
curved lips, he led me through his wonderful picture gallery,
showed me his tapestries, his enamels, his jewels, his carved
ivories, made me wonder at the strange loveliness of the
luxury in which he lived.

Whenever I imagine him posed, it is not naked or against a bare
wall. It is not with other people (other men) but, most characteristically, as a single man in a room, in an interior. It is not
just himself he composes and arranges. In the rooms of each of
my lovers or friends there is a singular collection of possessions.

And Wilde's house in Chelsea was full of possessions, objects
which composed elaborate interiors. He owned drawings by
Burne-Jones and by Whistler, by Monticelli and Simeon Solomon, china, a library of rare editions, signed copies of the works
of Hugo and Whitman, Swinburne and Mallarmé, Morris and
Verlaine.

And each of Wilde's heroes is a collector, a connoisseur. They
love to do nothing more than to recite the list of their treasures,
to sort and catalogue them. Imagine a room... *some dark antique
bronzes contrast with the pale gleam of two noble Christi Crucifixi,*

one carved in ivory, the other moulded in wax. He has his trays of Tassie's gems, his Louis-Quatorze bonbonnière with a miniature by Pettitot... one can fancy him lying there in the midst of his books and casts and engravings, a true virtuoso, a subtle connoisseur turning over his fine collection...

But he does not care what he collects. It is the activity of collecting itself that he enjoys. He will lead me from room to room, each one full. Dorian Gray hoards first jewels, then fabrics, then perfumes, church vestments. The individual items are as unimportant as they are costly. What matters is the cumulative effect of their sequence.

On one occasion he took up the study of jewels... this taste enthralled him for years, and, indeed, may be said never to have left him. He would often spend a whole day settling and resettling in their cases the various stones he had collected, such as the olive-green chrysoberyl that turns red by lamplight, the cymophane with its wire-like line of silver, the pistachio-coloured peridot, rose-pink and wine-yellow topazes, carbuncles of fiery scarlet with tremulous four-rayed stars, flame-red cinnamon-stones, orange and violet spinels, and amethysts with their alternate layers of ruby and sapphire. He loved the red gold of the sunstone, and the moonstone's pearly whiteness, and the broken rainbow of the milky opal. He procured from Amsterdam three emeralds of extraordinary size and richness of colour, and had a turquoise *de la vieille roche* that was the envy of all the connoisseurs.

He discovered wonderful stories, also, about jewels. ...When the Duke de Valentinois, son of Alexander VI, visited Louis XII of France, his horse was loaded with gold leaves, according to Brantôme, and his cap had double rows of rubies that threw out a great light. Charles of England had ridden in stirrups hung with four hundred and twenty-one diamonds. Richard II had a coat, valued at thirty thousand marks, which was covered with balas rubies. Hall described Henry VII on his way to the Tower previous to his coronation, as wearing "a jacket of raised gold, the placard embroidered with diamonds and other rich stones, and a great bauderike about his neck of large balasses." The favourites of James I wore earrings of emeralds set in gold filigrane. Edward II gave to Piers Gaveston a suit of red-gold armour studied with jacinths, a collar of gold roses set with turquoise, stones, and a skull-cap *parsemé* with pearls. Henry II wore jewelled gloves reaching to the elbow, and had a hawk-glove sewn with twelve rubies and fifty-two great orients. The ducal hat of Charles the Rash, the last Duke of Burgundy of his race, was hung with pear-shaped pearls, and studded with sapphires.

How exquisite life had once been! How gorgeous in its pomp and decoration! Even to read of the luxury of the dead was wonderful!

Then he turned his attention...

Something about this listing of treasures is unnerving. Why is such an effort being devoted to such a collection? What excessive energy and cost would have to be expended if it was to be realized — and even if it is "imaginary", what obsession has led to the hoarding of these obscure scraps of information? Can a list ever actually give us the pleasures it describes and promises, or can it only ever seek to choke the hunger that gapes beneath it by amassing a junkshop of unconvincing details? All its verbal luxuries actually achieve is to remind us that *this is not enough.* *Living in a city, you are always looking in shop windows, looking in magazines, being invited to want. Always you want more...*

Ah! You are not listening to me. Be calm. I — I am calm. I am quite calm. Listen. I have jewels hidden in this place — jewels that are marvellous. I have a collar of pearls, set in four rows. They are like unto moons chained with rays of silver. They are like fifty moons caught in a silver net. On the ivory of her breast a queen has worn it. I have amethysts of two kinds, one that is black like wine, and one that is red like wine that has been coloured with water. I have topazes, yellow as are the eyes of tigers, and topazes that are as pink as the eyes of a wood-pigeon, and green topazes that are as the eyes of cats. I have opals that burn always with an ice-like flame, opals that make sad men's minds, and are fearful of the shadows... I have sapphires big like eggs, and blue as blue flowers... I have chrysolites and beryls and chrysophrases and rubies. I have sardonyx and hyacinth stones, and stones of chalcedony, and I will give them to you, all, and other things will I add to them... What desirest thou more than this...

What desirest thou more than this?

The words, with which Herod vainly attempts to satisfy the abominable hunger of Salomé, seem to be as rare and precious as the things they describe. But in fact this exotic list is not a genuine antique at all. It is a reproduction. Wilde took both its form and its details from the *Art Handbooks* published by the South Kensington museums. Chelsea was overshadowed by the new museums, their giant interiors decorated with systematically organized collections of unique and precious objects, more alluring than the displays even of Oxford Street. His library doubtless featured the first volume of the *New English Dictionary*, the first that could claim to contain, in its heavy and crowded volume, all the treasures of the language. Each of these catalogues is haunted by the cry of Herodias when she hears Herod recite his list of riches: *As for you, you are ridiculous.*

What is the pleasure that these catalogues seem somehow not to include? What is it that Salomé desires, desires so fiercely that even this recitation cannot divert her? What more could she or we desire... ? I can show you a hidden book, an apocrypha, a catalogue that includes the true subject which this obsessed, repetitive, breathless phrasing seems always to hint. The book itself is part of the furnishings of a secret room. It is the rare and infamous *Teleny*, still locked (because it must be labelled both a treasure and a danger) in the Private Case of the British Museum. Come with me.

He led us through a dimly-lighted passage, and up a winding staircase into a kind of balcony made out of old Arab *moucharabie*, brought to him by his Father from Tunis or Algiers.

"From here you can see everything without being seen."

As I stepped in this kind of loggia and looked down into the room, I was for a moment, if not dazzled, at least perfectly bewildered. It seemed as if from this every-day world of ours I had been transported into fairyland. A thousand lamps of varied form filled the room with a strong yet hazy light. There were wax tapers upheld by Japanese cranes, or glowing in massive bronze and silver candlesticks, the plunder of Spanish altars; curiously wrought iron cressets of tortured and fantastic designs; chandeliers of murous, iridescent glass work reflected in Dutch gilt...

On faded old damask couches, on huge pillows made out of priests' stoles, worked by devout fingers in silver and in gold, on soft Persian and Syrian divans, on lion and panther rugs, on mattresses covered with electric cats' skins, men, young and goodlooking, almost all naked, were lounging there by twos and threes, grouped in attitudes of the most consummate lewdness such as the imagination can never picture to itself, and such as were only seen in the brothels of men in lecherous Spain, or in those of the wanton East...

From huge Chinese bowls rose costly ferns, dainty Indian palms, creeping plants and parasites, with wicked looking flowers from American forests, and feathery grasses from the Nile in Sèvres vases, whilst from above, ever and anon, a shower of full blown red and pink roses came pouring down, mingling their intoxicating scent with that of the incense which ascended in white cloudlets from censers and silver chafing-dishes. The perfume of that over-heated atmosphere, the sound of smothered sighs, the groans of pleasure, the smack of eager kisses expressing the never-satiated lust of youth, made my brain reel...

The text mimics the movements of Wilde's prose; the activity of the listing itself is erotic, while the boys themselves are effortlessly converted into objects, luxuries, additions to a fabulous collection. After the succession of furnishings and objets d'art, this is surely the missing chapter of *The Picture of Dorian Gray*, the chapter Wilde could never write, the key to Dorian's kleptomania, the true source of our hunger. We now know that Wilde himself collected and took pleasure in men just as he collected and enjoyed beautiful things. In the connoisseur's library, erotica and exotica are somehow indistinguishable.

These treasures, and everything he collected in his lovely house, were to be to him a means of forgetfulness, modes by which he could escape, for a season, from the fear that seemed to him at times almost too great to be borne.

I always knew that I had to live in a room of my own. We are all collectors. Our rooms are not decorated to announce our occupation or our family status; they are not really "domestic" interiors. They need reflect nothing but the tastes of their owner, the pleasure he takes in his life, his ability to choose and arrange his possessions. Think of the sequence of rooms through which your seductions have taken you, the living rooms, the bedrooms, and how their contents have impressed you, how they have been as sensual and as significant for you as their owners themselves.

1894. He... told me that luxury was nothing but a background, a painted scene in a play, and that power, power over other men, power over the word, was the only thing worth having, the one supreme pleasure worth knowing, the one joy never tired of, and that in our century only the rich possessed it.

Wilde, *An Ideal Husband*

1904. The armchair was placed directly in front of the fireplace, the ordinary garrett-coloured iron fireplace and mantel of a suburban lodging-house. To the grey wall above the mantel a large sheet of brown packing-paper was tacked. On this background were pinned photographs of the Hermes of

Herculaneum, the terra-cotta Sebastian of South Kensington, Donatello's liparose David and the vivid David of Verrochio, the wax model of Cellini's Perseys, an unknown Rugger XV, prized for a single example of the rare feline-human type, and the O.U.D.S. Sebastian of *Twelfth Night* of 1900.

F.W. Rolfe, Baron Corvo, *Hadrian the Seventh*

1915. Let us follow these bright Ornaments.
The rooms of their occupants are sometimes interesting.

Ronald Firbank, *Vainglory*

1922. They know how to arrange a drawing room, to compose "interiors".

Marcel Proust, *Sodome et Gomorrhe*

1933. The atmosphere of the room is one of luxury and fastidiousness. The owner is an artist in the sense that everything in the room has been chosen for its intrinsic value and given its absolutely right place in the general scheme of decoration... To the outsider, the room is artificial, but it excites curiosity about the owner. To him, it is a source of pleasure.

Mordaunt Shairp, *The Green Bay Tree*

1943. On the floor, Divine has put some threadbare rugs, and nailed to the wall... photographs of goodlooking kids, which she has stolen from photographers' display windows...

Jean Genet, *Our Lady of the Flowers*

1953. They're all queers, every damn one of them. The queer is the artistic arbiter of the age, chum. The pervert is the top guy now.

Raymond Chandler, *The Long Goodbye*

c.1963. ... the decor was decidedly flock wallpaper and red plush. The walls were decorated with framed photographs of stars — there was a stunning shot of Vivien Leigh...

Peter Burton, *Parallel Lives*

180

1978. ...a building on West 29th Street, filled by its landlord
with faggots, who fixed things up much prettier than straights...
built-in *banquettes* with huge patterned pillows of all colours and
friendly Oriental scatter-rugs and a tall armoire from Provence
and vases of flowers...

Larry Kramer, *Faggots*

1980. The money! The effort! One tenant mirrors everything,
the next panels the walls, the third lines them with mylar, the
fourth turns to *toile de Jouy*, the fifth to pegboard or handblocked
rice-paper.

Edmund White, *States of Desire*

Beautiful sins, like beautiful things, are the privilege of the rich.

Collectors are wealthy. In 1895, or now, London is a city obsessed
with the visible differences between rich and poor, and the
imagery of our rooms makes it clear that we have staked our
survival on upward social mobility. Simeon Solomon, John Gray,
Fanny and Stella, Clibborn and Atkins and the boys whose names
are listed in the trial transcripts all rose (albeit briefly; then as
now there was something hysterical, impermanent about the
imagery of "success") into wealthy and distinguished society. It
was precisely their entry into "homosexuality" that allowed them
to enter rich houses, the Savoy hotel, luxurious interiors. Now,
as then, disposable income is the prerequisite of a "gay lifestyle".
A collection of things, a décor, may appear to be an expression
of personality. It is always an expression of spending-power.
Dorian Gray and Oscar Wilde furnished and decorated their
houses at a time when most men in London lived in shared rooms
crowded with their families.

You seem to me to be living entirely for pleasure.

But why should we feel guilty? I always wanted to live in a room
of my own, and I always wanted the kind of style that is specifically

chosen, luxurious if you like. Material wealth and sensual pleasure have a very specific function for us; they compensate for other forms of poverty.

Hedonism is some kind of justification; Saturday night justifies the week. Our stylishness provides gratifying evidence of our ability to live well despite everything. Don't get me wrong; remembering what kind of city this is we live in, our assertion that we can and do enjoy ourselves is a profound one.

Of course, to one so modern as I am... the world will always be lovely.

To be a connoisseur is to be a member of an elite — not necessarily the elite of the wealthy, though always close to it in inspiration at least. We may no longer pose as aristocrats; but the crucial point is that we still see ourselves as somehow above or apart from the world of production, licensed to play. There is a new "aristocracy", bigger and easier to enter than the old one (you can do it), one of sensibility, by which I mean one that understands how pleasure works and how it can be obtained. When Wilde dedicated *The Importance of Being Earnest* as "A Trivial Comedy for Serious People" he was dedicating it to us, since we too, in all seriousness, wish to order the world so that the financial is trivial, pleasure is without cost, lies and deceptions without punishment. He was quite serious when he fantasized a world in which *the future belongs to the dandy. The exquisites are going to rule.* We have discovered (Wilde was one of the men who discovered it for us) a powerful solution to the pain or embarrassment of living in a culture which does not work — where things do not get to the people who need them. We replace "need" with taste, we abolish "use" and re-invent luxury. Taste and luxury together ensure the flow of pleasure from product to consumer. Welcome to the Pleasuredome.

The stereotype of gay culture as an irresponsible, hedonistic aristocracy, formulated in the nineteenth century, may have some accuracy still. Our possessions are of value and beauty only insofar as they are cherished by their owner. Our pleasures have no life of their own. They exist to reaffirm the life of their owner.

For them to function in this way they must be consumed again and again. The catalogue, the museum, the glance round the room, the familiarity of a personal collection, re-enacts this repeated consumption in its most immediate and gratifying form. (*In a house we all feel of the proper proportions. Everything is subordinated to us, fashioned for our use and our pleasure.*)

Repetition converts an appetite into an art.

The eroticism of a catalogue is not surprising. Pornography too is a catalogue. It lists parts of the body and their attendant fetishes just as a catalogue might list rare and precious things, with an identical effect of intoxication. It is a naming of pleasures. It too is mechanical in its operation, and we love it because it promises and gives us exactly what we want, with no effort beyond purchase. We enjoy pornography in exactly the same way as Dorian enjoys his jewels. Teleny's gaze moves without pause from object to body to object. The catalogue gives an object the vigour of a body, and a body the purchasability of an object. The list itself is satisfying. This is why we envy the power of pornographers. They abolish the effort and art of our sentences, our efforts to describe or capture, they make them seem ridiculous. In the same way, we are jealous of the man described by pornography, or the man who presents himself as a pornographic object and is thus able to ensure his purchase by an eager buyer. It is no accident that the very first homosexual pornographic story written in London begins with a scene in which trolling and shopping are confused:

> The writer of these notes was walking through Leicester Square one sunny afternoon last November, when his attention was particularly taken by an effeminate, but very good-looking young fellow who was walking in front of him, looking in shop windows from time to time, and now and then looking round to attract my attention. Dressed in tight-fitting clothes, which set his adonis-like figure to the best advantage... he had small and elegant feet, set off by

pretty patent-leather boots, a fresh looking beardless face,
with almost feminine features, auburn hair and sparkling
blue eyes, which spoke as plainly as possible to my senses,
and told me that the handsome youth must indeed be one
of the Mary-Annes of London who I had heard were often
to be seen. Presently the object of my affection almost
halted and stood facing the writer as he took off his hat,
and wiped his face on a beautiful white silk handkerchief.
The lump in his trousers had a fascinating effect on me. I
asked him to take a glass of wine. He appeared to com-
prehend that there was business in my proposal.

Sins of the Cities of the Plains or Con-
fessions of a Maryanne, 1881

I do not mean to suggest that this possession by description of
bodies or things is an inferior or inauthentic pleasure. The listing
of parts of the body or precious things may move us deeply. Its
expressions may employ the most cynical and professional of
languages — the salesman's catalogue, the pornographer's list of
stimuli — but nevertheless it is often indistinguishable from the
most spontaneous and intimate of languages — that of confession.

If on a dark night I whispered in your ear the most predictably
wild of sexual fantasies; if I could show you a shining shop-window
full of luxuries; if I could lead you through a silent museum
galleried with overwhelming gorgeousness, then your whispered
reply to my question would be, of course, *Yes, that is what I really
want.*

▷

The intoxication of possession, the importance of repeatedly
possessing things, is a characteristic pleasure of life in the city.
Shopping, cruising, advertisements, pornography. Because we
are people who have always been denied what we want, our
desire is justifiably insistent. However, "getting what you want"
is a process that must be endlessly repeated. Ending does not
feature on the list of pleasures; there is always another magazine.

Wilde was haunted by the novel À *Rebours*. He would turn to it restlessly and re-read it, its demonstration of the deadly infinitude of desire, its recitations of an appalling accumulation of luxuries which never seem to provide the longed-for *luxe, calme et volupté*. But he learnt nothing from his reading. The whole point of the book is that its hero, after all his collections have failed to bring him satisfaction, reaches a state of crisis, a decision, the concluding and conclusive paragraph of a moral tale. Wilde returned his Dorian to the beginning of the story, and made him repeat it. He made him an addict. Dorian is never satisfied by his possessions, and must always flee by night to the prostitutes of Whitechapel or the opium of Limehouse, which themselves prove endless, addictive pleasures. Whistler designed a room, the Peacock Room, which may stand as symbol of all fantastic city interiors, intoxicating and horrifying. It was the most fabulous interior of the age; it was meant to be the last word. It was redesigned again and again. Its walls were successively covered, stripped and recovered in silk, embossed leather and painted plaster, at enormous and futile cost. The customer was never satisfied.

Never before had he felt so keenly, or with such exquisite joy, the magic and mystery of beautiful things.

There is no magic, no mystery at all. The intoxication of the catalogue wears thin — at any moment the cadences of its prose become preposterous, too contrived. Worst of all its crucial element of repetition becomes repetitious, boring. The pointlessness of possession as a way of life is suddenly revealed. We are aware that the contents of a living room, or a museum, have been summoned not by magic, but with enormous contrivance and often at great expense. The idealism of our pleasure-seeking gives way. We are truly addicted, not to Beauty, but to Fashion. (What text is less convincing, less intoxicating than *The Complete Works* of Oscar Wilde — we know that his recitations of luxury saved neither him nor his creations from ruin.)

▷

There is a catalogue in *De Profundis*, the last catalogue he wrote, which is unlike all the others. In Reading Gaol where he wrote it, the connoisseur was truly alone in his room, with only imaginary or remembered luxuries to furnish a bare cell. The final humiliation of Oscar Wilde was bankruptcy; to pay the costs of his trial his house had to be opened to the creditors and auctioneers, ransacked. His collection of paintings, his library of first editions, his coterie of prostitutes and lovers had all been broken up and dispersed. His possessions were not to be cherished or preserved.

This final catalogue is unlike all the others because it conjures not pleasure but cost. It is, I think, the most moving passage in the letter:

> However, of course everything has to be paid for... the Savoy dinners — the clear turtle soup, the luscious ortolans wrapped in their wrinkled Sicilian vine-leaves, the heavy amber-coloured, indeed almost amber-scented champagne — Dagonet 1880, I think, was your favourite wine? — all have to be paid for. The supper at Willis's, the special *cuvée* of Perrier-Jouet reserved always for us, the wonderful *patés*, procured directly from Strasbourg, the marvellous *fine champagne* served always at the bottom of great bell-shaped glasses that its bouquet might be savoured by the true epicure of what is really exquisite in life — these cannot be left unpaid for, as bad debts of a dishonest client. Even the dainty sleeve-links — four heart-shaped moonstones of silver mist, girdled by alternate ruby and diamond for their setting — that I designed, and had made at Henry Lewis's as a special little present to you, to celebrate the success of my second comedy — these even — though I believe you sold them for a song a few months afterwards — have to be paid for.

Of course everything one does has to be paid for.

The pleasures we repeat, and repeatedly enjoy, are necessary to our lives. But the image of the bankrupt Wilde listing the trivial circumstances of his pleasure is a reminder that at any moment this repetition may cease to be effective. The appalled realization that the pleasure had come to an end is not simply the weeping of a rich man who has lost his possessions. Now that the reveller (the lover) is stone-cold sober, the vine leaves, the champagnes and the moonstones must be catalogued as all-too-accurate signs of the life he has led in this, his chosen city. *De Profundis* is a letter from a man who realizes that the method of his pleasure concealed the fact that pleasure has both origins and consequences, that it takes place within a specific economy and that it can, at any moment, be taken away. Perhaps we require of our pleasures that they conceal these facts. How could we enjoy ourselves if we worried too much that our whole culture is based on the consumption of pleasures, on the pleasures of consumption?

Conversation with a prostitute, 12 June 1984

"How was the job in Finchley?"

"It didn't take long. I went down to Selfridges and looked at washing machines, but six hundred pounds is a lot of money. I thought about buying a drier separately. I'll have to think about it. I keep getting these wants. I want a machine. If it wasn't a washer it would be something else. It's madness. It's the way we live."

Confession, November 1984

An out of town job will cost you a hundred plus fares. Your place will be twenty-five or seventy-five, that depends on what we do. A magazine will cost you five pounds, or more if it's under the counter stuff. Thursday night cost me two pounds to get in, say five pounds for drink and cigarettes, one pound ten for the night bus there and back. This jacket I'm wearing cost forty-six pounds, these boots cost sixty-nine pounds, I got these jeans for seventeen. I went to Covent Garden dressed like this. It cost me fourteen pounds and I met a beautiful man from Earl's Court. There was carpet from wall to wall, and mirror from wall to wall. He had several sorts of drugs, and a Goya print on his living-room wall. We had sex on a Chesterfield.

8.
PRETEXTS

Diary, 22 October 1983
The strangest thing is that it's so hard to tell if it's true or not.
My father always said, if you're not sure if it's the real thing,
then it isn't. In ten years time I suppose I'll be with someone
else, or on my own, or I'll have left the city, and I'll look back
and wonder how I could have believed that what I felt was real.
I've felt so much for so many men, I look into his eyes and
wonder if this is it. That's why I'm starting to keep this diary, I
suppose I just want to write down what is happening, against
the time when it isn't happening any more and I want to remember how and why I did all this.

Diary, 12 January 1984
Algernon: "Do you really keep a diary? I'd give anything to look
at it. May I?"
Cecily: "Oh no." (Puts her hand over it). "You see, it is simply
a very young girl's record of her own thoughts and impressions,
and consequently meant for publication."
The Importance of Being Earnest, Act II

I never found this scene funny. At the very moment when the
man she has been waiting all her life to meet (whether he *is* the
man she has been waiting all her life to meet is never made
convincingly clear) declares his love for her, Cecily at once

makes him repeat himself so that his words can be converted into a text, copied into her diary. "I have dared to love you wildly, passionately, devotedly, hopelessly," she writes. Does she think that his statement is true because she has written it down? Does it become any less true for being written down, instantly converted into the repeatable script of a sentimental comedy? Does it become any less true when, forty-six pages later in *The Complete Works*, in *Lady Windermere's Fan*, Lord Darlington turns, in all melodramatic seriousness to Lady Windermere and declares: "From the moment I met you, I loved you, loved you blindingly, adoringly, madly"? Does the fact that the words of love have been transferred from one voice to another make them inauthentic? After two hours of turning from text to text, looking up these reiterated phrases, I get confused, confused and frightened. To reassure myself that he means what he says, I turn to the letters; they seem more real. I look up the one where he declares to Bosie, *I love you, I love you, my heart is a rose!* But I can't forget that there was more than one man that he sent such letters to. I wonder, would the words become true if I dared to use them myself?

How can you tell if your feelings are real? Do I live like this from choice? Did I fall in love with him because he's handsome and kind, or because I needed, wanted to fall in love with a man like him?

▷

It is quite true. Most people are other people. Their thoughts are someone else's opinions, their lives a mimicry, their passions a quotation.

The most important thing about this theory is that the man whose story it claims to tell doesn't actually exist. Even the portrait which is supposed to authenticate his existence is a fake. But he has a name and a history, because we demand that he exist. We need him.

The theory in question is a footnote to one of the most picturesque controversies of English Literature, the one which proposes

THE PORTRAIT OF LORD A.D.

that Shakespeare's sonnets, which carry the famously obscure dedication "To Mr W.H.", were inspired by his love for a beautiful young man. The theory is expounded by Wilde in a short story, *The Portrait of Mr W.H.* I've read it again and again, trying to work out why it fascinates me, but I've never once read it trying to work out if this story of Mr W.H. is "true", if all of Wilde's literary detective work is historically accurate. We're not really even supposed to think about whether the theory is true. It is presented as a fiction, an intrigue of literary and erotic obsessions. It is initially told by one man to another as they sit and talk the night away, smoking too many cigarettes, watching the thin grey threads of smoke rise into the gaps in their argument. When the story is over, it is dawn.

The theory begins with the supposition that even though Mr W.H. may not and cannot be proved to exist, he is gorgeous. His face is both a symptom of desire, and a means of its transmission.

> It was a full-length portrait of a young man in late sixteenth-century costume, standing by a table, with his right hand resting on an open book. He seemed about seventeen years of age, and was of quite extraordinary personal beauty, though evidently somewhat effeminate. Indeed, had it not been for the dress and the closely cropped hair, one would have said that the face, with its dreamy, wistful eyes and its delicate scarlet lips, was the face of a girl.

In *Mr W.H.*, the portrait exists only because one Cyril Graham, a Cambridge undergraduate, became so infatuated with the theory that Shakespeare's sonnets are the result of a homosexual passion for a boy actor that he even went to the lengths of having a fake seventeenth-century portrait of the boy painted so as to prove his existence... In the end, despite Graham's research, as elaborate and exhausting as a love affair, he is unable to persuade the world that his theory is correct, and he kills himself. When Cyril Graham is dead, as dead and as fantastic as Mr W.H. himself, the portrait passes to his *great friend*, Erskine. This Erskine continues the scholarly search for Mr W.H., mixing academic and erotic passions, enduring a typical undergraduate romance. His search for the proof of the existence of the hypothetical Elizabethan beauty becomes indistinguishable from his devotion to his dead friend, of whom he always speaks with a catch in his voice — *I think he was the most splendid creature I ever saw, and nothing could exceed the grace of his movements, the charm of his manner. He fascinated everybody who was worth fascinating, and a great many people who were not.* Cyril Graham, "his very great friend", gradually becomes Mr W.H. in nineteenth-century dress, just as, of course, Mr W.H. is a nineteenth-century beauty in Elizabethan drag. Both men are gorgeous, effeminate, fatherless, talented actors. Cyril made a perfect Rosalind at Cambridge.

Erskine tells the tale of his research to the unnamed "I" who narrates the story, and he of course is obsessed, infected, so obsessed with *the secret of Shakespeare's heart*, the secret that hovers over the faces of these dead young men, that he repeats and elaborates the entire story for the benefit of the reader. And the reader, late in the night, pauses, only to light another cigarette, and then...

The story presupposes that its reader is ready to accept the suggestion of Mr W.H.'s beauty, ready to stand in line in this bizarre series of reincarnations. It presupposes that the reader, too, is a beautiful young man, a picture.

The "I" who narrates *The Portrait of Mr W.H.* is, of course, Wilde. Erskine, as it happens, is in fact Robbie Ross, Wilde's lover both before and after Reading Gaol. We can ascribe these names because one of Wilde's letters claims they worked out the plot together one night over a cheap dinner in a Soho cafe. Perhaps they were a little drunk. Between them they spun a whole fantasy of homosexual culture. If Cyril Graham is the reincarnation of Mr W.H., then the "I" who tells the story is somehow the boy's patron and lover, "Shakespeare", an older man contemplating his beloved, an artist whose homosexual passion for beauty is the foundation, moral and aesthetic, of his life and work. Shakespeare is to Wilde what Wilde has been to later cultures; *the* homosexual, our archetype. And Mr W.H. is not just another gorgeous boy, an individual erotic choice, a boy pulled from the Soho pavement just for one night. He is specifically the boy for whom Shakespeare created his great heroines, the boy who made sense of his life and work, he is the very boy whom (homosexual) Marlowe seduced away from Shakespeare to play (homosexual) Piers Gaveston to his Edward II. He is the epitome of a culture, the icon of a tradition; his smile comes right from the heart of London. As a setting for his languid figure, Wilde and Ross produced pages of quotations and academic arguments. They fantasized a complete history of the theatre in which he worked, rebuilding the garlanded or black-draped stage on which the beautiful boys acted out the emotions of their older, male patrons; the artists could glimpse between the satyr-carved pillars, in the performances of the boy-actors, the children they never had. They recited the names of Shakespeare's boys: Robin Armin, Sanford Cook, Nat Field, Will Ostler who accompanied James of Scotland; the lamented Salathiel Pavey, the famous Kynaston, James Bristow whom Henslowe bought for eight pieces of gold, Stephen Hammerton with his curious pale face. The list sounds just like the recital of boys' names which brought about the verdict at Wilde's trial; but here it is recited with reverence, not disgust. The two men are conjuring a whole trad-ition, a heady mixture of eroticism and erudition which made literary history into the justification and ennoblement of the love which was the basis of their own culture, the worship of beautiful boys. Around their café table they imagined a gathering of all their peers: the renaissance translators of Plato's *Symposium*; Michelangelo and his beloved Tommaso Cavalieri; Montaigne, in excessive and unlawful mourning for his friend Etienne de la Boëtie; the poet Richard Barnfield, who sang of the loveliness of anonymous Elizabethan beauties; Winckelmann, who was in-troduced to the pleasures of Greek Art by a romantic friendship with a young Roman; Hubert Languet, who wrote such passionate letters to the young Philip Sidney. All were invited to witness the recreation, the resurrection of Mr W.H.

Wilde and Ross remembered, in particular, that this theatre of which they are dreaming had been attacked and destroyed by "The Puritans" (those convenient all-purpose villains of English history — how would we explain ourselves without them). The homosexual artist, they claimed, has always been surrounded by

Philistines. They looked up from their table, looked out at the street and they thought: *this has all happened before.*

The Portrait of Mr W.H. was published in July 1889. I checked the dates, because I wanted to continue Wilde's erotic detection with work of my own.

In June 1890 the first instalment of *The Picture of Dorian Gray* was published in *Lippincott's Monthly* magazine. This story too features a brilliant, fatherless, beloved interpreter of Shakespeare's heroines, but this time the beloved is actually a girl, rather than a boy who dresses as a girl. She seems familiar, because she too has a flowerlike face, lips like a rose. Dorian Gray sees her playing Juliet (a part which Erskine conjectures Shakespeare had written especially for Mr W.H. at the height of his love) and falls in love with her. Just as Cyril Graham did, she transforms the horrid, squalid, Victorian theatre in which she must play. She, too, dies. Her name is Sibyl Vane. Sibyl Vane; Cyril Graham.

The features of the beloved can move freely from person to person. And this is not the only transposition. The man who actually paints the portrait of Dorian Gray, Basil Hallward, is deeply in love with his subject, and as he paints, the portrait of Mr W.H. appears again. Just as Shakespeare saw his boy as one *whose hair was like spun gold, and whose face was the meeting-place of the lily's white and the deep vermilion of the rose,* just as Erskine saw Cyril Graham, as Gray himself is to see Sibyl Vane, Basil sees Dorian as *wonderfully handsome, with his finely-curved scarlet lips, his frank blue eyes, his crisp gold hair.* He too sees this boy as the foundation of his art, his great friend, his point of entry into a great tradition. Dorian is his ideal, a platonic ideal in both the philosophical and sexual senses of the word. He is the model for whom he has been waiting all his life.

Wilde wrote in a letter, "Basil Hallward is what I think I am." So who was Dorian Gray?

Dorian Gray had gold hair, blue eyes, and rose-red lips. Lord Alfred Douglas, of course, was also blonde, blue eyed, lily white, and he had rose-red lips.

The point is, Dorian Gray was imagined in 1890. Wilde first

met Douglas in January or June 1891. He was the man for whom he gave years of his life, the man for whom he would have died, the greatest love of his life. He was his *type*.

He was a fiction, one that already existed in his books.

Diary, January 1985
Each of us takes on the ridiculous task of being historically original each time he begins a love affair. Every love affair begins with the certain knowledge that there has never been anything like this before. It is a truism that desire is prior to experience, but it is also true that a gay fantasy, an imagining of possible forms of desire, may be, quite possibly, that rarest of all things, a true fantasy. That is, something without any counterpart in real life, unlike, for instance, those heterosexual "fantasies" about power or possession which are not necessarily fantasies at all, but may be symbols of real power and real possession. Our desire is unimagined, unsocial, anti-social. We dream about men before we ever meet them.

And yet, and yet when we do meet them, our desire may take the most derivative, the most banal forms. The intense, condensed emotions of a brief encounter may feel alarmingly like a synopsis of that "falling in love" which heterosexual fictions so lavishly illustrate. We know that we can desire one man just because he looks like another man, or even like a picture of another man. And if I choose one man more and more often than the others it can still feel like "I want you to marry me", which I know isn't the point at all . It isn't what we mean to say at all. The shape of our desire seems always to come from somewhere else. I'm not sure, now, if my first "gay experience" was with that man, or occurred when I was a boy watching an old film on television, watching an actor ride a white horse through a river. I'm not sure which image provides the truest test by which I now evaluate my loves, which set of features I now remember and recognize.

> The hero... became to him a kind of pre-figuring type of himself. And, indeed, the whole book seemed to him to contain the story of his own life, written before he had lived it.

When I had finished my own pursuit of Mr W.H., when I had discovered that somehow Wilde's "real" love for Lord Alfred Douglas was the result, rather than the source, of his fictional loves, I was shocked. How could the portrait have been painted in 1890, if he first saw Douglas's face in 1891? How could I describe the gap between the features and their description; in what sense could I say that Lord Alfred Douglas "inspired" Dorian Gray, or that Dorian Gray, Sibyl Vane, Cyril Graham and Mr W.H. conspired in the creation of Lord Alfred Douglas? Like Erskine in his library I began to hunt for other texts, other evidence of the life of this fantasy. I knew all the time that like Erskine, like Wilde, I was scrutinizing an imagined historical London to see if it would reveal the face and ancestry of my own lover. When I sat there with the books, at midnight, I knew what I wanted from them.

▷

The decisive event in Dorian Gray's life is not an event at all, but a book. Erskine reads his own love story between the lines of Shakespeare's sonnets, a London romance; Dorian's book is an anonymous, untitled, yellow-covered text from Paris. It lies in wait for him until that moment of crisis when he is ready to read it, susceptible to its poison. Once it falls into his hands, he too stays up all night to read, and he too knows what he is looking for. It is, of course, given to him by an older man. Its hero describes how, as an archetypal nineteenth-century Parisian dandy, he tried to organize and identify his diseased life by imagining himself successively as a naturalist, a hedonist, a Catholic, with each identity requiring a different library of learning. Immersing himself in the suggestive narratives of the past, he christens himself Petronius, Tiberius, Caligula, Domitian, Elagabalus. The repercussions of this literary indulgence sound like an account of the sexual relations between a small group of old friends; each man is marked by the habits of old lovers, each connected by a chain of past intimacies. The Dandy imagines himself as a decadent Emperor; Dorian imagines himself as the Dandy; Wilde imagines himself as the susceptible Dorian. And as I read Wilde...

> ...one had ancestors in literature, as well as in one's own race, nearer perhaps in type and temperament, many of them, and certainly with an influence of which one was more absolutely conscious. There were times when it appeared to Dorian Gray that the whole of history was merely the record of his own life, not as he had lived it in act and circumstance, but as his imagination had created it for him, as it had been in his brain and his passions, He felt that he had known them all, those strange terrible figures that had passed across the stage of their world and made sin so marvellous, and evil so full of subtlety. It seemed to him that in some mysterious way their lives had been his own...

So I re-read the *Complete Works*, looking for my ancestors. To a young man alone in a library, all of Wilde's texts can begin to conspire, to imagine rather than record his life. He was continually imagining his own life under the guise of fiction. Certainly there are imaginary portraits to be seen in the guilty, guiltily heterosexual aristocrats of the stories and plays — Sir Robert Chiltern, Lord Illingworth, Lord Arthur Savile, the story of whose crime is subtitled "A Study of Duty", which might well have served as the subtitle for Wilde's married life. The stories not only record a glittering and disturbed past; they also predicted the details of a sordid and anxious future. In 1889 Oscar published one of his happiest stories, ostensibly a study of a lunatic murderer, a minor author, critic and criminal of the early 1800s, Thomas Wainewright. In the story, entitled *Pen, Pencil and Poison*, we learn that Wainewright was an exquisite with *pale, lemon-coloured gloves* whose enthusiams were exactly Wilde's: reproductions of renaissance masterpieces, Elizabethan translations, old china, French poets, Persian carpets. His favourite picture is *La Gioconda* (*The Mona Lisa*) whose face had inspired Pater to such ecstasies of interpretation and who is the true ancestor of the smile on the lips of the picture of Dorian Gray and the portrait of Mr W.H. He delights in glittering and artistic company, and he is a successful journalist and forger. His career, however, is shot through with a *strange sin*; he loves to poison people. He insists that his crimes are the result of deliberate perversity, not of any spontaneous malady, and Wilde notes with admiration that *his crimes seem to have had an important effect on his art*. Finally he is caught, tried and exiled — *The sentence now passed on him was to a man of his culture a form of death*.

This portrait of the author as a young criminal was written six years before Wilde himself was caught. Every detail of Wilde's life is there, under the guise of Wainewright's; every detail except the true name of the sin (the crime) with which Wilde is so evidently fascinated.

The tactic of attempting to find an identity through reworking the biographies of the past was not unique to Wilde. Other gay historians and fantasists were at work on more explicit but less public projects. Many of the writers catalogued here in chapter 5, "Evidence", wrote out their own lives in the personae of dead or foreign authors. They too sought inspiration and a sense of identity by taking a very particular view of their lives. They could not believe that theirs was a unique experience. Instead they subscribed to the opposite theory: the idea that one man's experience may be a repetition of another's.

They found their peers not in other men, but in other texts. John Addington Symonds, in 1891, went to Italy, and in the Casa Buonarroti in Florence, recovered and translated for the first time the correspondence between Michelangelo and his greatest love, Tommaso Cavalieri, which previous editors had managed to miss, mislay or mistranslate. He wrote:

> There is something inexpressibly pathetic in turning over the passionate letters and verses, indited by aged genius and youthful beauty, after the lapse of four centuries and a half.

Symonds found literal evidence of the ancestor of whom Wilde and Erskine had only dreamt. The experience was so moving because this lost text provided, at last, the justification of his own life. As a homosexual, he could justify his own hopes for a free life by claiming that, "the frank and hearty feeling for a youth of singular distinction which is expressed in these sonnets gave no offence to society during the period of the early Renaissance". This statement may not be historically true; but it is the true source of Symonds's own pioneering efforts to formulate the idea that perhaps homosexual relationships are not intrinsically antisocial. Simply, the letters provided him with the strength to make his effort; the fact that Michelangelo was at last proved to have "been a homosexual" meant that Symonds could be one too. More particularly, Michelangelo's texts could be made to justify Symonds's own position as an agonized and repressed artist, agonized and repressed for very specific reasons:

> It is not impossible that the tragic accent discernible throughout Michelangelo's love-poetry may be due to his sense of the discrepancy between his own deepest emotions and the customs of Christian society.

When the nineteenth-century poet interleaved the compassionate agonies of his own writings with those of his renaissance idol, he realized that it had all happened, in typically similar ways, before.

In 1897 Symonds wrote an (unsigned) autobiography as Case Study XVIII of Havelock Ellis's *Sexual Inversion*. There he recalled the time (March 1858) when he was eighteen, and he sat up till dawn, and in one sitting *he read the* Phaedrus *and* Symposium. *A new world opened, and he felt that his own nature had been revealed.* His nature somehow existed before he himself knew it, and it existed in a book. In 1886 the anonymous author of *Don Leon* learnt how to live from a book: *Thus with myself I reasoned; then I read / And counsel asked from volumes of the dead. / Oh! Flowery path, thus hand in hand to walk / With Plato and enjoy his honeyed talk.* In *De Profundis*, Wilde said that only someone who had read Plato could understand his letters to Douglas. In 1914 Forster's hateful Clive Durham, in *Maurice*, is allowed a moment of grace when he recalls that *he could never forget his emotion at first reading the* Phaedrus.

I bought my copy in 1977. It was the first book I ever bought because I'd heard (at school) that it was by a homosexual.

▷

Nowadays a broken heart will run to many editions.

For one who attributed such importance to individuality, to the personal and unrepeatable arts of lifestyle and conversation, to the exquisite, to the limited edition, Wilde seems to have shown remarkably little interest in being original . His life was *fashionable*, if fashion is the art and industry of making an imitation look like a novelty.

His successes were all other people's. The portraits he paints of himself are no more authentic than Erskine's portrait of Mr W.H. Originality is not a virtue in our culture; the most beautiful and successful men model themselves on other men. I never believe Wilde, not for a minute.

I discovered that nothing in the *Complete Works* is original. It's all from the library or the booksellers, not from the heart. *The Picture of Dorian Gray* is largely a reworking of Huysmans, Pater and Symonds, decorated with passages copied from such notable volumes as *The History and Mystery of Precious Stones* (1880), by Mr William Jones. The magpie was shameless; in April 1892 Mr E.W. Pratt of High Road, Lower Clapton wrote to Wilde wanting to know where he could obtain a copy of Dorian's favourite book, the book which reveals all, the Bible of perversion. Oscar wrote back: "Dear Sir, the book in Dorian Gray is one of the many books I have never written, but it is partly suggested by Huysman's À *Rebours*, which you will get at any French booksellers."

The presentation volume of *Poems* (1881) which Wilde tried to donate to the library of the Oxford Union was refused on the grounds that its contents were plagiarized from the work of Shakespeare, Sidney, Donne, Byron, Morris, Swinburne and "sixty more". Wilde did not create out of an intimate, heroic sense of himself as an individual or as a homosexual. He was prolific, public, commercial, promiscuous, shallow and repetitive. He was a plagiarist, like us, like me.

He was especially good at plagiarizing himself. Algernon, in *The Importance of Being Earnest*, says: "If I am occasionally a little over-dressed, I make up for it by being always immensely over-educated."

Oscar Wilde, in *Phrases and Philosophies for the Use of the Young* says: "The only way to atone for being occasionally a little over-dressed is by being always absolutely over-educated."

Lord Henry Wotton, in *The Picture of Dorian Gray*, says: "He atones for being occasionally somewhat over-dressed, by being always absolutely over-educated."

The first time you hear them, such epigrams seem to exist only by virtue of their exquisiteness; they are valuable because unique, uniquely appropriate. The profligacy with which they are scattered suggest an endless flow of wit, verbal riches. But the second time they appear, questions arise; the reader begins to feel cheated. If the words are so systematically re-used, the value of this currency must lie somewhere apart from "originality".

Wilde was almost obsessively repetitive; words reappear, just as the face of Mr W.H reappears. He seemed to have loved repetition for its own sake. Selby is the name of Dorian Gray's country house; and it is also the name of Lady Windermere's. A Lady Windermere appears in *Lord Arthur Savile's Crime*, and Arthur Savile is the name of one of the boy-actors in *The Portrait of Mr W.H.* Wilde also repeats his darker thoughts. Like us, he places them in different conversations, puts them into the mouths of different men. No sentiment was too serious to be re-used, rephrased:

"Still, the East End is a very important problem," remarked Sir Thomas, with a grave shake of the head.

"Quite so!" answered the young lord. "It is the problem of slavery, and we try to solve it by amusing the slaves."

The Picture of Dorian Gray

Kelvil: "Still our East End is a very important problem."
Lord Illingworth: "Quite so. It is the problem of slavery. And we are trying to solve it by amusing the slaves."

A Woman of No Importance

They try to solve the problem of poverty... by keeping the poor alive; or in the case of a very advanced school, by amusing the poor.

But this is not a solution: it is an aggravation of the difficulty. The proper aim is to try and reconstruct society on such a basis that poverty will be impossible.

The Soul of Man Under Socialism

The glittering phrases, which seem on utterance to be true because they are both spontaneous and unique, are reproduced, shifted from mouth to mouth and from text to text. Here is Wilde's most famous outburst, the speech that brought applause from the gallery, the one that can move us still, his answer to the question: *What is "The Love That Dare Not Speak Its Name"?* Delivered from the lower depths of the courtroom, this now reads as the truest of all his texts, because it is a naked appeal, an impromptu defence made on our behalf:

> "The love that dare not speak its name" in this century is such a great affection of an elder for a younger man as there was between David and Jonathan, such as Plato made the very basis of his philosophy, and such as you find in the sonnets of Michelangelo and Shakespeare. It is that deep, spiritual affection that is as pure as it is perfect. It dictates and pervades great works of art like those of Shakespeare and Michelangelo, and those two letters of mine, such as they are. It is in this century misunderstood, so much misunderstood that it may be described as "the love that dare not speak its name"', and on account of it I am placed where I am now. It is beautiful, it is fine, it is the noblest form of affection. There is nothing unnatural about it. It is intellectual and it repeatedly exists between an elder and a younger man, when the elder has intellect, and the

younger man has all the joys, hope and glamour of his life
before him. That it should be so, the world does not understand. The world mocks at it, and sometimes puts one in
the pillory for it!

Well that too is a quotation. At the moment of extreme emotion,
with all the attendant mannerisms of honesty, he was quoting
himself. He was combining, from memory, two unconnected
passages from *Dorian Gray*. They are not even spoken by the
same character. The first is put in the mind of Lord Wotton,
the second in the mind of Dorian.

> ...he remembered something like it in history. Was it not
> Plato, that artist in thought, who had first analysed it? Was
> it not Buonarroti who had carved it in the coloured marbles
> of a sonnet-sequence? But in our own century it was
> strange...

> The love that he bore for him — for it really was love —
> had nothing in it that was not noble and intellectual. It
> was not that mere physical admiration that is born of the
> senses, and that dies when the senses tire. It was such love
> as Michael Angelo had known, and Montaigne, and
> Winckelmann, and Shakespeare himself...

If this, the truest of all his speeches, is a quotation, or worse, a
quotation from his own work, then what answer can we hope to
have to our question, the only question we ever want to ask of
history, the first question we must ask of ourselves, *is this true?*

▷

Diary, August 1986
We too know the shameless pleasure of repeating our own clichés,
of making our lives a quotation. We too are profoundly unorig-
inal. It's not only in pornography that all men are the same. We
grow up invisible and alone, but then we characteristically move
from complete isolation into what feels like a complete culture

in a very short space of time. Do you remember entering a bar
for the very first time? Suddenly there are lots of you. We are
unafraid of admitting that we want to be like each other. Being
predictable is a small price to pay for sharing something, being
able to talk. When I was a boy, I wanted to grow up to be a
man, to be like other men. In 1977 I left home wearing platform
soles and a brown suit. My mother cut my hair. In 1984 I was
wearing Doctor Martins, 501s and, yes, sometimes a check shirt.
My lover now cuts my hair and I have a moustache. I look like,
or rather hope that I look like, a lot of other gay men. When I
was a boy, the thing I wanted most was to have sex with, or to
have power over, a tall dark man. When I was twenty-four, I
was getting what I wanted. When I was twenty-four, I wanted
to be in love with a tall, dark man with a moustache. At twenty-
eight, I am. When people ask me why I live in London, I say,
I've made a life for myself. But I haven't invented a life; I have
moved into, made a place for myself in a life that already existed.
It's quite true, I am other people. Tonight in the pub I listened
to two men trying to identify a man on the other side of the bar.
One said: "They all look the same, don't they?", and then the
other one said. "Don't tell me, he's the one with the short hair
and the moustache."

▷

The world is very stern with those that thwart her. She
lays down her precepts, and woe to them who dare to think
for themselves, who venture to exercise their own discretion
as to whether they shall allow their individuality and natural
characteristics to be stamped out, to be obliterated under
the leaden fingers of convention.

This text is part of John Bloxam's anonymous contribution to
The Chameleon of 1894, *The Priest and the Acolyte*. It seems
suddenly to imagine the possibility of a decisive escape from any
previous traditions. It explodes the whole anxious, repetitious
canon of Wilde's work with a single suggestion: in the struggle
to shape our identity, to recognize our own face, we must oppose

the individual to society, the natural to the conventional. In making this suggestion, Bloxam's story lays down the principles that have underlain our struggle for the past hundred years. His priest loves and dies for his acolyte in explicit defiance of the laws of his culture, and that love is sacred (true) because it is defiant. Through the unlikeliest of loves, that of an educated urban adult for an anonymous, inarticulate rural child, the long torture of the priest's life is brought to fruition; he finds his true self. Against a false world, we oppose a true love. Our loves do not, like others, confirm the status quo. They are, so runs the text, by definition personal, liberating and anti-social. Our very sense of identity is constructed around the idea of a unique self, and around the act of "finding yourself", making a practical distinction between our (gay) selves and the (oppressive) society which produced us. We are original.

The recent development of this tradition of thinking about ourselves has been to reject any stereotypes, roles or fictions, to refuse to be those people whom Wilde derided as condemned to relive the past, other people's lives, "their lives a mimicry, their passions a quotation". We have refused to act according to any given script; we have imagined that we need no pretext to live our lives. Or, as Frank O'Hara put it, more concretely, in 1960: *Well, but if you lust after someone / you must face it / your life, after all, must be real.*

But without a text, how can you tell if anything, much less love, is real?

Is it true that my experience of love, lust or anything else, is an inspired improvization? Is there really no text that I am quoting? Perhaps my life in this city is not so much individual and natural as collective and determined. In my search for something really true, in my hunt for the true portrait of Mr W.H., I find myself in a library of other texts, the world of other men. I didn't so much "come out" as "go in", since at the very moment at which we come out, declare our difference from the world, we immerse ourselves in a highly stylized, pressured, conventional society; gay society, Although the society I am part of is no more mixed than is any other part of British life (we may sleep together, but that does not mean that we share a life), I still feel, obscurely, that we are all the same, that we have a common identity, common interests. I have found that it is when we are most like each other, when we enter an economy based on the exchange of shared signs, that we have found our greatest strength. True individualists, our enthusiasms are vulgar, our passions commonplace, our venues familiar, our tastes predictable and our faces recognizable.

1894 (The Priest and the Acolyte)
He felt that here at last was something in the world that was really beautiful, something that was really true. Would the day come when those soft scarlet lips would have grown hard and false? When the soft shy treble would have become careless and conventional? His eyes filled with tears...

1984 (Diary)
I often lie awake at night and look at his face, and I watch him carefully because I'm sure that here is something beautiful, something really true. I suppose the time will come when his face will look different, but I have to believe that this is real. This body is real, these arms are real. These tears are real.

▷

One's past is what one is. It is the only way by which people should be judged.

Dorian Gray tells the deepest lie of his glittering career when he says, *I cannot repeat an emotion.* His whole life is a repetition; he lives entirely under the influence of others. His ancestors glare down from the walls and condemn him to a life of terminal debauchery and guilt. (Like us sometimes, he wonders: *Were his own actions merely the dreams that the dead man had not dared to realise.*) They predict his perversions, they are his pretext.

For Wilde, as for Gray, the past was a disaster, a horror. Its texts threaten and conspire. The fatal novel which Dorian reads is a prescription, a closure rather than an opening of possibilities; the leading men of *The Importance of Being Earnest* are hounded to their fate by a library of malevolent texts — diaries, letters, engraved cigarette cases, the manuscript of a three volume novel, baptismal certificates, bills, army lists, court circulars. Wilde's library seemed only to provide fatal inspirations; he too was pursued by texts. When he chose the script for his greatest and final performance, he felt compelled to play out the horrible comedy of Nero and Narcissus on the entirely inappropriate stage of nineteenth-century Soho.

At times the *Complete Works* reads as if he was writing night-marish burlesques of the very scenes that he was later to play out for real; Lady Bracknell is made to speak in such a *severe judicial voice* that Algernon and Jack pretend to shield the tender young ears of Gwendolen and Cecily *from hearing the details of a terrible public scandal.* Even she is not as terrifying a parody of the law as Herod in *Salomé*; if only Mr Justice Wills had stolen his final line for the conclusion of Wilde's trial, then we might imagine him pointing the accusing finger at Wilde and simply shrieking, *Kill that woman!* As it was, Mr Wills seems to have been barely touched by Wilde's bizarrely infectious prose. When all the details of Wilde's own Bunburying had been revealed, when all the discussions of the awful significance of stained sheets and late-night suppers of chicken salad and champagne had been completed, Mr Wills only found time to comment to the jury: *It is a condition of things one shudders to contemplate in a first-class hotel.*

The nightmare of confusion between text and action was com-plete.

For us, the past holds no terrors, if we are not afraid of joining, of being seen in the company of our "doomed", our condemned ancestors. For we may pick and choose from the riches of our history and of the city. Which traditions(s) do you place yourself in — by which I mean which style suits you best? Tell me which books you place on your shelves, and whose phrases appear in your diary... When you are old, who will ghost your memoirs?

Diary 14 October 1986

Last night I tried to convince him that the real theory being proposed in *The Portrait of Mr W. H.* does not concern the origin of Shakespeare's sonnets at all. The theory that Wilde is proposing is about our origins as homosexual men. At the very moment at which, historically, we begin to exist, he created a biography of a homosexual man in which the fake and the true are quite indistinguishable. He proposed that our present is continually being written by our history; that the individual voice can hardly be separated from the historic text which it repeats and adapts. If that is true, then we must choose our words with as much invention as care. I made him look me in the eyes and asked him if he would still love me if I told him I wasn't who I'd claimed to be, if I looked just like someone else, if I'd kept my face but changed my name, if I had been quoting someone else when I whispered in his ear. I was only half-serious, and of course, when the argument was over, we laughed, and then argued about which club to go to, and ran out of cigarettes, and fell into bed. I have a picture of Wilde hanging in my room. Perhaps I like the idea that we're being watched. I like the idea that he should see us, see how we boys now live in his city.

Sometimes when I look up at his face, I think there is really a great deal to be said for his theory.

9.
MESSAGES

Dear Oscar,
I know it's a bad habit to write late at night, especially
when you're drunk, but still.

When I went to Paris to put the flowers on your grave,
I made the gesture out of real love and respect. I got dressed
up. I made myself just as handsome as I could, so handsome
that the men would look at me on the journey. I made a
point of buying the roses from the florist in the Burlington
Arcade (remember?) and then when I got to Paris I walked
straight to the grave and laid them down with all the other
flowers looking just as strong as I could, stood there with
a smile on my face and I didn't cry once. I smoked a whole
cigarette for you and then turned and went. And then I
came back to London and started writing. Darling, it's all
for you. We're doing all this for you. I wish you could be
here to see us. The streets are not all that different — you
wouldn't get lost — but we are very different these days.
Can you imagine, tonight I walked down the Strand with
my lover, and we talked about which pub we would go and
drink in; we have a choice of places to go now, and the
chances are that when we get there no one will know us.
And then he put his arm round my shoulder. I suppose it's
gestures like that, public and unremarkable, that you could
never enjoy. I can't make it up to you, and it doesn't justify

what they did to you, but I wanted to tell you nevertheless. I think you didn't know things were going to change, and that really you weren't trying to change anything. You weren't thinking about us. The weight of a lover's arm on your shoulder is not a sensation you can ever enjoy now, nothing can ever be worth what was done to you, nothing can change that, but oh almost it does. We're walking your streets.

We're doing it all for you. It's all for you,

love,

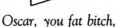

Oscar, you fat bitch,
Last night I dreamed your hand was on my face. You were there in the bed, big and fat like I've been told you were, lying in bed smoking and taking up all the room. It was quite funny at first. I tried to ignore you. I tried to get back to sleep, but I was uneasy about sleeping. I thought you might be watching. Sometimes, half-asleep, I'd roll over and knock against your body, our skins would rub together, and then I'd feel your hand on my face. I'd wake up and try to apologize. You said nothing but kept on smoking. I noticed that I didn't recognize either the smell or the brand of your cigarettes. I suppose you didn't have the same kind of cigarettes then. So I got up and put on the light and fetched you an ashtray and waited for you to talk. I realized that I had no idea what your voice would sound like. Once the light was on I wasn't embarrassed, really, by your body. You didn't try to cover yourself. You are old, and fat, and white, and you sweat slightly. You're an old queen; you are quite beyond being embarrassed by a younger man, quite capable of taking in the details of my body (I had half an erection swinging when I went to get the ashtray from the kitchen) without desire or inhibition. So I came back into the bed and sat close. I thought, having read about you, that you might want to run your fingers through my hair. I know I'm not blonde, and that I don't look like a boy

any more now that I've made myself look like a man, but I still thought that you might want to touch me. I thought you might want something from me. I thought I might have something to give you. I leaned against your shoulder and waited.

I wanted you to talk; I would have listened to anything you might have said. I would have held you if you'd wanted me to. I would have talked or listened all night. After all, I've done that for a lot of other men. I would have done anything; masturbated in front of you, or let you do anything you wanted.

And you said nothing, you didn't even look at me half the time. You smoked. Your eyes were dead, your fat white flesh was sweating slightly and quite dead. You used your right hand to bring your cigarette to your mouth with an absolute economy of effort. I supposed that they had finally managed to kill you. To reduce you to this. I couldn't talk, couldn't even ask you for a cigarette (that would have been something for me, you see, to smoke one of your cigarettes, to wake up with that taste in my mouth). I couldn't say what I wanted to say. I don't pity you. I don't even want to ask your advice, just to hear your stories; I'll work out what they might mean to me. Please, say anything at all to me, and I can use it. You old queen, you've got your hand on my face, I can't talk now.

Love,

10.
HISTORY

History (1) Do not be afraid of the past.

If we are ever going to get there, then surely it will be at half past one on a Sunday morning. When the music bites, when everyone you look at is so handsome, as the temperature rises, you can feel yourself sweat for joy. In the middle of town, in the middle of the night, the walls of Jericho are about to fall. Surely here, and now, the rules no longer apply. We are about to escape. The world is about to change.

All of our favourite experiences are deeply moving — ecstasy, intoxication, orgasm, romantic love, intimacy between strangers. We do not move forward, however; it is characteristic of all these pleasures that they move us up and down, not forward. Remember that after the lights of a night out (light in his hair, sweat on his shoulder), you walk outside, you turn up your collar, maybe you even let go of each other as you get on the bus, and then morning comes. We know that even after the darkest night, even if you can make Saturday night last well into Sunday afternoon, morning comes. Even after a night spent in his arms, morning comes. He has to get up and go to work. Even after the darkest sex (darkness of love, darkness of ordinary but well-executed lust), morning comes.

It is our commonest experience that after breaking the law we become law-abiding citizens. Literally, most gay men break the law. This has been a commonplace of our lives since 1885. It's both necessary and easy, the law being what it is. More significantly, and at greater cost, we break the "laws" of what is socially acceptable, since all our pleasures, both the obviously "extraordinary" ones like drag and fistfucking, and the ordinary ones like cocksucking, appearing in public together, crying on another man's shoulder, or being in love, are socially unacceptable. In other respects, however, we are indistinguishable from other citizens. We regularly watch ourselves turn into the most improbable of creatures, transform back again, then set off to the office or the dole office just like everybody else. And this is not just a question of appearances, of an awful truth lurking behind a bland exterior. The bland and the awful are harmoniously coexistent. One is not beneath the other; it does not threaten to erupt or disrupt. Morning does not disrupt the night any more than the glamour, the ferocity and wickedness of the night challenges or abolishes the day. We know that even if our coming out has changed our experience of the world, it has done nothing to change the world. After the moments of harsh intimacy with ourselves or with others we let the world fall back into place again. We acknowledge, with extraordinary calmness, given how much all this costs us, that there is no radical impulse beneath our radical acts. After Saturday night, another Saturday night, that's all. Morning comes.

We put the law together after we've broken it.

History can be a dark night too. It can move us. From its gallery of "characters" we choose those heroes who exert the greatest erotic or intellectual attraction — Saint Oscar, or the hardest, most anonymous boy. Then we place them against the background of a fantastic but solidly detailed city, a darkened version of our own London, since we have always lurked in corners. Our doorways have always been in the darker streets. Look over your shoulder tonight; the sculptures writhe on the Eros fountain or the strange lampstands of the Embankment, they catch the lime-light of the music halls, the shop windows of Liberty's blazing out over pavements of prostitutes. Socialist mobs are drawing blood in Trafalgar Square, and moving through the crowds, the rich men in evening dress, the scarlet soldiers, the poor men laughing together, making love after dark just like we do, their lives unbelievably courageous because those lives were, like ours, supposed to be impossible.

But all this history is quite useless. It doesn't get us anywhere, even if we are moved to tears. It may make us drunk with pleasure, but it returns us to the present uneducated. Even after all of this I can't say of Wilde that I got to know him; the information I have about him is distorted by the erotic and sentimental energies that distort any brief gay encounter. I read all night, but he's gone in the morning. Entering history like this can feel like entering a bar for the first time; it takes your breath away. Breathless, we could assemble a whole cast of new acquaintances, a whole library of costume dramas moving from, say, a drag party in 1725 to a uniformed wartime romance put into impressive chiaroscuro by the fires of the Blitz, finding in each place glamorous evidence of gay lives to make us feel that others have been here before us, that others have been oppressed, others have been as brilliant or inventive as us. If we were all ever to meet, surely it would be a wonderful party. But this history is not a record of change; the sensation it creates matches that of moving from one bar to another, one night to another. We abolish time and distance, difference, in exclaiming, *Oh! he's just like us.* We refuse the task (and pleasure) of identifying where he is like us, where he differs. We admire his face, but we don't want to talk to him in case he has the wrong accent. We wouldn't follow him along the street in case this familiar geography were to shift under our feet, in case we were to discover that we were not, after all, living in the same city. London is not always recognizable as London.

We are able to consider our history like this only if we imagine that history is at an end. History ends here. It is resolved, and dissolved, in our present.

You have always told me it was Ernest. I have always introduced you to everyone as Ernest... You look as if your name was Ernest. You are the most Ernest-looking person I ever saw in my life. It is perfectly absurd your saying that your name isn't Ernest. It's on your cards.

For Wilde history was a scandal, because it threatened to reveal us for what we are. Now times have changed, and I am eager to be a woman with a reputation, a past. I am baffled that I never acknowledged these acquaintances, that I never knew these men, that we always agree to part, that our intimacies are frequent but wasted, continually surprised by the fact that all this happened and was then forgotten. Why, each time, do we have to begin again, reinvent the wheel? For a moment we speculate.

But these are certainly dark times, and we must stay close together. (*I hear the awful syllable change, and see all things, qualities, impersonations, gliding from the embrace of their names* — Edward Carpenter.) Since I have my pleasures now, they must be enough, I must be exhausted by them and sleep contentedly at night. And more than that, how could we change? How could we ever change, now that we have become, at last, *homosexual*. We have invested everything not in doing something, but in being something. And it is literally everything that we have invested. Imagine the following: at a certain hour this evening your desires leave you; nothing else changes — not your face, your clothes, the company you keep or your conversations. They remain, but are, of course, now entirely devoid of meaning.

Having worked so long and so hard to achieve this identity, there is little reason to scrutinize it, to poke around in it for possible sites of adjustment and alteration. We remake history in our image, rather than looking to our history as a source of doubts and hopes. When you have sat for a portrait for so long, why blur or tear up the picture? Don't move; we have arrived.

You have always told me you were a homosexual. I have always introduced you to everyone as a homosexual. You look like a homosexual. You are the most homosexual-looking person I ever saw in my life. It is perfectly absurd your saying you want to change.

▷

History (2) For he, to whom the present is the only thing that is present, knows nothing of the age in which he lives.

And just when I thought I had finally arrived in the city, when I knew roughly what I wanted and where to find it, when I could finally walk the streets without map or guidebook, being sure of being recognized in some places, anonymous in others, just when I knew exactly how to dress and talk, everything changed.

In the heat of the past twenty years, sex has been the dynamic of our lives. It has validated our actions and our self-esteem. We have become handsome, masculine, demanding and unafraid of our pleasures, and the medium of all these victories has been sex. Sex organizes our relationships, our desires, our appearances, the styles and functions of our meeting places. Most of all, sex has been our Paradise. When the going gets rough, when we are forced to admit that we live in a culture which even now more or less hates us, we have still been able to reassure ourselves that for us sex is not only a true desire, but an available pleasure. We have been having a good time.

And now this sexual ease, the one thing that we have in common, has been taken from us. The arrival of a fatal, sexually transmissible disease, the perfect image to revive the most ancient and popular hostilities against us and within us, is rearranging the practical details of our lives, the imagery of our lives, our self-perceptions. Just when our culture was sensing its strength, its diversity of expression, we must now talk again of the all-importance of sex, reanimating the most reductive accounts of our lives. We have watched our most basic cultural metaphors suddenly change or lose their meanings; they have careered out of our control. Sex is no longer a harmless recreation or an affirmation; the permanent, casual promise of our sexual imagery now operates as a threat, a source of anxiety rather than of confidence. To come inside someone is no longer an act of sweetest intimacy but of violence. Pleasure is guilty again. To be attracted or attractive is now a problem rather than a delight; spontaneous, generous lust now looks dated. The handsome, single, fearless male now looks more like an old fashion than an erotic ideal or truth. Our most basic social formations sometimes feel as if they have lost their reason to exist; if you haven't come here to pick up a sexual partner, then why are we even in the same room? Maybe nothing holds us together. Everything has changed.

On a bad night, this précis of our crisis can be made to predict an end to our gay culture. But this map of our recent history is incomplete; the picture lacks perspective. The idea that this is simply an end is as false as the idea that ninety years ago, when Oscar fell from grace, gay life in London stopped or was stamped out. Certainly, the appalling image of a famous and brilliant man publicly and systematically destroyed must have made an impact. Specific ways of meeting or behaving must have been abandoned or shifted their ground; certain images, certain styles must have suddenly become useless or dangerous. But only ignorance could ever assert that in a period of threat our life stops. After 1895 the crowds of London were stirred by the patriotism of the Jameson Raid and The Jubilee. How did the gay people, recently cast by the press as abominations and outcasts, live in London during these celebrations? In 1982, during the Falklands war, London was the city of "our boys" — which gay pubs sang "Rule Britannia"?; and which gay men attempted to honour dead boy-friends and lovers at the official ceremonies of mourning? And in 1945, when London ceased to be the Babylon of the blackout, and men moved from the mobile, all-male environment of the army back onto streets full of watchful neighbours and families, how did their lives change? Why do we have such a short memory for our own culture?

What has happened is we have let ourselves believe, those of us who lived in, visited regularly or just aspired to the cities, that the seventies' transformation of our culture was in fact our apotheosis. We thought, for a moment, that we had finally arrived. The white, affluent, urban, male, butch, American style of the late seventies was, both as fiction and as reality, the real thing, the goal of all our struggles. (Not for nothing was our biggest discotheque opened under the name of *Heaven*.) It was a style that explicitly proposed a single culture. It offered to embrace everybody, to erase all differences in a generous, homogeneous, successful style. Commercially promoted on a mass scale, it seemed to absorb all the other, older styles. It arrived from elsewhere, fully developed and packaged, complete with a distinctive physique, costume, music and sexual code of practice. It could, quite genuinely, be bought; sometimes it felt as if nothing more was needed to become a successfully gay man than sufficient money to buy access to certain places, sufficient money to adopt a distinct image and thus a distinct peer group. It could be entered; the sense of having got there, of having arrived at a pre-existent destination, was literal. It specifically abolished, or appeared to abolish, the idea of ageing, of being of a particular age. It proposed an alternative to the attractions of wealth and class: sex. Its confidence was based on the revolutionary suggestion that the old life was history; finished. All this made it, for a young man just arriving in the city, an irresistibly powerful culture. Since I came out, or at least started to get some of the things I wanted, when this gay culture reached its height, adopting this style became synonymous with being gay. Wilde can have had no idea how true a prophet he was when he suggested that all missing persons would eventually end up in San Francisco. The image of a gay city became a reality: El Dorado. Since we persuaded ourselves that all our previous history had served to usher in the golden age, we now see the challenge that AIDS presents as a very particular kind of disaster: the end of the golden age.

There is a very specific gay sense of history in which nothing really happens until such time as you identify yourself as a gay man. We are born late. Much of my life didn't start until I was nineteen; J.A. Symonds said that he was "born" on Easter Day 1858, at the age of eighteen, when he kissed his first love, a schoolboy. For many of us "born" late, the lack of a past, of history, is not felt as a lack. Too eager for the future to look back. I used to think that I had no need of a history, no need to look to Wilde's London for information, for inspiration.

But now, as the attractive fiction of a promised land, a city of our very own, seems no longer credible, we notice that the older geography is still there for us to explore. Our history now becomes a way of understanding and exploring the change in our culture, not simply of reading it as an "end". I've begun to notice other parts of the city, and I realize that the men who live there are no more or less historic, part of history, than Oscar Wilde. They are expert in the complications of their own culture. They reassure me that we are not the first to have to fight for our lives.

▷

History (3) The one duty we owe to history is to rewrite it.

Oscar Wilde said that the one duty we owe to history is to rewrite it. Since I have no family photo albums, no christenings or weddings, no history lessons, no costume drama, no items about myself on the television news, a sense of history may be hard to come by. Mostly the work of our history will be the work of filling in silences. And when I begin to write or rewrite our history —

"What kind of man was he?"
  That is, what kind of men were we?
  It's true, ignorance is bliss. It's easier not to know too much. But ignorance is weakness too. If you don't know the stories, then how can you cherish your own life, hold it precious? What kind of respect can you have for all the men standing here? Never forget, all this has been taken away from us before. Never forget that it could be taken away again. We can only protect and enjoy it if we tell its stories, and tell them on our own terms. Watching that man in the high-heeled shoes, the black dress falling off one shoulder (it is late in the evening), I remember that he and his sisters have been making their own way as ladies of the night since 1870, when Fanny and Stella were doing the Strand. His frock is handed down, second-hand, part of a story, part of a tradition. And that man buying his younger boyfriend (slightly embarrassed, but happily drunk) another drink — I remember the bizarre twisting of mythologies that Wilde used to justify his adoration of young men, the mixing of a pastiche of Classical paederasty with a missionary zeal for "the criminal classes", the sense that they, not the boys he left sleeping in Chelsea, were his true sons — should I forget all that, should I be embarrassed myself? Should I look the other way? Should I dismiss all that simply because now, as then, one man is paying for another? Isn't there an attempt to create a new kind of relationship, an affair of the heart somehow appropriate to the meeting of two very different men? That's our real history, the one we're still writing.

"What kind of man was he?"

What does he look like, this man you're dreaming of, or this man you want to be? The image of an inflexible, redundant, "old-fashioned" past is a false one, caused by the fact that it is only preserved in texts and photographs. It might be easier to imagine this past if the picture could move, if the newsreel had captured, at the turn of the century, not the Great Queen's funeral but the dying of another queen, in a hotel bedroom in France: Oscar Wilde. As it is, those faces in the box of photographs are not immobile. For one thing, they are slowly fading. They are also alive. *The Picture of Dorian Gray* was alive, as meat is with maggots, its surface constantly changing, the composition corrupted and crawling with Dorian's restless and undefined sin. The picture remains restless, but no longer with sin. It comes alive again as I now scrutinize it, read into it and from it, make it give up new meanings as I attempt to use it as a mirror, a dictionary, an anatomy of my own, still nameless "sin". The face is still blonde and has blue eyes; irredeemably sentimental, a predictable fantasy. But it remains a sophisticated and true attempt to imagine an ideal, it still demands that I invest in its beauty, stand enraptured. The gaze is defiant but evasive, since like us it addresses two audiences at once. It is torn; it continually shifts between being a cryptic and an explicit portrait, guilty and courageous at the same time. Does it break or collude with the secrecy of its age — does it violate or epitomize the hypocrisy of its culture? Shall I forgive or accuse this beauty? How shall I return the smile on his lips; comedy or tragedy? I can take all this at face value, as an entertainment, or I can plunder it as a source of information about how, in 1891, a man could exist in the gaps between the East and West Ends, could explore the languages of fashion, the possibilities of a life after dark, could play with the Importance of Being Financially Independent, could ransack his city in an attempt to compose a portrait of that impossible creature, a homosexual man.

Wilde wrote about socialism, but was conservative. He was married, but made love to men. It is always difficult to describe or picture him exactly. The difficulty of description did not vanish with the turn of the century, when he became a "period figure"; nor when the word homosexual entered the dictionary to signify that the picture had been taken, the official portrait painted, the biography written. When someone asks you to describe your lover, each time you give a different account. He changes slightly, you continually struggle to bring the picture into focus, to select the right medium and pigments, to say what kind of man he really is. He does the same for you.

"What kind of man was he?"
   You'll never know what kind of man he was, or is, if he remains a picture on the wall, an icon. Apply to these men, to the attractions of history, the same practical methods that you would use in a variously populated bar. Admit your interest, your position, your hunger. Look at them carefully... history, too, is crowded; once you begin to look, the streets of London are busy, distracting, crowded with anecdotes and incidents. This room contains extraordinarily different men. You know that you are under no obligation to choose just one lover, or to compose one ideal body, or shape yourself in the embrace of a single role-model. Select, edit, rewrite, recompose; juggle your allegiances until you get what you want. Who catches your eye? Who are you standing next to? What attracts you and what repels you? Whose story intrigues you? That man is admirably stylish — do you find the style merely superficial, not a sign of true talent? Does he care what the other men are doing? Does he only enjoy mixed company when he is drunk? And tell me, don't you ever feel that everyone else in the room is insanely calm — doesn't anyone else smell burning? After all, at what point will this buying of pleasures, our real shared activity, stick in your throat? Which of these men is content to buy his pleasures and then return to the values of straight society? That return, perhaps, is one you'll choose to sympathize with, even support; but what if that door is closed? Closed, not from fear, since he has no real reason to fear anything more than the occasional loss of dignity, but because he believes (remember, this is being written in 1986) that only the "successful" have the right to pleasurable lives, that only those who are handsome, well-dressed and employed are worth remembering. He doesn't want to rock the boat. But whose boat? Whose

generosity is more than skin-deep, and whose courage? You can
see that several of the men here obviously feel little sympathy
for the "screaming" queens. They may allow them on public
holidays, or piously note their courage, their traditional roles as
fearless mascots, but will refuse any association with them on
the grounds that they are too loud, that they perpetrate an out-
dated and unfortunate stereotype. Forgive me for being so talka-
tive in a bar, but is it really true that old-fashioned effeminacy
is merely a stylistic affront to the masculine efficiency and hi-tech
grace of the modern (gay) man? Isn't it more to the point to
note that queens, especially drag queens, often come from the
wrong class? London's older drag pubs are working-class in style
and location; they are in marked contrast to the upwardly mobile
décor and ambitions of our more recent homes. And what about
the other men, for whom going down is an adventure, not a fall;
those men who are studying hard to be queens themselves, in
several different styles?

The conversation becomes too specific, my tone too strained;
the man I'm trying to talk to turns away. Of course sex, and a
vague sense that we belong together, will make us stay in even
the most uncomfortably crowded room. But what is it exactly
that would keep me, or you, standing by an old man who talked
too much, or by a racist, or a misogynist, or the man who just
turned his back?

How do you feel, on the streets of this city, in 1886, or a
hundred years later? How are you telling this story? What do
you make of your history?

▷

Those men at the end of the nineteenth century, those men who
in effect invented so much of the city in which I now live, had
very particular uses for history. Their rewriting was a very specific
project — they defined a hunger for the past which is now, again,
ours. First, they were in search of the simplest kind of history.
They wanted to believe that they had existed before. They
searched for proofs of their own existence, ransacking their lib-

raries with a scholarly enthusiam for Classical or Renaissance culture, reciting the names of their ancestors, proving their own existence. This is an effort which continues, though our search is no longer confined to the limits set by a Victorian public school education. Better still, they perfected the arts of a much less scholarly approach. They engaged in the inspired queenly assemblage of fragments of history. They were masters of allusion, suggestion, the misinterpretation and reinterpretation of images. Remember that while in one part of town Wilde was at his desk, recomposing the image of the Princess Salomé, in another all the princesses, queens, duchesses, ladies and plain Marys were also carving out characters for themselves. Between them moved all the anonymous men who pieced together their lives by visiting the bedrooms, studies, brothels and cafés in which the new texts and costumes of our culture were being created. They reduced the rules and models of culture to a fantasy in order to make it malleable to their own commands. They read between the lines of history, stole its best lines for their own use. They were magpies, thieves, *bricoleurs* for whom the past could be reassembled, given new and wicked meanings.

That effort continues; but under different circumstances. We now stand in a very different relation both to our own gay past and to the history of the dominant culture around us. Our lives, simply, have never been like this before. Our characteristic activity is not the consumption and recycling of the past; we are actively engaged in the production of our own culture on a large scale. The men of the nineteenth century — the gay people, homosexuals, Uranians, inverts, sodomites, MaryAnnes — were not silent, or passive, or uninventive, but they lived in a different city. Let me recite a list. None of these things existed in 1886: gay publishers; gay authors; gay discjockeys; gay entertainers working for a gay audience; gay plays; gay directors; gay bookshops; gay pop records and videos; gay magazines; gay newspapers; gay images on television; gay film; gay pressure groups influencing the funding and administration of the services and facilities of the city; the possibility of an organized response to threats to individual gays or to the freedoms of gay people as a whole. We now have public languages in which to rewrite ourselves. There is a huge difference between the experience of sitting alone, reading and re-reading a text by Wilde, filling it with imaginary if potent meanings, and the experience of walking into a bookshop and choosing from a shelf that spreads before you a choice of fifty contemporary gay fictions. All this does not mean that we have left behind the older city in which we were created. Many of its structures and languages remain just as surely as its streets and façades. We have not passed from a darkness, the darkness in which a fantasy of our future was bred, the fiction of our existence conjured, into the clear light of that future — our present — in which administration and politics replace history and artistry. We remain unlikely, fictional; we continue to produce and reproduce ourselves. Now, however, our power to imagine ourselves is of a different order. How shall we rewrite our history, our lives?

What is the exact meaning of the phrase *We are making history*?

Do you think it was a life like mine or yours that the men who gathered together on the appalling evening of 27 May 1895 imagined as they gossiped about the verdict passed on Wilde, on themselves? What did they imagine their lives were going to be like? What did they imagine their powers were on the evening of 14 February 1895, those rich men who could afford to be there, when Wilde took the curtain at the St James's Theatre on the first night of *The Importance of Being Earnest*, the glittering ruins of polite, heterosexual society lying at his feet like bouquets, the family and the law reduced to grotesque rubble by his vengeful comedy? Did they feel, on that evening ninety years ago, some kind of fragile victory? Later that night, what pleasures were celebrated by other men, who had no reason to care what the rich men up West were inventing? What did they think their (our) future would be? What was Wilde thinking of when, in December 1894, he published his deadly *Phrases and Philosophies for the Use of the Young*? He can have had no possible literary or commercial reason, because *The Chameleon* was merely an undergraduate magazine, and ran to only one hundred copies. He must have done it because the man he loved asked him to — Douglas knew the editor — because he wanted, dared to be associated with an (almost) homosexual project. It was a course he was to regret the following year, when it became part of the evidence against him. But in the summer of 1894, we were still testing just how far we could go. A Londoner was imagining a gay future. He said:

One should always be a little improbable.

and he said:

One should either be a work of art, or wear a work of art.

Thank you, Oscar, I will now take your advice. I will at the very least pretend to be free of the law, to imagine, to compose myself. I will make a real effort. Perhaps I could not only look different, but I could live differently, attempt the reconstruction of the city I live in... no wonder such advice could only be given in an epigram, in the language of theatrical comedy. Of course, the phrase suggests, no one would dare to be a work of art, to construct themselves according to a set of rules over which the law has no jurisdiction. Such a proposal is ridiculous. He can't have meant it.

Ninety years later, the words read rather differently. We are now able to measure them against realities which were never intended. We think of being rather than wearing as a real option. We know that being a work of art is much harder than wearing a work of art; the two activities are not really equivalent, and the symmetry of the epigram no longer suffices to yoke them together. But while an individual may calmly aspire to the very heights of fashion, which after all exists to make the acquisition of an "individual" image a relatively easy project, that same individual need no longer assume that being a work of art, being your own man, is an impossible or privileged occupation. In 1894, any such attempt could only be imagined as endangered, doomed, heroic, solitary, criminal. Now, together, our demand for a change in the production of "works of art" — the words, images and ideals that compose our lived experience — alters all that. We articulate a challenge which Wilde could not. We suggest that a gay culture is something to be struggled for, not dreamt or bought. At this point, our rewriting of history becomes a truly dangerous activity.

Ninety-two years after *An Ideal Husband*, ninety-six years after *The Soul of Man Under Socialism*, I'm still dreaming of what I want. In any formation of my desires, my sense of history has a very particular role to play. We are, in many obvious ways, written out of history. At the same time, we are acutely conscious of the shifting history of our own traditions, our heritage. We are offered a very particular and potent freedom of the city. Sometimes it feels like vertigo.

Don't be scared. We do it all the time.

▷

History (4) Five Personal Histories

1881. A fortnight ago I went down Whitechapel way, and dropped on such a nice, pretty boy. He was a shoeblack, and although only about thirteen years of age, beautifully formed and well hung with fine light golden hair, blue eyes and cherry lips. I fell in love with him. Whilst he was blacking my boots I asked a lot of questions about what he earned, etc, and soon found out that he lived in a refuge, where they kept nearly all he brought in every night to pay for his schooling and board etc, as he had no parents or relatives of any kind...

Here was a chance for NB, so I got him to promise to meet me near Moses shop in Aldgate in the evening, and the result was I brought him a rig-out as a page, had his ragged school livery made up into a parcel and sent back to the refuge, and took him off in triumph to my lodgings, a fresh place I engaged for that purpose that very afternoon. He was my page, and had a little bed made up in an anteroom next to my own bedroom. I had four rooms en suite at three guineas a week in a nice street in Camden Town...

He seemed delighted in the change in his prospects, and the jolly blow out of good things at every meal; so in the evening I asked him how he would like to go back to the Ragged School refuge again, as I did not think I should keep him very long. You should have seen the tears come into his beautiful eyes, as he threw himself on his knees and begged I would keep him, that he would die for me, and do anything he could to please me...

"Now I want to examine your figure," I said, "because I won't keep a boy unless he is well formed everywhere; so just strip yourself, my lad..."

I should not have thought he had so much sense of decency; but he blushed scarlet as the most delicately bred youth could have done, and the sight perfectly delighted me, as it was proof of his being a real virgin yet...

I could see he did not like it, but did it to please me...

He kissed me, and told me I might do anything I liked

with him, he loved me so...

At first I could make no impression. Being afraid his cries would be heard, I reached for a pocket handkerchief, and before he knew what I was about, had him effectually gagged. It was managed without losing my place, then with one hand putting a little cold cream onto my prick I gave a tremendous shove, and got a little further in. It must have been awfully painful for him, for he writhed and struggled to free himself from me, and went flat on the bed with a deep sigh, which would have been a scream but for the gag. The fact that I was inflicting awful pain only added to my lust...

From what I could see of his face, he was both laughing and crying in a hysterical state, so I thought I had better stop for that night at least, and it was a long time before I could bring him round to perfect sensibility...

I had him again the next night, but it was awfully painful for poor Joe; then I took him to Paris and sold him for a hundred pounds — he was so handsome I wouldn't take less...

▷

1983. I can remember when I was thirteen, before I came to the city. It was my very first time. There was a toilet on the way home from school. I used to go there, in my grey school uniform, and wait. One day there was a man inside. He was shorter, and older, than me. He had his cock out. I looked round and saw it. I was amazed. And then he said, do you want this, and I said, I put my hand around it, it was so big and so hot, and then I said yes. I can't remember what happened next. I think somebody else came in and I suppose I ran away, but I do remember that it was my very first time, and I remember him asking me that question, do you want this, and I said, I can remember I said, pardon, meaning, is that for me, is it really going to happen to me, at last. And then I said yes. My heart was going like mad, and yes, I said, yes I will, yes.

2 September 1985. I had that dream again. You know I told you I met a man whose friend, in 1937, had sex with Lord Alfred Douglas, and I keep thinking, it's not that long ago. And on Monday I read that story again, where the man picks up the boy in Whitechapel, makes him weep and bleed and then takes him to Paris and sells him. Well anyway in the dream I'm on the bus. I'm reading a book, some kind of history book. I get on at Trafalgar Square, and I'm going home, going East, it's the quarter to four bus, the one I caught home all through that summer of 1981, the first summer I lived here. There's sweat going cold on my back from the dancing. You're on the bus somewhere too, but it's empty. I look to see if you're watching, and you're asleep on my shoulder. You know I love you more like that than at any other time. And for once there's no one to look at us or laugh. I ride all through the West End. It's quite empty, all those big white streets on a summer's night, just the occasional man with dog's eyes, everything is distracting me from my book. They're always just at the end of the street, turning down an alley, looking with those dark eyes, always inviting me to follow with a turn of the shoulder. St Martin's, the Strand, St Mary's, Fleet Street, Ludgate, the dome. And then it's the City, all the banks are empty at night, on a summer's night. And then at Aldgate, suddenly, you know, where the City changes to the East End, the houses, it's teeming with people like fish, the Whitechapel pavement yellow with gaslight, and the women laughing like at the trial or in the film of "Oliver", and there, just by Tubby Isaac's, there is the boy. I drop my book. He has eyes like a dog too, he's like that boy we saw in the pub that night (the same accent). He has a t-shirt on; he looks a bit like me at thirteen, except I never looked that dangerous at thirteen, and you can tell from his expression that this isn't his first time. I drop my book, and he says, don't you want me baby? He grins, and he says, don't you recognize me?

I think I was really pleased to see him again.

1887/1985. "He turned on his heel, and hurried into the night.

"Where he went he hardly knew. He had a dim memory of wandering through a labyrinth of sordid houses, and it was bright dawn when he found himself at last in Piccadilly Circus. As he strolled home towards Belgrave Square, he met the great wagons on their way to Covent Garden. The white-smocked carters, with their pleasant sunburnt faces and coarse unruly hair, strode sturdily on, cracking their whips and calling out now and then to each other; on the back of a huge grey horse, the leader of a jangling team, sat a chubby boy, with a bunch of primroses in his battered hat, keeping tight hold of the mane with his little hands, and laughing... What a strange London they saw! A London free from the sin of night and the smoke of day, a pallid ghost-like city, a desolate town of tombs! He wondered what they thought of it, and whether they knew anything of its splendour and its shame, of its fierce, fiery-coloured joys, and its horrible hunger, of all it makes and mars from morn to eve... he envied them all they did not know.

"By the time he reached Belgrave Square the sky was faint blue, and the birds were beginning to twitter in the gardens."

I didn't go out last night after all. I wonder if the boys missed me. I sat up all night instead, reading the Wilde stories again, all those stories where men stagger home late at night. I always love that bit where he meets the boy with the flowers in his hat. I could cry, because it's true, isn't it, that's the only hour at which you can imagine the city is innocent, when things seem about to start again and the streets, perhaps, are ours. Between two and five anything could happen. When I finished reading the sky wasn't pale blue, but dead white with fog at first, and then pale yellow. I went out of the front door and looked out at the sun rising over all the new buildings. For once, everything was quite still. I wanted to call you.

1986. So much can happen. In 1895 these were the streets where the journalists came looking, trying to find the place where Dorian had smoked his opium. Those streets have gone now, although some of the pubs are still there, and you can still see some of the cobbles. Earlier I think Carpenter must have known someone round here, because he tells a story about a boy and a sea captain from the docks, and he says they used to meet in a pub just off the Mile End Road. And in 1944 there was one pub here (I got this story from one of the men from the steam room at the Baths) which stayed open all night, all through the Blitz. *It was terrible,* he told me. *You could do anything you wanted.* And when I moved here, the pub on the Dock Road, before they did it up, was like something left over from an earlier city, all the grey-haired affairs holding court for their boys, someone sitting with his mother, everyone watching the drag acts, and perhaps one solitary beauty drinking alone, drinking before going into town. And now there's a gay bar right next to the tube station. Walking there on a Saturday night, I hear as many insults as if this was still the city in which crowds collected outside Bow Street to abuse Wilde. But when I get inside (I have to pass the bus stop, crowded for the last bus of the night, to get to the door) everyone's there, it's a different world, a world which the people at the bus stop could not imagine, a world which none of us could have imagined twenty years ago. I hardly know which city I'm in, you don't feel as if you're in London any more.

At two o'clock the classical music comes on and we all go home, all over London. Sometimes I go and sit by the river; the lights on the water in the dead of the night look the same now as they must have done then. What kind of city is this? Sometimes I sit in my room, after a man has left, or I'm walking to meet a friend, or I'm waiting to get on a bus to come and see you and I wonder, if just once, if just once we tell each other what our lives have been like, what would happen?

History (5) You must not dream. It is only sick people who dream.

History (6) The only real people are the people who never existed.

History (7) What did it matter, what happened to the coloured image on the canvas. He would be safe.

The Picture of Dorian Gray *ends when Dorian, on the last page of his story, picks up a knife and slashes to ribbons the image which has haunted his life.*

NOTES

The frontispiece and endpiece show flowers on the grave of Oscar Wilde in the Père Lachaise Cemetery, Paris, autumn of 1987.

Epigraphs: Walter Benjamin, *A Berlin Chronicle* in *One-Way Street*, NLB, London 1979.

     Edward Carpenter, *Towards Democracy*, John Heywood, Manchester 1883.

Dedication This dedication is incomplete. I would also like to thank all those who provided support and inspiration for the work in progress: Rick Bébout at TBP, the organizers of the "Sex and the State" conference in Toronto in 1986, Miss Whitmore, Nicolas, John Steer, Edmund White, Mr Hughes and Gene Paul Rickard. This book is for me and Mr Jones.

TO BE SUGGESTIVE FOR FICTION IS TO BE OF MORE IMPORTANCE THAN A FACT

       Oscar Wilde; the last sentence of *Pen, Pencil and Poison*
         in *The Complete Works of Oscar Wilde*, Collins,
          London and Glasgow 1966, p. 1008.

Abbreviations used throughout:

WILDE: *The Complete Works of Oscar Wilde*, Collins, London and Glasgow 1966.

HYDE: H. Montgomery Hyde, *Famous Trials 7: Oscar Wilde*, Penguin, London 1962.

Tell me your story: the opening of my text is in fact the opening of *Teleny or the Reverse of the Medal: A Psychological Romance of Today*, London, 1893 (republished in 1986 by GMP, London). An anonymous questioner interrupts an all-male after-dinner conversation and asks Camille des Grieux to describe how he met his lover.

Villiers Street: WC2. This is where all good boys go to 'Heaven', London's biggest gay disco. Villiers Street runs off the Strand, down the side of Charing Cross. It is therefore on the edge of the West End cruising grounds of the late nineteenth century, close to the Albany, the Savoy Hotel (where Wilde took his tricks), the Haymarket, Piccadilly and Leicester Square. So then, as now, men would have been walking up Villiers Street to the pleasures of the West End; some of the street's façades still survive from 1891. When Wilde was editor of *Woman's World* he would reach his office on Ludgate Hill by taking the underground from Sloane Square and then walking up the Strand. So he knew this corner well.

We gay men: This book was written by a gay man, born in 1958, living in London from 1982-1987. I hope it is clear that it is not about any other time or place, and is in no sense a "representative" gay text, a text about "being gay". The geography and obsessions of this particular male are peculiar, not typical. The word *gay*, throughout the book, is not meant to be equivalent in meaning to *homosexual*, any more than it is meant to be equivalent to *Uranian* or *invert* or any of the other words used.

Oscar Wilde's sexual inversion: HYDE, p. 27. Although the attitudes of H. Montgomery Hyde's edition of the trial transcripts are dated (the first edition was in 1948) they are always clear, and this remains the most informative book on Wilde.

Paris version of Dorian Gray: The catalogue in which this and *Teleny* are advertised for sale is in the British Museum, CUP 364g48/42 and 25.

Pink lampshades: HYDE p. 249. Wilde hosted and paid for a dinner party for Alfred Taylor and his friends. Cross-examined about the festivities, he found time to mention that they "were amused by the little luxuries of Kettner's, the pink lampshades and so forth". Kettner's is still in Romilly St, Soho. Dorian Gray passes a night in Dockland on p. 141-2 of *The Complete Works*, and Lord Arthur Savile sees the Garden at night on p. 176.

Solferino: Where Charles Parker and Alfred Taylor met Wilde (HYDE, p. 171). After a champagne dinner Oscar declared, "This is the boy for me", took Parker to the Savoy, fucked him and gave him £2. Dorian Gray also dined there (WILDE, p. 67) before crossing town to see Sibyl Vane play Juliet.

Many similar cases: HYDE, p. 268.

Simeon Solomon: The rise and fall of the artist whose unapologetic survival of "disgrace" is an instructive contrast to the moral neatness of the fable of Oscar Wilde is reliably recounted in the illustrated catalogue to the Jeffrye Museum (London) exhibition of 1985, *Solomon, A Family of Painters*.

C.M. Otis : Otis was a thirty-six-year-old man who was psychoanalyzed by Dr L. Eugene Emerson in 1911. His case is reconstructed and reconsidered by Martin Duberman in *The View from Christopher Street*, Chatto and Windus, London 1984.

Strange flowers : Pater, *Studies in the Renaissance*, 1873 (conclusion).

Flowers glass hid: Theodore Wratislaw, *Orchids*, 1896.

They are unhealthy: Wilde, *Pall Mall Gazette*, 1885, reviewing Marc-André Raffalovich, *Tuberose and Meadowsweet*.

The aromatic odours: Charles Kains Jackson's translation of Ernest Raynaud, *"Antinous"*. *The Artist*, 1893.

Red rosebuds: J.G.F. Nicholson in *The Artist*, 1892.

His hand an orchid gave: Percy L. Osborn in *The Spirit Lamp*, 1893.

Illustrations to *Flowers* by John Nugent Finch, from *The Orchid Album*, B.S. Williams, London 1882.

I dreamed I stood: the opening of *The Two Loves* by Lord Alfred Douglas, in *The Chameleon*, Oxford 1894. It is in this garden that the "Love that dare not speak its name" makes its appearance.

Beardsley: Aubrey Beardsley's illustrations to Wilde's *Salomé* are the only adequate criticism of the text ever made. They depict the Princess three times; as a failed New Woman of the 1890s; as a terrifying, imminently sexual adolescent of indeterminate gender, icily abolishing the comedy of The Law; and as a fashionable exercise in London Art Nouveau. Her different guises make an uneasy wardrobe of contradictions.

Nazimova: In 1905 Alla Nazimova (b. 1879) worked in Whitechapel for J.T. Grein. She spent the summer with Emma Goldman in New York. In 1916 she became famous for her anti-war vaudeville skit, *War Brides*. In 1921 she considered playing Hamlet on film, but then decided to play Camille opposite Valentino. They wore matching *maquillages* designed by Rambova. In 1923 she ruined herself by financing, directing and starring in *Salomé*. She played the princess as a fourteen-year-old girl surrounded by flaming homosexuals and hunky eunuchs. The peak of her career was reached in 1931, when she played the Mother in the original six hour version of *Mourning Becomes Electra*. She was still gorgeous and still making films in 1940. She died in 1945.

Nora: The first London performance of Ibsen's *A Doll's House* was staged by J.T. Grein in 1889. The Princess Salomé (1891) is therefore in deliberate contrast to the other heroines of the intellectual drama dealing with the "New Woman" — Ibsen's Nora, Pinero's Second Mrs Tanqueray. Archer, in 1893, called the Princess "an oriental Hedda Gabler". Lest we should forget that her story is a serious investigation of current social themes, the text not only repeats the themes of Wilde's comedies (the wicked woman; the troublesome wife; the social power of the men cancelling the theatrical power of the women) but also bizarrely transfers many of their incidental details into an oriental setting. *Salomé*, in fact, is as much a domestic comedy as *An Ideal Husband*, while *Lady Windermere's Fan* is as anxious and guilty a melodrama as *Salomé*. Sir Robert Chiltern cries, 'Put out the lights!' at the end of Act One of *An Ideal Husband*, and a single beam of light falls on a tapestry; Herod cries, 'Put out the torches!' at the end of *Salomé*, and again a single beam of light falls on the allegorical figure of a woman. Herod commands that carpets be laid out on the terrace (WILDE, p. 561) and so does Lady Windermere

(WILDE, p. 387). Herodias, like Lady Windermere, has a fan with which she strikes out at crucial moments in the party (WILDE, p. 565). A concordance to the phrases, images and proper names which Wilde transferred from one text to the other, with little or no alteration, would be almost as long as *The Complete Works* itself.

She is like: Salomé, WILDE, p. 553.

You will do: Salomé, WILDE, p. 557.

A foreign city: London after the theatres have closed, the city after everyone else has gone home, is a recurrent image in Wilde's texts, as it must be in the imagination and experience of many gay men. The Young King (WILDE p. 226) looks out over a jasmine-scented version of the city, with "the huge dome of the cathedral looming like a bubble"; but this oriental dome is in London, because Lord Arthur Savile sees it too (WILDE, p. 190), cooling the dangerous night, "the huge dome of St. Paul's loomed like a bubble through the dusky air". We should imagine that Herod's palace is in Belgrave Square. The Baptist's cistern is somewhere in the London underworld, anywhere where a Princess may flee late at night from a crowded bar or 'party, and find a dark street hiding the blossom of a beautiful and sexually available male body.

Roses: Lady Windermere's are on p. 385, and Dorian's on p. 80 of *The Complete Works.*

The Green Bay Tree: By Mordaunt Shairp. First performed in London in 1933, revived 1950, reprinted by Methuen in *Gay Plays* ed. Michael Wilcox, 1984. Mr Dulcimer (Dulcie) is the main character, an authentically Wildean corrupt and corrupting dandy.

Monsieur Venus, Roman Matérialiste: By Rachilde (pseudonym of Mme Alfred Valette) and Francis Talman, Brussels 1884. Wilde read it (Brocard Sewell, *A Footnote to the Nineties,* Cecil and Amelia Woolf, London 1968), and so did John Addington Symonds (*Modern Ethics,* 1891, p. 19).

Charlus: At the opening of *Sodome et Gomorrhe* Baron de Charlus meets Jupien, and Proust draws exact and extensive parallels between the functioning of the vegetable kingdom and that of the dispersed kingdom of the Cities of the Plain. A bee enters an orchid at the very moment their eyes meet, and in the flower-laden first chapter of *The Picture of Dorian Gray* a bee also enters a flower at the very moment when the act of (homosexual) fertilization takes place; "... the bee flew away. He saw it creeping into the stained trumpet of a Tyrian convulvulus. The flower seemed to quiver, and then swayed gently to and fro... they turned to each other, and smiled." (WILDE, pp. 32-3).

Dandies: Rosy lips and joys occur endlessly in Wilde's letters.

Buttonholes: Lord Goring summarizes the Wildean philosophy of the buttonhole in Act Three of *An Ideal Husband* (WILDE, pp. 522-3); Dorian Gray chooses an orchid, 'a marvellous spotted thing, as effective as the seven deadly sins' (WILDE, p. 147), and Lord Illingworth rediscovers the same monstrosity blooming in the conservatory in *A Woman of No Importance* (WILDE, p. 438). Algernon chooses (*The Importance of Being Earnest,* WILDE, p.344) a pink rose in preference to the suggested Maréchal Niel; and the penultimate page of *The Complete Works* (1205; *Phrases and Philosophies for the Use of the Young*) reminds us that, "A really well-made buttonhole is the only link between Art and Nature."

For me, flowers: WILDE, p. 955.

Lilac and laburnum: De Profundis, WILDE, p. 954.

Out of his mouth: Ballad of Reading Gaol, WILDE p. 855.

It is superbly sterile: O.W. letter fo R. Clegg, April (?) 1891.

Homosexuality: J.A.Symonds in a letter, 21 October 1892, to Havelock Ellis.

Beauty forsakes itself: The Portrait of Mr W.H., WILDE, p. 1166. Wilde's rephrasing of Shakespeare's warning to his beautiful young man, Mr W.H.

Childless men: WILDE, p. 1175.

Oscar was very bulky: Michael Gambon, *Radio Times,* 23 March 1985.

He slipped a green carnation: Robert Hichens, *The Green Carnation,* R. Smythe, London 1894. Lady Bracknell, ransacking the library in the final scene of *The Importance of Being Earnest* for a clue as to Ernest's true identity (WILDE, p. 383) finds a copy of Hichens's book. "This treatise, 'The Green Carnation', as I see it is called, seems to be a book about the culture of exotics." The book was a commercial success, but was withdrawn from publication in the spring of 1895, when anything hinting at homosexual connections became very unfunny and very unfashionable.

Three quotations: The title should be *A Few Maxims for the Instruction of the Overeducated*, WILDE, p. 1203.

Narcissus: Dorian Gray, WILDE, p. 88.

Ma Bichette Cherie: The letter is from F. Carlier, *Les Deux Prostitutions*, in *Études de Pathologie Sociale*, Paris 1889. M. Carlier's book is a dressing-up box full of precious first-hand records of the life of Parisian queens of many species — slang, frocks, affairs, letters, names, affectations. It is reassuring to know that a queen now, as then, may be betrayed by her "passion pour bijoux voyants" or by her "amour immodéré du verbiage". Javotte and Zerline's circle of friends included Louise la Misère, la Salope, la Femme Colosse, Mlle la Fanchonette and la Poudre de Riz. Zerline's reply to Javotte was:

> London, February 7 1865.
> Ma bien chère Zerline,
> Your letter was a treat; they'd told me that you'd gone to Africa, I was so afraid for you amongst all those lions and leopards, not to mention the arabs, who are just crazy for blondes and have such big teeth, so *sharp*.
> Things are better now on the boulevards and the Champs Elysées, even if they're not quite without their dangers; you look after yourself, ma gazelle, there have been such misadventures amongst the ladies in the last six months, I can hardly tell you... Oh! us poor girls, struggling against *such* a prejudiced world. Is it true that la Fortin is dead? The fuss all that caused here in court — it was terrible. She was so charming, so sweet. Who gets the pearls?
> I haven't heard a word from La Princesse since she got to Rome. She's playing *la belle indifférente* in the arms of her lover, who's quickly gone back to beating her up again.
> I fear it *won't* all turn out for the best.
> La Champlumé is in Switzerland, a little bit depressed and itching to get back to Paris. I think she's out of bread and has to play Cinderella to her family. Her last letter really cut me up. She just hasn't got what it takes to make a good woman happy.
>
> > votre ami,
> > Javotte.

One of Carlier's more fascinating observations is that despite constant police harassment, the queens were accepted on the streets in drag at Carnival in Paris. Did London offer any similar acceptance in the 1860s, when the life of queens as described by Fanny and Stella (see below) was remarkably similar to that of Javotte and Zerline? Carlier published his account of his campaign against the queens as part of a campaign to criminalize homosexuality in France, to bring French legislation in line with the English Labouchère Amendment.

Private Flower: I didn't make this up. The newspaper article was transcribed from *Galignani's Messenger*, probably June 1833, by the man who compiled the appendix to *Don Leon*, Anon. 1866.

Watch that man: was the title of the B-side of Lulu's recording of "The Man who Sold the World", produced by Bowie and Ronson for Polydor in 1974. She appeared on *Top of the Pops* dressed and sounding exactly like a diminutive Bowie; a woman dressed up by a glam bisexual to look like a drag queen playing a straight man. I was sixteen when I watched it, and amazed.

Look at your past: WILDE, p. 953. *De Profundis.*

But the picture: WILDE, p. 78. *The Picture of Dorian Gray.*

It has been said: HYDE, p. 27. Major General Hector MacDonald, D.S.O. was born in 1852, and spent his early life as a draper's assistant in Dingwall. He joined the Gay

Gordons, and saw distinguished service in Afghanistan, in North and South Africa, and on the Nile Expedition of 1885. He became a Scottish hero, and earned a reputation among military outfitters as the most fastidious dresser in the British Army. He was stationed in Ceylon when recalled to London on grave but unspecified charges. On 14 March 1903 the papers reported that after a sudden mental collapse he had shot himself in a hotel room in Paris. The scandal was such that his mother refused permission for a public military funeral; nevertheless thirty thousand people turned out to pay their respects at the Dean Cemetery, Edinburgh, and the Scottish press was full of eulogies eager to scrub away any stain on the Idol of the Scottish Nation.

> No perfumed, pampered, jewelled lordling this,
> But fashioned grandly — every inch a man;
> Let slimy creatures mouth and meanly hiss
> Malevolent venom — speak the truth you can.
>
> W. Stewart Thomson in David L. Cromb, *H.M. MacDonald, A Memoir,*
> Eneas Mackay, Stirling 1903.

> The career of General MacDonald is one of the most interesting and romantic of any that adorn the pages of our military annals... it will doubtless be referred to through many a succeeding generation in order to excite the enthusiasm and stimulate the enthusiasm of youth.
>
> Mark Lovell, *Soldiers of the Queen: Library No. 5,* Ed. A. Egmont Hake,
> London Publishing Co., 1900.

MacDonald is included here because he is listed among the homosexual suicides in Xavier Mayne's *The Intersexes.*

   Up until 1873 *Simeon Solomon* was an artist, albeit one with a reputation for appearing at parties with over-handsome young men. In 1873 (on the evening of February 11) he was arrested while having sex with Mr George Roberts (61) in a public toilet off Oxford Street. After 1873 he was therefore a homosexual. He became an alcoholic tramp, but was by all accounts peculiarly happy. He continued to produce paintings and drawings, visionary and obsessive attempts to portray homoeroticism in the context of complete literal and cultural poverty, until his death in 1905.

   John Addington Symonds: drawn by Carlo Orsi.

   That face: The Sphinx without a Secret, WILDE, p. 215.

   Phillip and Gerald: How to defend your boyfriend from an older man's unwanted attentions; the lovers from E.I. Stevenson's *The Ordeal of Phillip and Gerald, or Left to Themselves,* 1893. The original caption reads, "How dare you! Don't you touch him again!"

   Henry ("Harry") Scott Tuke, RA: painting a boy somewhere near Falmouth, featured in *The Studio,* Vol. 5, London 1893. Tuke made his name with open-air studies of Cornish boys pretending to be Endymion, Leander, Perseus etc. His most famous painting was *August Blue* (1893) whose soft-focus rough trade inspired a whole school of white-on-blue "Boys Bathing" homoerotic poetry. His favourite model was one Johnny Jacker, who remained a friend even after he had grown up, got married and played football at the Olympics for Britain. Their relationship was described in a cautious biography of 1937: "Harry inspired devotion in many people, who were ready to be his willing slaves if called upon, and yet he never made the smallest effort to produce this effect. I think John would have allowed himself to be flayed alive if it could have done Harry any good" (M. Tuke Sainsbury, *Henry Scott Tuke, A Memoir;* Martin Secker, London). Tuke's house was called *Pink Cottage,* and his boat *Nijinsky;* he had seen *La Spectre de la Rose* in 1923 and decided that the dancer was "the most beautiful thing in the world." In 1929 he was still exhibiting naked adolescents at the Royal Academy, justifying his visions of youthful beauty with titles like *Sunburn.*

   Gustavus Cornwall: Secretary General of the Post Office, Dublin, made the front pages of *The Illustrated Police News* on 26 July 1884. See EVIDENCE for details of the scandal.

One of the boys from Cleveland Street: *Illustrated Police News*, 11 January 1890. The defence got them off with nine months hard labour by arguing that they had been seduced and corrupted, i.e. that they were not really *like that*.

The Duke: a.k.a. *Lord Euston*, an important client at Cleveland Street, *Illustrated Police News*, 4 December 1889. He was first taken there by Jack Saul, who gave extensive descriptions of the ducal sexual habits during the trial. He got dragged into the scandal when Ernest Parke, editor of the *North London Press*, claimed that Euston was part of "a foul and widespread plot to poison the morals of the community and make the name of England a hissing and reproach in Christian Europe". Euston sued him unsuccessfully for libel. Full details in L. Chester, D. Leitch and C. Simpson, *The Cleveland Street Affair*, London 1976.

Fanny and Stella: from *The Illustrated Police News*, 14 May and 19 June 1870.

Horatio Herbert Kitchener: by Sir Hubert von Herkomer, 1890.

Frederick Gustavus Burnaby: by J.G. Tissot, 1870.

Hugh Mundell: was arrested while escorting Fanny and Stella to the Strand Theatre on the night of 29 April 1870. "They informed me that they were men dressed up in women's clothes. I said it was a good joke, and did not believe it." Well, was he lying? Was he actually looking for a night out with two gay women, in our sense of the word? Or was he one of the still unclassified men, the London gentlemen who are not homosexuals, but who like to buy a drink for a man in a frock?

The Pederats: This picture is sadly missing from my collection. It is listed in a catalogue of pornographic snapshots in the British Museum (CUP 363 g 48, Album 7). The other lost faces listed there include: *Two finely built young men, wearing lace-trimmed lady-knickers and corset to enhance sweet illusions*; *The Sin of the Priest — Newest and rarest collection for Pederasts*; *a stout licentious monk cooling his passion with a young negro*; *l'amour fin de siècle*; *Tommy Atkins at the Transvaal*.

Mr Gibbings: who acted as Hostess at drag balls at Haxell's Hotel, made a fearlessly camp appearance in the box at the trial of Fanny and Stella.

Charles Hammond: (*North London Press*, 30 November 1889) lived with Jack Saul at 19 Cleveland Street and was the madam there, keeping the aristocratic clients supplied with uniformed telegraph boys and soldiers. He was allowed to escape to America, which prompted Henri Labouchère to claim that the Salisbury government was eager to cover up possible involvement of the Prince of Wales in the scandal. The Prince had asked Salisbury not to prosecute the case so as to protect his son, Prince Albert Victor, and his Assistant Equerry, Lord Arthur Somerset.

Whitman: The frontispiece to a London edition of 1886; this is the face all those moved by the poems could have put to their dreams. *Anne de Joyeuse* is mentioned in *Dorian Gray* (WILDE, p. 107). He was, before he was promoted and married off to the Queen's sister, one of the *mignons* of Henri III. At the wedding, the King and the bridegroom appeared in identical frocks. This snippet, with many other scandalously interesting anecdotes, is to be found in Isobel Murray's notes to the 1981 OUP edition of *Dorian Gray*.

Marc-André Raffalovich: photograph courtesy of Emmanuel Cooper.

'E'll 'ave 'is 'air cut: HYDE, p. 273

Edward Hamblar: The caption which accompanied this picture of Hamblar in drag was printed in *The Illustrated Police News*, 26 October 1889. It is reprinted in EVIDENCE.

Lord Arthur Clinton: What did Stella see in him?, *The Illustrated Police News*, 16 June 1870.

I do not say you are it: Queensberry's reply when Wilde asked him, "Lord Queensberry, do you seriously accuse your son and me of improper conduct?" HYDE, p. 73.

Piccadilly Vultures: was the original caption to this image from *The Illustrated Police News*, 25 January 1890. The readers were presumably meant to know that the Dilly was a popular pick-up spot for gay prostitutes, and to recognize a stereotype image of a queen.

Wagner: Dorian Gray, WILDE, p. 107.

Oscar Wilde: Caricatured by Aubrey Beardsley in the frontispiece of John Davidson's *Plays*, published 1894. The Overweight Pleasure Principle.

At first sight Simeon Solomon's engraving for the *Leisure Hour*, 1866, is a straightforward vignette from a series depicting Jewish ceremonies. Look again, and you see a picture of two Jewish homosexuals and their culture — excluded, unobserved, unembarrassed; and of their relationship with each other — it is the "man" (then as now) who does the looking, and the "boy" who gets looked at. Or am I reading too much into a very ordinary magazine engraving? Obviously the editors of the magazine didn't.

A young man photographed lying face down by Baron Corvo (Frederick Rolfe) and used as decoration in *The Studio*, 15 June 1893.

Sir Richard Burton: painted by Frederick Leighton, 1876. Lady Burton wrote to the *Morning Post* of her destruction of her husband's translation of *The Scented Garden* when she found it in his papers after his death; "...it treated of a certain passion. Do not let anyone suppose that Rd Burton ever wrote a thing from an impure point of view. He dissected a passion from every point of view, as a doctor may dissect a body, showing its source, its origin..." Quite; the question isn't whether he was or he wasn't, but *how* he was. Burton might stand as the very model of a modern homosexual, if we can accept the idea that our ancestors were pioneers and connoisseurs, not just perverts.

Clients arriving at Cleveland Street: *Illustrated Police News*, 25 January 1890.

Sin: Basil Hallward to Dorian Gray, WILDE, p. 117.

Simeon Solomon: Both photos of Solomon from Bernard Falk, *Five Years Dead*, London 1937.

Bosie at Oxford: The Border Standard, 15 December 1923.

None of us: Lady Windermere's Fan, WILDE, p. 399.

Mere words: The Picture of Dorian Gray, WILDE, p. 117.

Oh, the shame of it: Lady Windermere (rising), WILDE, p. 420.

Declarations of love: Basil Hallward spends most of two pages (WILDE, pp. 93-4) trying to explain to Dorian how he feels; he talks about worship, jealousy, domination, of secret emotions, but even though we now want him to come out and say it, he never once uses the word love. Wilde's declaration was written in a letter dated March 1893 from the Savoy Hotel.

Jewelled style: Wilde on French Symbolism, WILDE, p. 101. This language, like slang and like talking dirty, combines indecent suggestiveness with technical accuracy.

Keep your horrible secrets: Alan Campbell stops his ears when Dorian blackmails him into disposing of Basil Hallward's body, seduces him into being party to his crime. We are never told what secret from his past Gray threatens to reveal.

Expressions banales: Jean Genet, *Notre Dame des Fleurs*, Folio, Paris 1976 (first published 1948) p. 36.

Reprenant ma vie: Notre-Dame, p. 37.

Walk home at dawn: The journeys which Wilde's characters make as dawn breaks over the city of dreadful night are remade into truly gay odysseys in *Notre-Dame*, when Divine, Gorgui and Our Lady (in a pale blue frock edged with white lace) descend the Rue Lepic in Paris at five in the morning with no one to watch them, and Our Lady sings *Taraboom ti-ay* to the trashcans.

I went as far: De Profundis, WILDE, p. 882.

When to Lie and How: The Decay of Lying, WILDE, p. 990.

This great friendship: The Portrait of Mr W.H., WILDE, p. 1167.

Why do you seem: from the opening of *Sins of the Cities of the Plains, or Confessions of a Maryanne*, London 1881.

Drag: The second quote is from a letter to Stella, read out in court during the trial of Boulton and Park, 1871. The trial transcript is in the Public Record Office, PRO File DPP/4/6/1871.

It is very painful for me to be forced to tell the truth: The text continues: "It is the first time in my life that I have ever been reduced to such a painful position, and I am really quite inexperienced in doing anything of the kind." *The Importance of Being Earnest*, WILDE, p. 366.

Could it be: Lord Arthur Savile's Crime, WILDE, p. 174.

It is perfectly monstrous: A Woman of No Importance, WILDE, p. 436.

It is quite true: The Picture of Dorian Gray, WILDE, p. 82.

The Intersexes: By Xavier Mayne. Privately printed Naples, 1909. Mayne also wrote a novel, *Imre*, 1908, which chronicles a romance with a soldier in the Balkans. It has a few moments of tenderness — "Not till he was nude, and one could trace the ripple of muscle and sinew under the fine hairless skin, did one realize the machinery of such strength. I have never seen another man walk with such dignity... It was a pleasure to see him simply cross the street" — but its main concern is to illustrate the brutal division of the homosexual world proposed by *The Intersexes:* into masculine and effeminate races. The masculine homosexual (preferably uniformed) is seen as doubly male, forming with his passionate brothers an enlightened vanguard of society, a militaristic version of the politicized army of lovers imagined by Carpenter; the queen, however, is a disgrace, perverted, debauched, often upper-class, and deserves all the humiliation he receives. This association of masculinity with "real" or innate homosexuality, and male values, and of effeminacy with "false", perverted homosexuality remains with us. The question still is, are you a real man? Are you a good or a bad homosexual, acceptable or unacceptable? We still value ourselves according to whether we are an invert or a pervert. A pervert is one who has been seduced by the urban subculture into adopting "unnatural" excesses of behaviour — drag, leather, promiscuity, political activity, going on demonstrations, anything in fact, which erodes our sexual ease and makes us in any way different or distinguishable (beyond what we do, in couples, in our private beds) from other, i.e. heterosexual people. An invert is "just like that". This judgement is made by us as frequently as it is made by those outside our culture. Two typical passages from *Imre*:

> In every feature and every line and sinew and muscle, in every movement and accent and capability, we walk the world's ways as men. We hew our way through it, with vigour, success and honour. We plough the world's toughest seas as men. We rule its states as men, we direct its finance and commerce as men, we forge its steel as men. We fight in the bravest ranks of its armies as men. So Super-Male, are we not the extreme of the male, its climax of the aristocratic, the All-man?

> Ah! those patently deprived, noxious, flaccid, gross, womanish beings! Perverted and imperfect in moral nature and even in their bodily tissues! Those homosexual legions that are the straw-chaff of society; good for nothing except the fire that purges the world of garbage and rubbish! ...the painted male-prostitutes of the boulevards and twilight-glooming squares! The effeminate artists, the sugary and fibreless musicians! The Lady-Nancyish rich young men of higher or lower society; twaddling aesthetic sophistries; stinking with perfume like cocottes! The second-rate poets and neurasthenic *precieux* poetasters who rhyme forth their forged literary passports out of their mere human decadence; out of their marrowless shams of all that is a man's fancy, a man's heart, a man's love-life! The cynical debauchers of little boys; the pederastic perverters of clean-minded lads in their teens; the white-haired satyrs of clubs and latrines! ...What a contrast are these to great Oriental princes and to the heroes and heroic intellects of Greece and Rome...

The narrator of *Imre* undergoes a classic coming out; his adolescence is troubled by dreams of a "Friend"; he tries to find a Doctor who will cure him; he attempts marriage; he meets an ideal "friend" but he turns out to be straight; he reads German, Italian, French and English books which inform him of his true nature of his "simisexualism"; he confesses his true feeling to his "friend", who responds with; "Society needs more policemen than it has, to protect itself from such lepers as you!" He travels, hoping to discover his "true simisexual Masculinity". His struggle is ended when he confesses to

Imre, and finds his love returned.

Public opinion: The Critic as Artist, WILDE, pp. 1055-6.

Boulton and Park: All this information is taken from a broadsheet entitled *Stella: Star of the Strand*, London 1870, and from *The Times*, April and May 1870. There is a summary of the case in William Roughhead, *Bad Companions*, W. Green, Edinburgh 1930, and the trial transcript is in the Public Records Office. A fictional account of the drag ball attended by Fanny and Stella at Haxell's Hotel is given in *Sins of the Cities of the Plain*. The ball was hosted by Mr Gibbings, who, when Fanny and Stella were arrested, broke into 13 Wakefield Street and stole most of their drag to prevent it falling into the hands of the law. The account occurs in the part of the text which purports to be by Jack Saul. Since Saul, Gibbings, Boulton and Park were all real, documented gay men, the text must have been written by someone who was very close to the subculture of the 1860s.

A letter purporting to be from Lord Arthur Pelham Clinton was published, posthumously, in *The Times* of 20 June 1870 appealing "to the common sense of the community, whose calmer judgement cannot possibly exert itself until the merits of prejudice, naturally excited by the enormity of the offence charged against me, shall have been dispelled by the full light of a free and impartial trial." The letter was prepared by a solicitor, and signed by Arthur on his deathbed. It was accompanied by an announcement that he had died of exhaustion, resulting from scarlet fever. Lest this seem a little unconvincing, the story was repeated on 24 June, authenticated by evidence from the *Lancet*.

Illustrated Police News: 14 December 1889. The reports in *The Times* also provide ample evidence of the fact that Fanny and Stella were merely the ones that got caught; in May 1870 it attributes the exceptional crowding of the court to "the notoriety acquired by certain young men who, for years past, have been in the habit [of cruising in drag]"; and on 23 May, as the popularity of the trial as entertainment increased, it thought it its duty "to add that in all other cases of a similar character heard by Sir Thomas Henry, for many years past, the court has invariably been cleared of all persons excepting the reporters…" The other queen was Edward Hamblar — see Evidence, October 1889.

Scandal: Ernest Parke had used the Ripper murders of the summer of 1888 to boost the circulation of the *Star*. In 1889 he moved to the *North London Press*, and as editor used the Cleveland Street scandal as a platform for his anti-Government polemics.

Mayhew's categorization of prostitutes in in Volume 4 of *London Labour and the London Poor*, 1862.

James Greenwood, *Unsentimental Journeys, or, Byways of Modern Babylon*, 1867. *The Wilds of London*, 1874. *Odd People in Odd Places*, 1883.

Andrew Mearns, *The Bitter Cry of Outcast London*, in *Pall Mall Gazette*, October 1883. London Babylon also reappears in the title of the articles William Stead used in the "morality" campaign that led to the Labouchère announcement: *The Maiden Tribute of Modern Babylon*, July 1885. If Mayhew didn't meet any male prostitutes, Stead did; but he didn't publish any accounts of these encounters, made during his researches into child prostitution, but passed them privately to Henri Labouchère.

Richard Rowe: the repetition of apparently unique, first-hand documentary accounts of the underworld was common. This particular opium den, in Bluegate Fields, appears not only in Greenwood, Rowe and Wilde, it also, Rowe notes, provided the model for the opium den-keeper in Dickens's *Edwin Drood* (1870).

Adrian Singleton: Dorian Gray, WILDE, p. 143.

Dreadful socialistic days: "You know the Savile girls, don't you? — such nice, domestic creatures — plain, dreadfully plain, — but so good — well, they're always at the window doing fancy work, and making ugly things for the poor, which I think so useful of them in these dreadful socialistic days." The Duchess of Berwick, *Lady Windermere's Fan*, WILDE p. 391. For a different perspective on London's times of trouble, try Gareth Stedman Jones, *Outcast London*, London 1971, or John Quail, *The Slow Burning Fuse, The Lost History of the British Anarchists*, Granada, London 1978, both of which describe and analyse the unrest which I have merely noted.

He laughed at me: Jack Saul's evidence to Frank Lockwood (later Solicitor-General during the Wilde trials), trial of Ernest Parke, 1890.

I know that there are men: An Ideal Husband, WILDE, p. 501.

All the details from the *three trials* of Wilde are taken from H.M. Hyde's edition of the trial transcripts.

Love that dare not: The moment when Wilde was asked to identify this love continues to reverberate in our history. There can only be one answer to the question; we must always affirm our identity; yet there can be no one answer to the question, since there is no single, unspecific love to be described.

Just explain to me: Lady Windermere's Fan, WILDE, p. 390.

The first letter is from Oscar on holiday in Devon; the second is *De Profundis*, WILDE, p. 889. Douglas had sent Oscar a sonnet entitled *In Sarum Close* in January 1893.

Shame: Marc-André Raffalovich, "Piers Gaveston", in *Tuberose and Meadowsweet*, 1885.

This edited version of the cross-examination of Wilde is from p. 113 of HYDE. The quotations from *Dorian Gray* only appear in the *Complete Works* in an adapted form; the version quoted in the trial is from the first version, *Lippincott's Monthly Magazine*, 1890. In the revised version Basil does not say that he never loved a woman.

Neo-platonism: The allusion to academic history is both obscure and precise. Wilde was certainly serious about the relationship of Basil and Dorian Gray being a nineteenth-century version of the neo-platonic relationships typified by Shakespeare and Mr W.H. Dorian, by virtue of his beauty, inspires the older man with both awe and devotion; he incarnates his aesthetic ideal, and enables the artist to express his love in works of art. Wilde is in fact developing the iconography of the tradition in an alarming and radical direction. Dorian Gray does not represent an ideal at all; his nature is not revealed by the artist (Basil) in a definitive form, although that revelation is bitterly parodied in the final appearance of the portrait. His restless nature is not educated by the lover so that it reaches its perfection (the Platonic education whose narrative underlies biographies like those of Symonds, of Ronald Heatherington, (the priest in *The Priest and the Acolyte*), or of Mayne (in *Imre*), where another man brings out, realizes the obscure longings of the homosexual in their final form). Instead, Dorian is portrayed as perpetually change-able, subject to influence, devious, eclectic and elusive. He is always becoming someone else, while always feeling that he is trapped by an obscure destiny or identity. His picture thus defines, precisely, the image of a homosexual in the late, English, urban nineteenth century.

The homosexual version of Platonism was not only familiar to the erudite, however; things Greek were regarded with popular suspicion. Swinburne, in a letter to George Powell referring to Simeon Solomon, (Swinburne, *Letters* ed. Phyllis Grosskurth p. 492) noted that *Platonist* was understood to be "at once accurate as a definition and unobjec-tionable as a euphemism". And Gilbert's lyrics for *Patience* (1881) had referred to love "à la Plato".

Admission must cease: Sir Frank Lockwood, Solicitor-General, HYDE, p. 258-9

Details: Lady Windermere, in *Lord Arthur Savile's Crime*, WILDE, p. 173

I am a boy: Towards Democracy, Edward Carpenter, 1883.

It is a terrible thing: The Importance of Being Earnest, WILDE, p. 383

It was his duty: "The world would simply say that he was mad. They would shut him up if he persisted in his story..." Dorian's final meditation, with its familiar logic, comes just before he decides to destroy the last piece of evidence against him, the picture itself. WILDE, p. 166.

The crime of which: HYDE, p. 272.

Guilty: HYDE, p. 272.

I remember: De Profundis, WILDE, p. 947.

If one tells the truth: Phrases and Philosophies for the Use of the Young, WILDE, p. 1205.

A forger: Pen, Pencil and Poison: A Study in Green, WILDE, p. 993.

The first duty in life: *Phrases and Philosophies for the Use of the Young*, WILDE, p. 1205.

The fool, the fraud: " ...we — the fool, the fraud, the knave —" *The Ballad of Reading Gaol*, WILDE, p. 850. That *we*, in 1898, indicates Oscar's understanding that *one of them* can also be *one of us*.

He was entirely lacking in wholeness: *Pen, Pencil and Poison*, WILDE, p. 993.

One can fancy: ditto, WILDE, p. 1007.

The O'Flaherty [sic]: *The Artist*, 1 Sept. 1893.

Adult baptism: WILDE, p. 377.

One name: Mrs Arbuthnot (the Woman of No Importance herself), WILDE, p. 455.

Insincerity: All his life, from *Salomé* to *De Profundis* to *The Importance of Being Earnest*, Wilde was trying to find an alternative to sincerity as the philosophical alibi for his life in London. The quote is from *The Critic as Artist*, WILDE, p. 1048, and reappears, when the narrator refers to himself as I, in *Dorian Gray*, WILDE, p. 112. "Is insincerity such a terrible thing? I think not." Insincerity may not be terrible, but letting go of sincerity, of the alibi of *real feelings* in favour of perversion, triviality and invention is terrible.

A new life!: "That was what he was waiting for. Surely he had begun it already." *Dorian Gray*, WILDE, p. 165.

Posing as a somdomite (sic); Queensberry left this misspelt message on a card for Wilde at the Albemarle, and thus successfully goaded him into legal action.

The secret of life: Lady Hunstanton, Mrs Allonby and Lady Stutfield in *A Woman of No Importance*, WILDE, p. 464, articulate the philosophy of a specific gay life with peculiar accuracy:

Lady Hunstanton: Ah! those things are very sad no doubt, but I believe that there are admirable homes where people of that kind are looked after and reformed, and I think on the whole that the secret of life is to take things very, very easily.
Mrs Allonby: The secret of life is never to have an emotion that is unbecoming.
Lady Stutfield: The secret of life is to appreciate the pleasure of being terribly, terribly deceived.

Who wants to be consistent?: *The Decay of Lying*, WILDE, p. 971.

To invent anything at all: *The Importance of Being Earnest*, WILDE, p. 375. Our ability to reinvent our lives, especially in dark times, continues to be heroic. But consider the rest of the quotation: "Upon the other hand, to corroborate a falsehood is a distinctly cowardly action". Our forgery, our artistry, is always close to lying. In 1895 Wilde was lying to Constance Lloyd (Mrs Wilde). Now we may lie when we insist on passing as men, as members of the society of Real men.

Possessions: Nothing in this chapter can claim to be an original thought. These ideas are all to be found in *The Complete Works*, and in particularly abrasive form in Walter Benjamin, *The Work of Art in the Age of Mechanical Reproduction* (section iv, 1936, in *Illuminations*), which ends with the following astonishing admonition, which has animated all of my reading of Wilde ever since I realized I couldn't justify my fascination with his texts by saying that he was a "good writer": "But the instant the criterion of authenticity ceases to be applicable to artistic prodution, the total function of art is reversed. Instead of being based on ritual, it begins to be based on another practice — politics." (trans. Harry Zohn, London 1970).

A bazaar: The epigraph from R.L. Stevenson of *The Chameleon*, 1894.

Time: the present: The opening stage direction of *The Importance of Being Earnest*.

I remember so well: Sir Robert Chiltern, a respectable husband, recalls how as a young man the sinister and strangely sexual Baron Arnheim seduced him into committing the financial indiscretion which later threatens to ruin his marriage and his career.. *An Ideal Husband*, WILDE, p. 505.

Interior: This sense of the word is first cited by the OED from 1864.

Imagine a room: This particular interior was constructed by Thomas Wainewright,

WILDE, p. 996.

The study of jewels: Dorian Gray, WILDE, p. 107. Edward II, Piers Gaveston, Charles the Rash, James I and his "favourites" were all "homosexual".

These treasures: Dorian Gray WILDE, p. 111.

Beautiful sins: Dorian Gray, WILDE, p. 69.

Pleasure: A Father's Rebuke: An Ideal Husband, WILDE p. 490.

Hedonism: "Oscar Wilde is one of Paul's heroes", *Observer* magazine, London, 16 September 1984. The Paul in question is Paul Rutherford, (gay) dancer with Frankie Goes to Hollywood, a man of our times. In 1984 he stopped being on the receiving end of Thatcherism, left Liverpool, got dressed up and helped create some of the hardest dance music of that summer. Just for the moment it seemed that we were going to be happy when "Relax" came on with the lasers. The record was a huge success, because it captured exactly (and failed to challenge) the contradiction inherent in the glittering marriage of pleasure to consumerism. By all means inspire journalists and dancers with the hope that "living well is the best revenge"; mention Dorian Gray and recite the name of Baudelaire three times on your record sleeve; let your publicist say that "one of the main jobs of advertisers in this conflict between pleasure and guilt is not so much to sell the product as to give moral permission to have fun without guilt", but I still don't believe it. Even if Rutherford, on the stage at the Hammersmith Odeon, was the most beautiful man in London, I still don't believe it. Or rather, I only believe it for the duration of the song. The music is forgotten, a new product is offered us, and the doctrine of endlessly repeated, endlessly elusive pleasure as the only solution to our poverty goes unchallenged.

To one so modern: De Profundis, WILDE, p. 954.

The future belongs to the dandy: "It is the exquisites who are going to rule", Lord Illingworth, as he seduces Gerald, his illegitimate son, in *A Woman of No Importance*, WILDE, p. 459. Wilde is nowhere more serious, and the measure of his seriousness is that we are still caught in the exact trap which he described in a character as obnoxious as Lord Illingworth. We believe, modern as we are, in the ambiguity of *All Art is Quite Useless* — the final sentence of the preface to *Dorian Gray*, WILDE, p. 17. We have it both ways. Of course, we know it isn't true, but of course we know it is true. We play as privileged comedians, selecting, consuming and discarding as wilfully as we please, literally reducing our culture to the production and consumption of (pleasurable) rubbish. Simultaneously, we genuinely believe in the importance of wealth and taste, that through our consumption we genuinely master our experience of the world.

In a house...: The Decay of Lying, WILDE, p. 970.

Repetition: the quote continues: "Each time that one loves is the only time one has ever loved. Difference of object does not alter singleness of passion. It merely intensifies it." *Dorian Gray*, WILDE, p. 149. This may apply equally to desired objects or bodies or persons.

Repetition: The most appropriate description of London's gay nightlife as I experience it is in *Dorian Gray*, where the prose of the book that sets the pattern of Dorian's life is described as being characterized by "subtle monotony... complex refrains and movements elaborately repeated." (WILDE, p. 101). Repetition is the basic formal principle of our desire. We repeat sex, we repeatedly compare bodies (whether we touch them or not). We look like repetitions of the same form. We shape our romances (brief or long) by talking of One who will end the sequence of Numbers. We go *regularly* to places of entertainment. Our music is repetitious. It is the apotheosis of repetition. It operates as Wilde's prose operates; it is beautiful, but only because of beauties of phrasing, not beauty of original sentiments; it is erotic, but always obliquely, pornographically; it is sentimental, it repeats sentiments; it is mechanical, repeating certain phrasings and images to mechanically guaranteed effect. It mimics the splendours of orgasm and grand emotion, but the heights of this music are only reached because we invest it with energy and pleasure in exact proportion to its acknowledged banality. It demands that we invest it with meaning; it announces that it is replaceable.

Shopping: shopping and cruising become interchangeable activities in the city when Young Wilson (aged 16) describes his habits in *Sins of the Cities*: "(I) am living with my Father and Mother at Greenwich and only come to the West End to look about and see the shops and swells. If a gentleman is very pressing I never consent to anything unless he asks me to accompany him to his house or chambers." Cruising is like window shopping. The boy, like a purchase, begs to be chosen and taken home.

Never before: *The Young King*, WILDE, p. 226. The Young King's story is as moral as Dorian Gray's. He is a homosexual connoisseur, one for whom only luxury can redeem his life. In a series of nightmares he sees how his bejewelled, perfumed, upholstered city (a thinly disguised nineteenth-century London) coexists with the dark, hungry city of the proletariat who labour and die to produce his luxuries. After a nights of anxieties and imminently radical sympathies, he does not instigate a revolution, however. On waking he turns to the higher and newer pleasures of Religion. Wilde attempts to dissolve the guilt which is built into the gay mythology of pleasure in exactly the same way as Frankie Goes to Hollywood did, with the dance floor of "Heaven" replacing the Cathedral as the heart of the City, the site of its salvation.

De Profundis, WILDE, p. 952.

It is quite true: *De Profundis*, WILDE, p. 926.

The hero: *Dorian Gray*, WILDE, p. 102.

One had ancestors: WILDE, p. 113. Algernon, in *The Importance of Being Earnest*, has an imaginary friend, Bunbury, who is his alibi when he wishes to disappear and do unmentionable things. Dorian Gray also has "mysterious and prolonged absences" (WILDE, p. 102). Basil Hallward says, "When I leave town I never tell my people where I am going." (WILDE, p. 20). All of Wilde's characters lie about their lives all the time. We too say to our straight acquaintances, innocuously, "I'm going out tonight."

There is something inexpressibly pathetic: John Addington Symonds, Letter to George Dakyns.

The frank and hearty feeling: John Addington Symonds, *The Life of Michael Angelo Buonarroti*, London, 1893.

Broken heart: *Dorian Gray*, WILDE, p. 25.

The Love that dare not: The repetitions do not make the answers to this question lies. The repetitions are signs of experiments in rephrasing, definition in shifting contexts. The first version is on page 41 of the *Complete Works*, the second on page 97.

Frank O'Hara, *Lines During Certain Pieces of Music*, *The Collected Poems of Frank O'Hara*, Alfred A. Knopf, 1971, p. 383.

One's past: *An Ideal Husband*, WILDE, p. 500.

I cannot repeat: WILDE, p.90.

Were his own actions: *Dorian Gray*, WILDE, p. 113.

When he chose the script: Wilde cast his history as a comedy in *De Profundis* (WILDE, p. 879), for once writing himself into the text of heterosexual mythology, admitting that there were to be other versions of his story besides his own: "For with that grotesqueness of effect that is as it were a Gothic element in history, and makes Clio the least serious of all the Muses, your (Douglas's) Father will always live among the kind pure-minded parents of Sunday-school literature, your place is with the infant Samuel, and in the lowest mire of Maleboge I sit between Gilles de Retz and the Marquis de Sade."

Which tradition: In Larry Kramer's play *The Normal Heart* (1985) the main character brings the audience to tears with a speech that begins: "I belong to a culture that includes Proust, Henry James, Tchaikovsky, Cole Porter, Plato, Socrates, Aristotle..." The speech is part of a long gay tradition, in which a gay "let us now praise famous men" is recited in order to prove that we are noble, distinguished and mighty, not simply over- or erroneously sexed. The nineteenth-century version can be found, for instance, in Xavier Mayne, J.A. Symonds, or Oscar Wilde's *Mr W.H.* What happens if the speech begins: "I belong to a culture that includes Edward Carpenter, Jean Genet, Simeon Solomon, Ernest Boulton, Samuel M. Steward and William Burroughs..."; or if it begins: "I belong to a culture that includes the very best of Disco music 1972-78, Lewis Leathers, George

Platt Lynes, hundreds of anonymous pornographers and drag artists, all my friends and lovers, and all the gay politicians in London."?

Do not be afraid: The concluding section of *De Profundis*, WILDE, p. 956.

Morning comes: I wrote this passage at the suggestion of a lover, and then realized I was repeating a passage from *Dorian Gray*, WILDE, p. 105: "...we watch the dawn remaking the world... Nothing seems to us changed. Out of the unreal shadows of the night comes back the real life we had known. We have to resume it where we had left off, and there steals over us a terrible sense of the necessity for the continuance of energy in the same wearisome round of stereotyped habits, or a wild longing, it may be, that our eyelids might open some morning upon a world that had been fashioned anew in the darkness of our pleasure, a world in which things would have fresh shapes and pleasures, and be changed, or have other secrets, a world in which the past would have little or no place."

1725: In 1725 a Molly House (the eighteenth-century predecessor of a gay bar — a tavern and boarding house used exclusively by homosexual and bisexual men) in Covent Garden was attacked, and the mollies, many of them in drag, fought back. Given the symbolic importance of drag queens from the Stonewall Bar from the Stonewall riots of 1969, this detail, from David Bray's *Homosexuality in Renaissance England* (GMP, London 1982), assumes extra piquancy. It's nice to know that drag culture has always been a focus of resistance — always, that is, if you accept the thesis that the turn of the seventeenth century into the eighteenth marks the beginning of a recognized homosexual culture in London.

You have always told me: The Importance of Being Earnest, WILDE, p. 325.

I hear the awful syllable: Edward Carpenter, *Towards Democracy*, 1883.

For he, to whom the present: The Critic as Artist, WILDE, p. 1040.

Symonds refers to 1860 as a year when "I was two years old," (Phyllis Grosskurth's biography, 1964 p. 121). He was actually born in 1840.

The one duty: The Critic as Artist, WILDE p. 1023.

1881: Sins of the Cities of the Plain.

1983: Diary.

2 September 1985: Letter.

1887/1985 The Wilde quotation is from *Lord Arthur Savile's Crime*, WILDE, pp. 176-7.

1986: Diary.

You must not dream: Salomé, WILDE, p. 565.

The only real people: Decay of Lying, WILDE, p. 975.

What did it matter: Dorian Gray, WILDE, p. 88.

Endpaper *God save the Queen*: Wilde to Ross, Letter, 13 October 1888.

God Save the Queen.

9 781852 421236